HIDDEN HEROES OF
THE BIG SANDY VALLEY

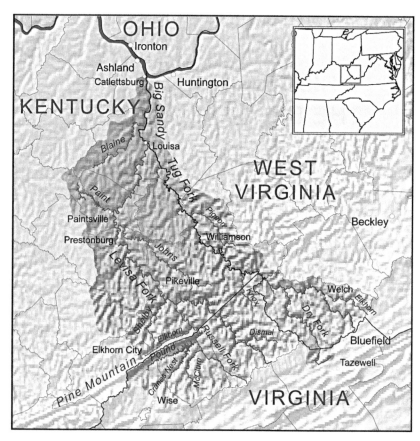

The Big Sandy Valley of eastern Kentucky.

HIDDEN HEROES OF
THE BIG SANDY VALLEY

Compiled and edited by

James M. Gifford

JESSE STUART
FOUNDATION
Ashland, Kentucky
2015

ISBN: 978-1-938471-35-3

Published by
Jesse Stuart Foundation
4440 13th Street
Ashland, Kentucky 41102
(606) 326-1667
jsfbooks.com

DEDICATED TO

Julianne "Judy" Willams Perry,
the inspiration for this book and a true
hidden hero of the Big Sandy Valley.

ACKNOWLEDGMENTS

From the conception to the completion of this project, I have enjoyed the steadfast encouragement and assistance of Julianne "Judy" Williams Perry. Several of the essays required extensive revisions. Diane Blankenship, Laurie Cantwell, and my administrative assistant Judith Kidwell typed dozens of drafts for me, and Judith also played a major role in indexing and proof-reading this book. In the summer of 2014, I received excellent assistance on all aspects of the project from Nicole Wells, an editorial intern who is currently pursuing an advanced degree at Eastern Kentucky University.

I want to thank the following individuals, institutions, and businesses for providing photographs: The Kentucky Highlands Museum & Discovery Center; University of Kentucky Libraries; Lexington Herald-Leader; Filson Historical Society; Hindman Settlement School; Karen Daniel, Johnson County Public Library; Mike Duncan and Amy Smith of the Inez Deposit Bank; Caroline Wilson; and Steven Pettaway, Photographer, Supreme Court of the United States. Many of the authors supplied photos of their subjects.

When the manuscript was completed, Adam VanKirk paged and designed it into a beautiful book that truly credits the hidden heroes who are profiled here and the authors who have worked with me to create this important book.

James M. Gifford
Ashland, Kentucky
August 2015

CONTENTS

John Cannon	Paula Kopacz
Harry M. Caudill	Clyde Pack
Cathy Corbin	Edwina Pendarvis
Kevin Coots	John David Preston
Linda Scott DeRosier	John Sparks
Brenda Evans	John Howard Spurlock
James M. Gifford	Ernest Martin Tucker
Loyal Jones	Nicole Wells
Jonathan Jeffrey	

INTRODUCTION

The Big Sandy Valley, a geographical corridor approximately 120 miles in length, stretches from Pikeville to Cattletsburg along the Kentucky-West Virginia border. The valley is a function of the Levisa Fork and Tug Fork rivers that flow through southeastern Kentucky. The two rivers are approximately twenty-five miles apart and flow north in parallel fashion until they converge at Louisa and flow into the Ohio River near Cattletsburg. The Big Sandy Valley is almost 5,000 square miles of mountainous land that includes the counties (going from north to south) of Boyd, Lawrence, Johnson, Floyd, Martin, and Pike counties, along with the southeastern sections of Magoffin, Knott, and Letcher counties.

The Big Sandy Valley — sometimes called Kentucky's last frontier — was shaped by a series of historical events. Settlement in the seventeenth and eighteenth centuries was difficult because of Indian hostilities and the formidable geography of the region. In the nineteenth century, the small population was divided by the conflict of the American Civil War. After the Civil War, the region was joined to the outside world by steamboats that plied the rivers from the 1830s to the beginning of World War I. Early in the twentieth century, the colorful steamboat era came to an end as railroads pressed south into the valley, running parallel to the rivers, and facilitating the extraction of the region's valuable timber and coal. The repeated boom and bust cycle of eastern Kentucky's coal industry is reflected in out-migration literature and music. Regional spokesmen like Harry Caudill decried the "brain drain" of the region as many young people left their Appalachian homes for secure employment in the auto industries and school systems of Northern states. Running a parallel course to this out-migration was the initiation of federal legislation that created a welfare society among many of the area's poor and unemployed.

From the beginnings of Appalachian history until the present, outsiders have defined Appalachian people and Appalachian ways in negative terms. As early as the 1720s and 1730s, William Byrd's travel writings about the southern mountains defined a "back country" where lazy people lived a primitive lifestyle. By the twentieth century, these negative impressions were reinforced by cartoons like Lil' Abner and Snuffy Smith and later by televisions shows, *ad naseum*, including "The Dukes of Hazard" and "The Beverly Hillbillies," which combined with print journalism, showed mountaineers as childish, backward people, more comic than threatening, people living in a land that became a missionary field for America's churches.

In 1964, President Lyndon Johnson launched the federal government's war on poverty from Tommy Fletcher's front porch, near Inez, in Martin County, Kentucky. That iconic image of the President and his wife talking with people who were obviously very poor played to the mainstream image of the Big Sandy Valley. That image has been reinforced by "documentaries" and fictional presentations like A&E's popular mini-series on the Hatfields and McCoys. Today, we live in a world of cultural awareness and sensitivity to other people's unique differences. And yet that cultural sensitivity never seems to extend to the people of Appalachia, who remain the punchline of an American joke.

For more than two centuries, politicians, novelists, journalists and scholars have "discovered" and written about Appalachia with the same analytical success enjoyed by the three blind men who went to see the elephant. For example, in 1899, William Goodell Frost defined the people of Appalachia as "our contemporary ancestors;" seven decades later, minister Jack E. Weller defined Appalachians as "yesterday's people." However, the cruelest assessment was rendered by the great English historian, Arnold Toynbee, who compared the people of Appalachia to the "barbarians of the Old World" and observed that we were a people "who had acquired civilization and then lost it." One of the truths of life is that often, even when we know something is wrong, we still don't know what is right. That's the purpose of this book: the people who are profiled in this book are true representatives of millions of people who have populated the Big Sandy Valley for more than two hundred years. I invite you to read their stories and discover the reality of a great regional people.

James M. Gifford, Ph.D.
CEO & Senior Editor
Jesse Stuart Foundation

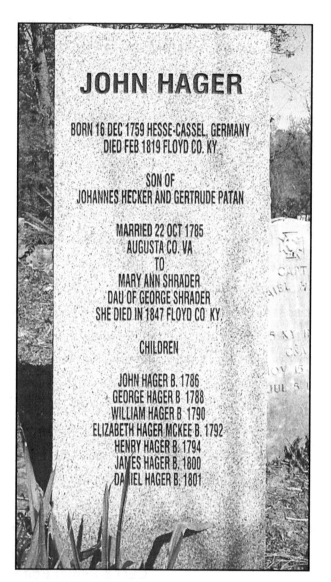

JOHN HAGER

BORN 16 DEC 1759 HESSE-CASSEL, GERMANY
DIED FEB 1819 FLOYD CO. KY.

SON OF
JOHANNES HECKER AND GERTRUDE PATAN

MARRIED 22 OCT 1785
AUGUSTA CO. VA
TO
MARY ANN SHRADER
DAU OF GEORGE SHRADER
SHE DIED IN 1847 FLOYD CO. KY.

CHILDREN

JOHN HAGER B. 1786
GEORGE HAGER B. 1788
WILLIAM HAGER B. 1790
ELIZABETH HAGER MCKEE B. 1792
HENRY HAGER B. 1794
JAMES HAGER B. 1800
DANIEL HAGER B. 1801

The gravestone of John Hager, in Floyd County, Kentucky.

MARY SCHRADER HAGER:

DAUGHTER OF THE REVOLUTION

By John Sparks

Long before Rosie the Riveter empowered American women during World War II, patriotic women were serving in capacities traditionally assigned to men during wartime. School-books mention the stories of Molly Pitcher, Margaret Corbin and Deborah Samson, all of whom acquitted themselves in Revolutionary War battles with heroic deeds of which the so-called weaker sex was not often thought to be capable. And it so happens that the Big Sandy Valley of eastern Kentucky has its own unsung hero of the American Revolution: Mary Hager, the matriarch of the Hager family of eastern Kentucky, was not only a pioneer of American home-front defense workers but an individual who challenged every prejudice about a woman's proper "place."

Mary Schrader, born in a German settlement somewhere on the Virginia/Maryland boundary about 1755, was a tall, plain girl; nothing about her was petite. Her father, believed to have been named George, was a millwright, and Mary labored in the fields and assisted her father and brothers at the mill as well. She could pick up heavy sacks of corn and wheat and bear them with ease, and she could outwork any man who had the temerity to challenge her speed or endurance with the heavy "grain cradle." These feats did not endear her to local men, who were threatened and unnerved by her physical prowess.

When her father and brothers all joined the Continental Army, Mary assumed the responsibility of managing her father's mill alone, a task she bore up with courage. Virginia military quartermasters were among her best customers at this time. On one occasion a sutler, a large, powerful young man missing his right hand, came to the mill with three wagons and a party of soldiers to purchase grain. He gave orders for the grain he wanted in each of the wagons, and of course Mary helped load it. She kept her eyes open, though, and afterward she noted that one soldier had taken one sack too many. Even nowadays most young women would be intimidated, and with good reason, by a squad of rough soldiers in the lawlessness that is a fact of life in wartime—but not Mary. She hefted the sack onto her shoulder and took it back to the mill.

The soldier slapped her hard across the face, and in most cases he would have gotten away with the act of violence — but this time he was dealing with tough young Mary Hager. He'd been better off to have saved his aggression for the British. The sutler was now some distance apart, and on hearing Mary's heavily-accented shout and her tussle with the thief he ran back to see what was wrong. He apologized to Mary for the soldier's behavior and then ordered that the thief be tied to a wagon wheel. He then gave the man a severe horsewhipping, applying the lash with his left hand due to his disability. It was probably the very first time in her life that Mary Schrader had had a man come to her rescue, and though she remained proud and independent throughout her life she never afterwards forgot the young disabled officer.

After the war ended and her father and brothers returned, Mary relinquished her leadership role at the mill. Still, her strength remained undiminished, and the fact that she could outdo any man who doubted her abilities with a grain cradle may have amused her. But finally, a young man challenged her to a reaping contest and he proved to be of different mettle than the others. Not that he could beat her, of course, no man could; but instead of being humiliated by her, he was attracted to her.

This was John Hager, newly arrived to the area from the southern frontier. John was an immigrant from the Old Country, courtesy of the elector of Hesse-Cassel and the British Government. An apprentice blacksmith known in his native province by the name of "Johannes Hecker," he had been conscripted in 1778 at age eighteen along with two of his brothers to serve in the Hessian contingent in America. Knowing that he would probably never see his parents or his remaining brother ever again, he became so embittered against the British while on his sea voyage that he resolved to desert and throw in his lot with the Americans. He managed this after his regiment landed at Charleston, South Carolina and marched inland to the Broad River. Early one morning he left his sentry post, enduring a difficult two-day trek through forest and swamp during which he could easily have been caught by the British and shot as a deserter or caught by the Americans and shot as a Hessian, before reaching the camp of Colonel Thomas Sumter. Sumter, anxious to muster any and all men to the patriot cause that he could, took young Hager on, and for the remainder of the war John fought with distinction under Sumter and Generals Francis Marion and Nathanael Greene. He bore the scar of a saber cut on his cheek as a testimony of his service.

After the war, John probably came to Virginia from South Carolina to join General Anthony Wayne's Indian campaign simply because he was young, penniless, and without family. After the Indian action in the South, he drifted north toward the German settlement where the Schraders lived, and as luck would have it he had tried to match Mary at reaping and gotten beaten soundly. Though the scenario was hardly the stuff of a romance novel, as so few real lives really are, this reaping contest appears to have made John Hager decide that Mary Schrader was the woman he wanted for his wife. He began to pay court to Mary, she accepted his proposal of marriage, and the two were wed at Staunton, county seat of Augusta County, Virginia, on October 27, 1785, when she was thirty and he nearly twenty-six.

John and Mary began their married life in Amherst County, Virginia, and here their children were born: Katherine, John Jr., George, William, Elizabeth, Henry, James, and Daniel. John was a small farmer and blacksmith, and although he and Mary were literate enough to read a German Bible, they never learned to read or write English. When Daniel was a baby, the family migrated westward to Kentucky. Settling on land known as the

Blockhouse Bottom near the present Johnson-Floyd County border, near where John's Creek empties into the Levisa Fork of Big Sandy, they became one of the new territory's more prosperous clans. There is no way that we can judge their lifestyle by modern standards. They were small-scale slave owners, and their slave labor was supplemented by that of indigent white orphans and juveniles bound to them as indentured servants by the Floyd County Court. They lived by the standards of their time and place and accepted them as the status quo. Because of the hardships that they had faced during the Revolution, though, we might hope that John and Mary both tried to be fair to their black and white servants. For all that, though, it is almost certain that the couple regarded one another as equal partners in their marriage much more than was then common. Their children often heard John speak fondly about the reaping contest years before in which Mary had not only beaten him but captured his fancy, the tale perhaps being followed with a chuckle from Mary.

During her life in Floyd County, Mary also established a reputation as an herb doctor and probably a midwife as well. Her experiences as a wife and mother had taught her a great deal about medicinal plants and remedies. Her house calls and homespun prescriptions, given in the broken English that remained on her tongue all her life, were in demand for miles up and down the Big Sandy River — and she never asked for payment for her services.

John Hager died in February 1819. A few months later, James married and moved away, giving the stream on the other side of Big Sandy known as Hager Branch its name before settling finally on Greasy Creek in Johnson County. Of the older children, Katherine had already married James Layne of a prominent Floyd County family, John Jr. had moved near Paintsville, George to Indiana and then back to Kentucky's Greenup County, William to Tennessee, Elizabeth to Mississippi, and Henry to Nashville. Finally, the youngest son Daniel married and moved his bride Violet to the Blockhouse Bottom farm.

Mary Hager was then in her mid-sixties. Not long after the government began granting pensions to surviving Revolutionary soldiers, an old man named Thomas Brown came up the Levisa Fork of Big Sandy looking for fellow veterans. He had heard that John Hager had fought in the Revolution, and although he didn't anticipate any direct assistance he wanted to ask Mary if she knew any other local veterans who could testify at his pension hearing. Mary received him graciously, but with a slight shock. Brown looked strangely familiar, and he had no right hand.

Noting Mary's reaction, Brown explained that he hadn't been injured in the war, but in a boyhood accident at a frontier house-raising. The injury had relegated him to duty only as a sutler. Her sense of *déjà vu* growing, Mary offered that she had operated her father's mill near the Maryland-Virginia line during the war, and Brown replied by recalling a visit to just such a mill in that area. A soldier under his command had tried to steal grain from a German girl at that mill, Brown had exercised the rough Army discipline of the times... and as he spoke, tough old Mary Hager did something that her children, and possibly her husband as well, had never seen her do. She fell on Thomas Brown's neck and wept, and he, finally recognizing her, embraced her and wept with her. The two old independence fighters, having lived for years unknowingly within sixty miles of each other, were finally reunited. Mary's testimony won Thomas Brown his Revolutionary pension, with no doubts expressed by the commissioner hearing the case; if he had questioned Mary's word, he might have had a fight on his hands.

Mary Schrader Hager died in 1847 at Blockhouse Bottom, by then the nucleus of a community still known as Hager Hill, Kentucky. Her descendants have scattered nationwide from the family cradle of the Big Sandy, and they include not only farmers, miners, and housewives, but physicians, merchants, and attorneys—and many have followed in the footsteps of Mary's stalwart Hessian husband to serve in America's military. Mary achieved her own independence generations before most American women even allowed themselves the thought of it. She was a true eastern Kentucky pioneer for the Equal Rights Amendment. And yet, when we consider where she came from, the river valley she helped to settle and civilize, what she accomplished in her ninety-two years—and perhaps if the poet Edgar Lee Masters had penned a *Big Sandy River Anthology* rather than the *Spoon River Anthology* for which he is so justly famous—we might yet wonder if Mary Hager would dismiss our modern world with a wry smile, an indulgent wave of her work-callused hand, and the words Masters put into the mouth of his fictional Lucinda Matlock:

Degenerate sons and daughters,
Life is too strong for you;
It takes life to love life.

White Squaw
The True Story of Jennie Wiley

Arville Wheeler

White Squaw is a junior book version of the Jenny Wiley story.

JENNY WILEY

By James M. Gifford

Thomas and Jenny Wiley pioneered land on Walker's Creek in Bland County, Virginia. On October 1, 1789, while Thomas was away, a small band of Indians, seeking revenge for a recent defeat at the hands of white settlers, attacked the Wiley cabin and killed and scalped Jenny's three older children and her brother. Jenny, seven months pregnant, was taken captive along with her baby son, Adam.

She then began a nightmare flight through the wilderness into the dark Kentucky hills to westward. Jenny's only hope for survival was to keep pace with her captors. On the third day, a Cherokee Chief snatched the sick child from its horrified mother and smashed little Adam Wiley's brains out against a tree. Evading rescue parties, the Indians moved northwest into the Big Sandy Valley of eastern Kentucky. Unable to cross the flood-swollen Ohio River, they retreated to a series of winter camps in present-day Carter, Lawrence, and Johnson counties.

With only a rock bluff for shelter, Jenny spent the winter

laboring as a slave. She gave birth in a cave, but three months later the Indians killed and scalped the infant, after it failed to pass their test of courage. After almost a year in captivity, Jenny escaped, miraculously evading pursuit as she made her way to a small settlement at Harman's Station on John's Creek. From there, a hunting party returned Jenny to her home in Virginia.

After Jenny was reunited with her husband Thomas, they had five more children. Surprisingly, the family left Virginia in 1800 and settled in the Big Sandy Valley — the land where she had been held in captivity for almost a year. Thomas died a decade later and Jenny lived until 1831. Her gravesite is in Johnson County and she is memorialized by two highway markers and a state park that bears her name and perpetuates her legacy through an annual outdoor drama.

Jenny Wiley's ordeal as an Indian captive was not unique. From the very beginning of America's history, women and children from the northern colonies had been captured by Indians. Between 1675 and 1763 approximately 1,641 New Englanders were captured by Native Americans. Some, like Jenny, escaped. Others were purchased from bondage by their families. These accounts of women and children held captive by "heathen" Indians became the first "bestsellers" in American literary history. Stories of "proper" Christian women brutalized as slaves and raped or forced to marry Indian men was the same formula for book sales that often creates bestsellers today — sex and violence. Mary Rowland's story, published in 1682, was widely read and a classic example of captivity narratives that stirred the fears of English colonists in North America.

Jenny Wiley, the daughter of Hezekiah Sellards, was born around 1760 in Pennsylvania. She married Thomas Wiley in 1779, and they built a home on the Virginia frontier. Like most eighteenth century women living in the English colonies, Jenny had heard dozens of stories like Mary Rowland's.

Women who were Indian captives often witnessed, as Jenny did, the murder and scalping of husbands, sons, and brothers. They surrendered their propriety to the harsh circumstances of slave labor and captivity. They were no longer able to wear clean or "proper" clothes and often surrendered much more than their modesty to their Indian captors.

When Jenny Wiley dictated her story in 1831, the last year of her life, and when Harry Caudill published it in 1969, they both saw the story as a dramatic episode in Kentucky's frontier history. Today Jenny's story is part of a genre of American literature: the Indian captivity narrative, and it is being examined within the broader context of postmodern literary and cultural analysis. What follows is a more detailed assessment of *Dark Hills to Westward: The Saga of Jenny Wiley*.

THE SAGA OF JENNY WILEY

Kentucky's pioneer history has provided fertile ground for writers of literature as well as for historians. Nineteenth century writers of historical fiction like John Alexander McClung, Robert Montgomery Bird, and James Weir paved the way for twentieth century novelists like Joseph Alexander Altsheler, Janice Holt Giles, and Elizabeth Maddox Roberts.

In *The Great Meadow*, perhaps the best novel ever written on Kentucky frontier life, Roberts describes the opening of the land beyond the Appalachian mountains as an American epic, observing of Daniel Boone and his contemporaries that "there were giants in the earth in those days." The same might be said of the generation of authors that followed her onto the dark and bloody ground of Kentucky's frontier fiction. Certainly one of those giants was the late Harry M. Caudill, a highly respected statesman and, at times, a controversial polemicist.

Best known for non-fiction works like *Night Comes to the Cumberlands* and *The Watches of the Night*, Caudill also wrote fiction, including *Dark Hills to Westward: The Saga of Jenny Wiley*, first published in 1969. A preacher sat down with Jenny Wiley in 1831 and wrote out her story, and although Jenny may have embellished it many times, it is the only first-hand account we have.

It is also the basis for Caudill's novel. He traces Jenny's year in captivity — a time when she saw her babies murdered and a white captive tortured to death — and tells the thrilling story of her escape. It is not a story for young children or the faint of heart! His vivid prose presents a clear picture of Jenny's courage, and offers keen insight into the physical fatigue and psychological stress of her ordeal. As the late William S. Ward observed in *A Literary History of Kentucky*, Caudill does more than tell Jenny Wiley's story: "He achieves a picture of a time and place in history when toughness, courage, and resourcefulness were essential human qualities if one were to survive." Jenny was a survivor.

Immediately upon its publication in 1969, *The Saga of Jenny Wiley* was hailed as a significant contribution to the body of literature and lore that surrounds this frontier heroine. Among the kindred studies useful for background information are *Jenny Wiley, Pioneer Mother and Borderland Heroine* by Henry P. Scalf of Prestonsburg, and *The Founding of Harman's Station and the Wiley Captivity* by William Elsey Connelley, with four additional chapters by Edward R. Hazelett of Paintsville.

When Caudill published *Jenny Wiley*, he was already nationally known as the author of *Night Comes to the Cumberlands*, a study of Appalachia and he was seen as an expert on the region's economic and social problems. This reputation prompted immediate interest in his novel, which was widely reviewed.

While the reviewers praised *Jenny Wiley*, they also found fault with Caudill's venture into historical fiction. The book received criticism for poor character development and unconvincing dialogue, but the harshest criticisms concerned Caudill's treatment of the Indians as simply bloodthirsty savages. Tom Bethell's detailed and insightful review in *The Mountain Eagle* (Whitesburg, Kentucky) offered a middle-ground assessment: "The treatment of Indians weakens this book; but it is still a first-rate piece of storytelling — occasionally in a class with Mark Twain and Kenneth Roberts and always unraveled with the kind of persistent enthusiasm that makes Harry Caudill well worth listening to, and well worth reading."

So, be forewarned. If you are looking for a "politically correct' version of race relations, you will not find it here. Like the great fireside storytellers that Harry M. Caudill descended from and represented, he tells a searing story from the perspective of Jenny and her white contemporaries. Readers should keep in

25

mind that Caudill did not write the book as an historian, but as a storyteller, and his goal was to tell Jenny's story as she experienced it.

Several changes have been made in the 1997 edition of *The Saga of Jenny Wiley*. The book has been completely redesigned, with larger page size and print size for easier reading. A lengthy historical Introduction has been moved to the end of the text and re-titled "Author's Historical Afterword." The spelling of "Jennie" has been changed to "Jenny" to conform to general usage, and there are some other stylistic modifications. At the request of his widow, Anne F. Caudill, the text of the book stands as Harry Caudill wrote it more than twenty-five years ago.

The 1997 edition has been greatly enhanced by Anne Caudill's Epilogue, which provides background information on the research and writing of *Jenny Wiley*. It also includes Mrs. Caudill's personal insights into her late husband's life and accomplishments.

Dark Hills to Westward: The Saga of Jenny Wiley would be useful in college-level courses that deal with Women's History or Appalachian History, or it would be an excellent supplementary text in American History survey courses. It is a must for adult readers who want to learn more about pioneer life in Eastern Kentucky.

DANIEL WILLIAMS

PIONEER PREACHER OF
EASTERN KENTUCKY

By John Sparks

Blessed are the people that know the joyful sound: they shall walk, O Lord, in the light of thy countenance.

> *—Psalm 89:15, sermon text taken by Elder Daniel Williams at the first annual meeting of the Burning Springs Association of Baptists, October 1813*

In the middle of an early summer day in 1820, the body of an obscure backwoods preacher was laid to rest on a point a few ridges over from the Big Sandy Valley by his family, neighbors, and fellow church members. The larger world took little, if any, note of the minister's passing; but if Ralph Waldo Emerson's observation, "I am a part of all that I have met," is true for all of us, the small crowd of eastern Kentucky settlers buried not only their community's spiritual leader, but a crucial link to the outside world, which in some of its aspects would not be renewed until

Elders John "Racoon" Smith, 1784-1868 (left), and Jeremiah Vardeman, 1775-1842, successors of Daniel Williams to the pastorate of Lulbegrud Church.

our own modern era. For in his youth in the Bluegrass Region of central Kentucky, Elder Daniel Williams had known and worked with makers and shapers of history before moving to the eastern mountains and creating a bit of history of his own. And if he was, like Emerson, a part of all he had met, he was a complex character, a mix of erudition and superstition, joy and sorrow, faith and doubt, and reassurance and perplexity, that is still very much a part of the religious world of the Big Sandy Valley in the twenty-first century.

One of the more prominent points of disagreement among genealogists about Daniel Williams is his ancestry. It is generally agreed that his father was named Edward, or Ned, but some local pedigree buffs swear by their honor that he was actually the son of Isaac Williams, whom they rename "Isaac Edward" and who was the first husband of Jefferson Davis' paternal grandmother

— making Daniel Williams, as it were, a half-uncle of the first and only President of the Confederate States of America. In truth, similar grandiose tall tales are not uncommon in the older genealogies of the pioneer families of both central and eastern Kentucky, which has more Colonels in it than any other state in the Union. It is likely that this legend got started during or in the aftermath of the Civil War, when partisan passions ran high in most eastern Kentucky counties and one of Daniel Williams' grandsons was a Confederate militia leader of some regional renown.

Another, more down-to-earth, story would hold that Daniel's mother's maiden name was Jemima Anderson, daughter of one "Captain John Anderson" and sister of Nicholas Anderson, the latter of whom was in fact closely associated in court and other records with Edward Williams. The assumption seems to have been made that Jemima must have been a sister of Nicholas Anderson, thus explaining the close links between Edward's and Nicholas' families over several years. Whatever Edward Williams' and Nicholas Anderson's partnership entailed, though, at this writing the best historical evidence compiled by the most competent genealogists tells us that Daniel Williams was born some time in the spring of 1763 in Prince George County, Virginia, near present Quantico, and was the son of Edward and Jemima (Carter) Williams — Jemima being related in a collateral line to a prominent Old Dominion planter family from that area and Edward perhaps coming from Quaker stock in Pennsylvania and migrating to Prince George County.

What is certain, though, is the record of Edward and

Jemima Williams' and Nicholas Anderson's church relationships. A Regular Baptist congregation was gathered on Chopawamsic Creek in Prince George County on November 22, 1766 by the ministers William and Daniel Fristoe, and Edward Williams and "Niclos Antherson" were received into this fellowship by profession of faith and baptism a little over a year later, on November 24, 1767. Nine days after Edward's and Nicholas' baptisms, "Jemiah Williams" was immersed and admitted to membership in the church as well. The Williams and Anderson conversions took place in the heyday of the Great Virginia Baptist Revival of the late 1760s, when the other major sub-denomination of the Baptists in the American colonies, the Separates under the leadership of Elder Shubal Stearns in North Carolina, began to move into Virginia to hold revival meetings. Before then, the Regular Baptists had been rather staid and formal, believing, like the Presbyterians, that salvation was limited to a certain number of "God's elect;" but the loud and boisterous Separate Baptists were more inclined to believe in a salvation that was available to all through repentance. Thus at this point in time, under the influence of the musical, hypnotic "New England Holy Tone" preaching cant brought south by Shubal Stearns and copied by virtually all the younger preachers led by him, Virginia's Regular Baptists had suddenly become almost as emotional and evangelistic as the Separates.

Though the descendants of Edward Williams have sometimes claimed that he was one of the first settlers at Boonesborough with Daniel Boone in 1775, court records indicate that neither Edward Williams nor Nicholas Anderson brought their families to the Kentucky territory until 1779, when the two men secured land grants on Lulbegrud Creek some miles east of Boonesborough in what is now Montgomery County (first Fayette County, then Bourbon, then Clark). This is not to say that Edward and Jemima Williams and their children were not pioneers in every sense of the word, however. Kentucky was a completely wild land in those days, and although the town of Lexington, forty-odd miles to the west of Lulbegrud Creek, soon came to boast of itself as "the Athens of the West," no settlement in the Kentucky territory would be free from the danger of Indian attacks until at least 1794. Edward and his sons, including young Daniel, had to clear away giant virgin timber to make "new grounds" for farming, often with loaded rifles or muskets and bullet pouches and powder horns slung from their shoulders. Though there is no certain record of it, the teenaged Daniel is also said to have participated in the last battle of the Revolutionary War as well: the bloody 1782 Battle of Blue Licks in present Robertson County, Kentucky, occurring months after Cornwallis' surrender at the Battle of Yorktown because news traveled so slowly. The fray pitted settlers against a combined force of British and Indians, and Daniel Boone's son Israel was one of the many fatalities.

For all the rough-and-tumble violence implicit in Kentucky living in that day and time, though, civilization was coming. A year or two before the Blue Licks battle, the first Baptist churches in the territory had been organized. The members of at least one of these, located on Gilbert's Creek south of the Kentucky River, had migrated together from Virginia into the new land, and the year after Blue Licks another "traveling congregation" from the Old

Dominion stopped, settled, and built a church house from the region's native limestone between Boonesborough and Lulbegrud Creek, complete with firing slits chiseled in the building's sides as a precaution against Indian attack. This building still stands on a secondary road off Kentucky Route 627 between Winchester and Boonesborough, the turnoff marked by a Kentucky Historical Society plaque. The fellowship styled itself as the Providence Church, and many of the charter members came from Orange County, Virginia although others seem to have joined up during a stopover along the Wilderness Road at a settlement known as Wolf Hills (present-day Abingdon in southwestern Virginia's Washington County). The flock's pastor was Robert Elkin, a minister who had begun to preach in 1771 at the Dan River Separate Baptist Church in Pittsylvania County, Virginia under the leadership of its pastor, Dutton Lane, and who later linked up with the church's organizers in Orange County to move to the new land with them.

Although a great number of Virginia's Separate Baptists became Regular Baptists after they migrated to Kentucky, adopting the Regular Baptist creedal statement known as the Philadelphia Confession once they got to the new territory, Robert Elkin's Providence Church was perhaps the largest and most powerful Baptist congregation in the Bluegrass Region that still held to Separate Baptist principles: no creedal statement but the Bible itself, salvation available to all, and the musical, emotion-inspiring New England Holy Tone preaching cant. The Kentucky Regular Baptists organized two new associations in the territory in 1785, known as Salem and Elkhorn and both of which adopted the Philadelphia Confession, but those churches wishing to remain Separate Baptist stayed apart until 1787 when they organized the South Kentucky Association of Separate Baptists. Robert Elkin assumed and effectively continued in a leadership role for this group until the two Baptist factions joined together to form the United Baptists in 1801.

Oddly, Edward and Jemima Williams and Nicholas Anderson and their children seem to have bucked the trend, as it were, religiously: whereas many if not most Separate Baptists became Regular Baptists after moving from Virginia to Kentucky, the Williams and Anderson families converted the other way, from Regular Baptists to Separate Baptists. The records of Elkin's Providence Church indicate that Edward, Jemima, and Nicholas all applied for membership and were received "by experience," without having to be re-baptized, on September 8, 1787. A month later, twenty-four year-old Daniel Williams was received "by experience and baptism" at Providence as well, and then a month after that his sister Winifred, or Winnie, was baptized and joined also.

We cannot be certain as to exactly who officiated at Daniel Williams' baptism. It could have been Robert Elkin himself, in his role as the church's pastor, but by 1787 another noted Virginia Separate minister, Andrew Tribble, had joined at Providence as well. A veteran of persecution and imprisonment in the Old Dominion for preaching and holding religious assemblies without a license from his county's court, Tribble claimed to have been "the fifty-third Baptist [converted] north of the James River," and his subsequent work with Daniel Williams might indicate that the younger man could have chosen Tribble to baptize him rather than Elkin. Regardless, Tribble gathered another Separate Baptist church on

Tate's Creek, south of the Kentucky River in Madison County, and here he pastored and preached with Daniel Boone's brother Squire, an "occasional" speaker or exhorter. Some claim that, when Daniel Williams married a young pioneer girl named Violet Crouch some time in the mid-1780s, Squire Boone officiated at the wedding ceremony, but there is no evidence that Squire Boone was ever actually ordained as a full minister, much less granted license by the Madison County Court to perform marriages.

And so Daniel and Violet Williams spent the early years of their married life going to church at Providence, and listening to the exhortations of Andrew Tribble and Robert Elkin; but about the year 1789 a controversy arose between the two senior preachers, and before it was resolved it had split Providence Church effectively in half. We cannot now know exactly what the topic or topics of dispute were, although a guess may be hazarded that it might have had something to do with an attempt at union between the Regular and Separate Baptists in Kentucky near that time. Tribble was much more willing than Elkin, at this point, to work with Regular Baptist ministers who preached election, fore-knowledge, and predestination to salvation, and one of the key issues the Regulars held against the Separates was the latter group's contention that "Christ tasted death for every man." The Tribble faction of Providence Church built a new meetinghouse on Four Mile Creek, a short distance south of Providence's meetinghouse on Howard's Creek, and known, ironically, by the name of "Unity." Andrew Tribble continued to serve here until he became entangled with a lawsuit with one of his members, resigning his pastorate and taking his membership finally to Tate's Creek. He was one of the principal organizers of the Tate's Creek Association, the first Kentucky Separate Baptist group to unite with the Regular Baptists in 1794, and likewise the first Kentucky Baptist body to assume the name of United Baptists. Yet even so, his daughter Nancy, who had married a young preacher at Unity named David Chenault, remained behind with her husband at the Unity congregation rather than follow her father to Tate's Creek.

Thus "the joyful sound" to which Daniel Williams hearkened in his younger days and about which he was to preach so memorably in years to come, involved a great deal of spirited singing, shouting, hugging, and handshaking against a backdrop of loud, musical preaching, all of which he would have believed deeply were the evidences of walking in the light of the Lord's countenance — counterbalanced, sadly, by the periodic dissonance of arguments, "broken fellowship," and schisms. This sort of give-and-take was to be part and parcel of his church experience for the rest of his life. And so in late 1793 or early 1794, when enough settlers finally warranted land and began to farm on Lulbegrud Creek and it was decided that the community was big enough to support a church of its own, one was gathered as an "arm" from Robert Elkin's Providence congregation, although a few Regular Baptists may have been involved in the new congregation as well. The church was organized not under Elkin's supervision but by Andrew Tribble and Thomas Ammen, both of whom at that point were in the active process of withdrawing from the South Kentucky Separate Baptist Association to organize the new Tate's Creek United Baptist Association. Edward and Jemima Williams were among Lulbegrud Church's charter members and the couple was chosen as deacons for the congregation in March 1794. Daniel was chosen to act as an Elder at the new church two months later, but neither he nor Violet transferred their own memberships from Providence to Lulbegrud until December of that same year. Even then, for some reason Daniel may have still preferred his older church home to his new one, since he "moved his letter" back to Providence in April 1795 and remained there one more year. This could have been for the sake of his ordination as a preacher, as he was recognized by the Clark County Court as qualified to perform marriages as a minister of the Gospel on September 22, 1795. He moved his membership back to Lulbegrud in April 1796.

Edward Williams appears to have remained a member, and a deacon, at Lulbegrud for the rest of his life. One of the last times he is mentioned in the church record book, in 1804, the year of his death, is especially poignant: in failing health, the old pioneer had to avail himself of what simple medications he could, and one of the few medicines available in those early days was whiskey. He was cited by the church at least once for drinking too much, but his fellow members ultimately decided that he should merely be "tenderly admonished and restored to his former standing." One more gross misconception about Edward and Jemima that has been maintained by some genealogists uninformed about early Kentucky law is the notion that the two were estranged from one another in their old age. The fact is that in those days women had no property rights apart from their husbands or guardians, but even so, county clerks were required by law to speak to wives "separate and apart from their husbands" and explain each of their husbands' property transactions to them before any such deeds could be registered, so that no land could be sold without the wives' knowledge. And so when Edward Williams began to deed his property to his children, including Daniel as well as his brothers Caleb and Joshua, in the days of the old woodsman's final illness, the clerk of the Montgomery County Court had to take Jemima "separate and apart" from Edward and make sure that she knew exactly what was happening. But the words *separate and apart* in connection with Jemima in the deed records stuck out, causing some researchers to speculate about a divorce that never occurred.

For his part, Daniel Williams and his growing family had left the Lulbegrud Creek area about 1798 or 1799 to settle on Sycamore Creek, several miles to the southeast, and near the present community of Jeffersonville, Kentucky. He was succeeded in the Lulbegrud pulpit first by Moses Bledsoe, then by David Barrow, and after Barrow by Jeremiah Vardeman. Williams thought so highly of this latter minister that he named his youngest son for the preacher. But at Sycamore Creek, Daniel raised up another Separate Baptist church named for the watercourse near it, and his new neighbors, including an exhorter named Ambrose Jones and several members of the Hopper, James, Lykins, Coffee, Trimble, Lacy, and other families, joined in the fellowship's constitution. At the time, Sycamore Church was one of the few organized Baptist congregations anywhere near the eastern Kentucky mountains, and some early settlers from the eastern hills may have occasionally made the journey to Jeffersonville to visit and worship at Sycamore Church. One other similar church that existed then was located on Bald Eagle Creek, a tributary of the lower Licking River in present Bath (then Bourbon) County, and attended by, among others, the families of William Ferguson and Josiah Fugate including Fugate's son Randall, daughter Sarah, and her husband Archibald Prater. This church had been led for a brief time by one Elder Samuel Hannah, a Pennsylvania veteran of the Revolutionary War who had settled, married, and been raised up to the ministry among the Separate Baptists in Bourbon County. However, Hannah had grown impatient with the difficulties he encountered in obtaining clear title to the lands he clamed in Kentucky, and for a while had moved to what were then known as the "Northwest Territories," where he had helped raise up another early church just across the Ohio from the mouth of the Kentucky's Little Sandy River. But even so, Hannah evidently still liked the Bluegrass State and eventually brought his family back to it, perhaps even at the urging of the Fugate, Ferguson, and Prater families.

While all this moving, settling, re-settling, and church organizing was going on, Kentucky found itself in the midst of the greatest and most dramatic religious revival that the state has ever known. Beginning among the Presbyterians in western Kentucky in late 1799, the so-called Great Revival spread to the Methodists and finally the Baptists in the year following and by 1801 all three groups were gaining converts, many in the thrall of the "barks," the "jerks," and other bizarre phenomena, by the hundreds. In the heyday of the Revival too old Robert Elkin finally got the concessions he wanted from the Regular Baptists, that is, terms that included the article that "the preaching [that] Christ tasted death for every man, shall be no bar to communion," and so on these so-called Terms of General Union the Kentucky Regular and Separate Baptists finally joined forces, dropped their respective names, and became the United Baptists at a meeting at Elkin's historic Providence Church in late 1801. It's quite likely that Daniel Williams, living only a few miles to the southeast, would have attended this meeting, but whether or not he did, it is certain that for the next two years or so he entered into his most active period among the central Kentucky United Baptists as a whole. His coworkers and acquaintances included some of the giants of both Kentucky and American Baptist history: John Gano, David Barrow, Ambrose Dudley, Jeremiah Vardeman, Jacob Creath, John Taylor, William Vaughan, John Price, and many others. Williams found a great deal of good, and certainly good intentions, within the new United Baptist organization — but sadly, as the Revival spirit, as it were, died down, he also discovered a great deal that was much less than perfect, unless one considers the idea that the Kentucky General Union of United Baptists was the perfect place for some very human Christians to behave very humanly.

The last act of the old South Kentucky Separate Baptist Association before its union with the Regular Baptists was the division of itself into halves, to be called North and South District Associations. Both Lulbegrud and Sycamore Churches as well as Robert Elkin's Providence flock wound up in the North District, and when this new association met for the first time, at Unity Church in October 1802, the venerable Elkin was perhaps naturally elected the group's first moderator. Among his duties was to appoint members to draft a constitution for the group, as well as appointing messengers to visit and bear "letters of correspondence" to the other Baptist associations that were in the new Union, and Daniel Williams was among his appointees for both jobs. In addition to helping write the constitution and presenting it for the association's acceptance, he was picked, along with Moses Bledsoe, to represent North District at the Elkhorn Association's 1803 meeting at the prestigious Town Fork Church in the city of Lexington. This church was very much the Lexington First Baptist of its day and time. Local legend has it that its members used the chapel of Transylvania University for their meetinghouse for a period, and for its pastor the flock boasted one of the most famous Regular Baptist ministers then known in America: John Gano, a New Jersey native who had preached and done mission work in virtually every one of the American colonies, served as moderator of the historic Philadelphia Baptist Association, and had pastored New York City's First Baptist congregation before pulling up stakes in his old age and moving to the Bluegrass State with one or two of his younger sons.

Unfortunately, Gano was an extremely strong predestination-and-foreknowledge man as well, believing and preaching even such unpleasant extensions of the doctrine as the eternal damnation of non-elected babies. After the 1801 Baptist Union he and his pastoral assistants, who included John Price and Absalom Bainbridge, began to express loud dissatisfaction with the Terms of General Union and the idea that the former Regular Baptists might get corrupted by the influence of the Separates — and this, even though John Price had been one of the Terms' signers from the Regular Baptist side. So at this summer 1803 Elkhorn Association, with both Daniel Williams and Moses Bledsoe in attendance as messengers from North District Association, Town Fork Church called for a resolution that every church in Elkhorn Association be bound to the group's "constitutional principles" regardless of the 1801 Union. It passed, and the entire proceeding was pretty much a slap in the face to every ex-Separate Baptist guest present at Town Fork for the occasion, including, of course, both Bledsoe and Williams.

At least Moses Bledsoe must have bitten his tongue and smiled, but evidently not so his traveling companion. We cannot be exactly sure what Daniel Williams voiced in response to the Town Fork resolution, but we can say with a fair degree of certainty that it must have been disapproving, blunt, and to the point. A month or so later, when North District Association convened for its 1803 annual meeting at Bethel Church in Montgomery County, John Price and fellow Town Fork member Henry Payne tagged along with Elkhorn Association's regularly appointed messengers and made sure that a complaint about Williams was presented too. Accordingly, old Elkin appointed Price, Payne, and three visiting minsters from the Tate's Creek Association along with himself personally to "look into the difficulty occurring in the church at Sycamore, and report next association."

In short, Daniel Williams suddenly found himself up to his nose in Kentucky Baptist ecclesiastical politics, simply for being outspoken about an honest opinion that his old mentor Elkin himself shared and had upheld for many years. The composition of the committee the North District moderator sent to Sycamore

Church gave the secret all away, even though Elkin more than likely included himself in it to try to give Williams a bit of discreet defense: Price and Payne were there to present the complaint, and Elkin invited the three Tate's Creek ministers, who had been working under a partial acceptance of Regular Baptist beliefs and practices for some years, along as a sort of buffer between Williams and the two Town Fork visitors. Though the men all reported at the 1804 North District meeting that the "difficulty" had been "amicably settled," the whole experience couldn't have left a good taste in Daniel Williams' mouth: one of the biggest and most prestigious "town" churches in the Bluegrass had been allowed to invade and disrupt his little flock at Sycamore, and Robert Elkin, Moses Bledsoe, and the rest of North District's leading ministers had allowed it to happen for the sake of the status quo. Williams himself didn't even bother to attend the 1804 Association meeting, although his friend Ambrose Jones did as a representative from Sycamore, and the extant records indicate that Williams attended only three more such annual North District gatherings in his life — each, apparently, because for one reason or another he thought he had to be present.

Williams' case was hardly isolated. The same year that the controversy at Town Fork occurred, South District Association split into "Jeremiah Vardeman" and "John Bailey" factions over another political fight after not quite two years of existence, with the larger (Bailey) group reassuming the name of the South Kentucky Association of Separate Baptists and which is still extant and active in south central Kentucky to this day. In addition to providing a home base for the Town Fork controversy, Elkhorn Association itself

42

kicked out a few churches and preachers that had begun to advocate Unitarian principles — among them even James Garrard, who was the sitting Governor of Kentucky. After John Gano died, Town Fork Church went to war once again, this time over a business disagreement between the new pastor, Jacob Creath, and a member named Thomas Lewis, and so odious to modern sensibilities one wonders now how two professing religionists, let alone ministers, could have been involved in it. The men had swapped slave girls, with Creath giving Lewis a promissory note for the difference in value between the two slaves, and when Creath's new slave girl died, he refused to pay off the note. Other Elkhorn churches started taking sides with one or the other of the two Town Fork factions, using the slave-swap story as a cover to disagree (once again!) over election and predestination; and before the nasty little conflict was over, Elkhorn had divided itself into two associations, with the minority, calling itself the Licking Association of Particular Baptists, becoming one of the immediate antecedents of the later "Primitive Baptist" movement. And then to cap it all off, in 1805 a new association known as Bracken presented North District Association with five "charges" against Elder David Barrow, Daniel Williams' successor in the Lulbegrud pulpit, for preaching that slavery was wrong and that slaveowners should begin gradually emancipating their human chattel. For this "abominable heresy" and "delusion" he was expelled from his seat in North District and his pastorate at Lulbegrud, and he went on to organize a small abolitionist Baptist association that called itself "The Friends to Humanity." To make a long story short, within a decade after the Great Revival was over, the Kentucky United Baptists had split into six different factions, and the main group had become a lot more skilled about what proclaiming it was *against* than what it stood *for*.

These weren't controversies that Daniel Williams simply heard about from afar. In Montgomery County, only forty- to fifty-odd miles from the seat of Bluegrass politics of both secular and religious types, they were the sum and substance of his conversations with other preachers, and often, no doubt, with his church members. We can only imagine his discouragement, especially since he'd been personally involved with one of the first post-Union fights. It is recorded that he was present, with Ambrose Jones, at the 1805 North District session where Bracken Association visitors cited David Barrow for preaching emancipation, but we should pause to remember that it was very near this point in time, according to local historians, that Daniel Williams first came to the eastern Kentucky hills, "hunting and preaching," as it were, because he so loved "solitude and the wild woods." A preacher he was, and a hunter he had to be, but this particular hunt to the east may have been more for peace of mind than anything else. A surprising number of his neighbors moved southeast at very near the same time, from both Sycamore and Bald Eagle Churches and ultimately including Williams' own brother Joshua and even his mother Jemima; we may never know how many of these Montgomery County United Baptists were simply looking to settle new territory, or how many sought the same kind of respite from church politics. To put it another way: the joyful sound, and the light of the Lord's countenance, must have seemed to Daniel Williams and a good many of his members to be leading east, towards the direction of the Big Sandy and upper Licking Valleys.

Daniel Williams apparently remained as pastor at Sycamore until at least 1809, no doubt returning to Jeffersonville one weekend a month for the church's scheduled meetings. He was then succeeded in the Sycamore pulpit by a young exhorter named William Vaughan, from the nearby Friendship Church in Clark County, and after a few years Vaughan went on to become one of the most famous Kentucky Baptist evangelists of his day, dying finally in 1876 at the age of ninety-one. He gave a detailed account of his conversion experience to Kentucky Baptist historian John Henderson Spencer, who published it in 1885 as part of his *History of Kentucky Baptists* and in the process gave an interesting look at how Baptist preachers conducted worship services and exhortations in those early days, and in his memoirs Vaughan even recalled a little about his preaching tenure in Montgomery County at Sycamore. But while the younger man was settling in at Jeffersonville, Daniel Williams was pouring his own energy into preaching and forming Baptist congregations in the eastern Kentucky mountains. The South Fork Church near present West Liberty, for the first three years or so of its existence known as "Poplar Meeting-House," was gathered as a so-called "arm" from Sycamore and organized in late 1808. Samuel Hannah had returned to Kentucky from southern Ohio a little before this, and Williams helped him organize Burning Springs Church a year and a half later at present Salyersville, principally from his fellow former members at the old Bald Eagle Church to the northwest. Williams was the first pastor of both these congregations.

Even further to the southeast, along the upper Big Sandy, ministers were entering and churches were being organized as well. Young Methodist circuit-riders, who as a rule were worked so hard by their presiding elders that their life spans averaged out only to about thirty-three years, made inroads perhaps even before the Baptists. These included Benjamin Edge, John Johnson, and Marcus Lindsey, the latter of whom became so well-known throughout the Big Sandy Valley and adjoining watercourses that the first name "Linzie" or "Linzey," initially associated with the preacher, became common throughout the nineteenth and twentieth centuries (though now perhaps it is more popular as a girl's name). But among the Big Sandy Valley Baptists, the other earliest preachers were Simeon Justice, a corpulent, very nearsighted old preacher originally from Holston Association's Little Ivy Church in Buncombe County, North Carolina, his younger colleague William Salisbury, and Electious Thompson, a Maryland native who had converted to the Baptist Church from Roman Catholicism. Justice and Salisbury gathered the Stone Coal, Mud Creek, and New Salem Churches on tributaries of the Big Sandy, and Thompson organized a congregation at the Indian Bottom in present Perry County. Yet another group of immigrants, this one from the St. Clair's Bottom Baptist Church in southwestern Virginia — actually, according to Virginia Baptist historian Robert Baylor Semple, a factional split-off over two strong and opposing pulpit personalities, one a former Regular Baptist and the other an ex-Separate — settled near the conjunction of the Big Sandy with Paint and Buffalo Creeks close to present Paintsville and organized a church in 1805. This congregation, initially known as Buffalo Shoal and later as Paint Creek and then Old Union, was first under the leadership of minister William Brundage, the "Regular Baptist" of the St. Clair's Bottom controversy; however, Brundage soon moved on to Ohio, and his place was taken by Samuel Hannah and Basil Lewis. Later on Hannah's and Lewis' efforts were aided by a larger crop of new exhorters including James Wheeler, Henry Dixon, Caleb May, and Ezekiel Stone.

For whatever reason, though, of all these varied personalities Daniel Williams seems to have been recognized as something of a natural leader by everyone. The frontier ministers had to have met more or less by chance on the banks of the Levisa Fork of Big Sandy at Prestonsburg, county seat of the enormous eastern Kentucky area then known as Floyd County and where all these new congregations were developing. Perhaps they became acquainted with one another by bringing in names of brides and grooms they had married to the County Clerk, Alexander Lackey, himself a Baptist, or perhaps while recording property transfers, or maybe simply by falling into conversation on "Court Day," which was regarded as a holiday and an excuse to make a trip to town by nearly all the early Big Sandy Valley settlers. One of the first recorded attempts at the eastern Kentucky Baptist preachers' working together involved the ordination of Ambrose Jones as a minister at South Fork (then still known as Poplar Meeting-House) in 1811; Daniel Williams made sure that his church clerk, John Lykins, wrote a letter to "Brother Jesttis" (Simeon Justice) to invite him to come and participate. Despite Williams' troubles with North District Association, both of the earliest churches he helped organize in eastern Kentucky became members of the body, Poplar Meeting-House in 1809 and Burning Springs in 1810, though Williams himself attended only the 1810 Association meeting as a messenger from Poplar Meeting-House. In 1812 he and Hannah convinced the Buffalo Shoal Church to join them as members of the association, and so that year delegates James Wheeler, Walter Mankin, and William Meek traveled all the way from Big Sandy to Robert Elkin's old Providence Church near Boonesborough to "lay in their letter" with North District. The Stone Coal, Mud Creek, and New Salem congregations headed by Justice and Salisbury remained independent of an association for the time being, though Electious Thompson's flock at Indian Bottom applied for membership in and joined the Washington District Association of southwest Virginia after it was organized in 1811.

But finally, in the midst of another dramatic revival in which Daniel Williams baptized 78 converts at South Fork and 24 more along with Samuel Hannah at Burning Springs, and during which the other eastern Kentucky churches must have grown dramatically as well, the far-flung, remote eastern Kentucky Baptist congregations became resolved to organize and maintain an association of their own. They sent representatives to a "conference" at South Fork Church in late 1812; Williams read and explained the Terms of General Union of the Kentucky Baptists and the Constitution and Rules of Decorum of North District Association to them, they agreed to accept all three documents, and then resolved to send messengers to organize the new association at Burning Springs Church in October 1813. South Fork,

Burning Springs, and Buffalo Shoal Churches all obtained letters of dismissal from North District that summer, the churches headed by Justice and Salisbury sent their delegates northward, Electious Thompson's Indian Bottom Church transferred from Washington District, two newly-organized fellowships (one from Buffalo Shoal, located on Big Blaine Creek and gathered by Basil Lewis, and the other at the head of Red River, formed from South Fork by Daniel Williams and Ambrose Jones) chipped in, and thus was born the Burning Springs Association of Baptists. And after preaching the introductory sermon for the new group's initial meeting — the occasion for his discourse on the text quoted at the beginning of our story — Daniel Williams was chosen as its first moderator.

The joyful sound that Daniel Williams sought, the light of the Lord's countenance that he searched for diligently in spite of all the unholy quarreling he had seen and would continue to see to the end of his days: from it can be traced the beginnings of almost every native religious body in the Big Sandy Valley. United Baptists, Old Regular Baptists, eastern Kentucky's Primitive Baptists, mountain Free Will Baptists, "Enterprise" Regular Baptists, Churches of Christ and Christian Churches, and even, in part, the two organizations known as the Churches of God as well as unnumbered independent so-called "non-denominational" congregations, can all be traced back to the early work of Williams and his colleagues. Daniel Williams never lived to see any of them except of course the United Baptists in their oldest form, and indeed most of their subsequent histories are far beyond the scope of this work. Yet Williams might have had a tiny inkling that at least one such body was coming: that group originally known as the Reformers, and now as Disciples of Christ, Christian Churches, and *a cappella* Churches of Christ. The success of this movement in eastern Kentucky can be traced in large part to the untiring efforts of "Raccoon" John Smith, one of Daniel Williams' successors to the pulpit of the old Lulbegrud Church and the victim of as much unfair Baptist political treatment as his older counterpart, and certainly more intense personal grief than Williams himself had ever known. The idea that *something* divine must exist above tawdry denominational scraps and squabbles, and that it was his bounden duty to find it and proclaim it, was in large part the impetus for Smith's own fiery preaching, and among his most loyal and dedicated supporters was the congregation of the Red River Church mentioned above, and its pastor after Daniel Williams' death, Joseph Nickell. Smith, Nickell, and old Samuel Hannah's nephew and namesake Samuel Jr. were the pioneer preachers of the Christian Church, or Church of Christ, Reform movement in the Big Sandy Valley, and in fact the very first individual that Daniel Williams had baptized after the consti-tution of the old Poplar Meeting-House, back in 1809, Joseph Nickell's uncle Isaac, became a charter member of the White Oak Christian Church that Raccoon John Smith and Joseph Nickell gathered in the heyday of the Reform. It is not known whether Daniel Williams would have agreed entirely with Raccoon John Smith's altered theology, but it's fairly certain he would have appreciated the difficulties that had caused Smith to change his theological positions — and for all we know, this very well may have been one reason that Joseph Nickell, who had grown up in the ministry under Williams' pastorship at Red River, was so eager to listen to Smith in the first place.

Though Burning Springs Association, still extant and active, is at present affiliated with the Primitive Baptists, as was Lulbegrud Church a few years before it became extinct and North District Association until its final meeting in 1960, of the original congregations Daniel Williams worked with in both North District and Burning Springs, the Big Blaine, Buffalo Shoal (now Old Union) and Burning Springs Churches are all United Baptist; the New Salem, Stone Coal, and Indian Bottom congregations are Old Regular Baptist; Sycamore and Red River both became Christian Churches, Sycamore later being identified with the *a cappella* Churches of Christ; and insofar as can be determined, Mud Creek Church followed this latter course as well. The reader might take note here that the United States' largest Baptist sub-denomination, the Southern Baptists, has not been mentioned so far, and in truth, if one looks at Baptist associations from a sort of genealogical or pedigree standpoint, as many traditionalist Baptist groups in this region do, the Big Sandy Valley's Southern Baptists come from an almost completely collateral "family line." Whereas Burning Springs Association was organized from North District Association, which in turn was formed from the old South Kentucky Association and its Separate Baptist antecedents in Virginia and North Carolina, eastern Kentucky's Southern Baptists originated with the Greenup Association, the first "Missionary Baptist" body on Big Sandy. Greenup Association was organized in 1841 from the Ohio Association on the southern border of that state, and Ohio Association's immediate ancestor was the Teay's Valley Association of present West Virginia. In turn, Teay's Valley

Association had been formed from the Greenbrier Association further eastward, and Greenbrier was formed jointly from Ketocton Association, one of the earliest American Regular Baptist bodies, and the New River Association, originally a Separate Baptist group. Not that any of these differences in and of themselves would have been particularly important to Daniel Williams personally, however: in 1814 Burning Springs Association formed a correspondence with the Teay's Valley Association, and for the rest of Williams' life and some years afterward the two bodies regularly exchanged yearly letters and "shared the stand" with each others' ministers at association meetings. And in 1815, this relationship between Burning Springs Association and the groups that would come to identify themselves as "Missionary Baptist" brought the most exotic visitor to Daniel Williams' cabin that the old preacher would ever know: Luther Rice, a former Congregational missionary who had been converted to Baptist principles and immersed and ordained by no less an historical personage as Rev. William Carey at the Lall Bazaar Baptist Church in Serampore, India, and who, along with Adoniram Judson, had been appointed by the eastern seacoast Baptists' Board of Foreign Missions as one of their own first missionaries.

Luther Rice and his young assistant, Bluegrass native James Welch, visited the Burning Springs Association at its third annual meeting, held at South Fork Church in October 1815 as one stop in an extended fundraising tour of Kentucky. They had missed attending North District Association by a few weeks, though Montgomery County Judge David Trimble — a member at Sycamore Church, by the way — arranged for Rice to preach in the courthouse there, and he collected a handsome sum for Adoniram Judson's brand-new mission in Burma (now known as Myanmar). Perhaps Trimble himself, who had a son, Mark, who lived in the eastern hills and was a member at South Fork, informed Rice and Welch about the upcoming Burning Springs meeting, but in any case, Rice borrowed a fresh horse from one of his hosts in the Bluegrass and set out with Welch for the mountains. The two arrived at the association site on Friday before the body was to convene on Saturday morning, and in Rice's journal for that year, preserved and housed in the Gelman Library of George Washington University in Washington, D.C., he recorded that they spent the night with Daniel Williams and his family. Williams in fact took them to church at South Fork that evening, where they met Elder John Young from Little Sandy River, a minister and visitor from the Teays' Valley Association, and a man who would prove to be an important contact for them in the future. Next day when the Association formally convened, Rice was allowed to speak and present his case for the support of Judson's mission; and not only did Williams and his flock agree to open a correspondence with the Baptist Board of Foreign Missions, they requested Rice, Welch, and John Young to preach on Sunday, followed up with an "exhortation" by Williams. And somehow, in a part of the country where hard money was as scarce as hens' teeth, on that autumn Sunday Rice managed to collect $9.82 — an enormous amount in those days—from the hill people visiting Burning Springs Association. Rice and Welch spent their second night in the mountains with South Fork member Daniel Peyton, and next day headed back for the larger world.

But as fate would have it, although John Young and Teays' Valley and later, the Ohio and Greenup Associations, all eagerly embraced Rice and his message, Burning Springs Association's correspondence with the Baptist Board of Foreign Missions was short-lived. There can be no doubt that Luther Rice was a tireless worker for the Missions Board, but he — and for that matter, James Welch, John Mason Peck, and several of the younger missionaries — sometimes behaved in ways that plain hill people such as Daniel Williams and his Big Sandy church brethren found hard to swallow. In 1819 Bluegrass Baptist minister and historian John Taylor recorded the typical climax of one of Rice's missionary sermons in a pamphlet entitled *Thoughts on Missions:* "[Rice] had the more pathos the nearer he came getting the money, and raising his arms as if he had some awfully pleasing vision, expressed without a hesitating doubt, that the angels were hovering over the assembly, and participating in our heavenly exercise, and just ready to take their leave, and bear the good tidings to heaven of what we were then about, in giving our money for the instruction and conversion of the poor heathen; and as if he had power to stop Gabriel's flight, in the most pathetic strain cried, 'Stop angels, till you have witnessed the generosity of this assembly!' About this time, perhaps twenty men, previously appointed, moved through the assembly with their hats…"

We can't say for sure that Rice carried out this same piece of stagecraft at Burning Springs Association in the fall of 1815, but if he did, we might wonder if Daniel Williams — more or less compelled by his position as moderator to round up men to pass around their hats for the missionary — would have been more surprised, annoyed, confused, embarrassed, insulted, or a combination of all. At least the display was probably not quite so bad as Tetzel's hawking indulgences in medieval Germany, or the fare one sees regularly nowadays from certain television evangelists. There's really nothing new under the sun. But for reasons good or bad, the Burning Springs Association dropped correspondence with the Baptist Board of Foreign Missions in 1819, two years longer than North District remained connected with the entity, while Teay's Valley Association steadfastly maintained its relationship with the Board. And strangely enough, neither Burning Springs nor Teay's Valley Associations felt behooved to quarrel about this particular difference between them for nearly twenty years more. Now, the descendants of both groups continue to worship up and down the shores of Big Sandy, still disagreeing over the issues John Taylor articulated all the way back in 1819, but one set as committed as the other, each in its own individual way, to carry out the commission they feel they were given by the Lord.

By the time Burning Springs Association severed its relationship with the Foreign Missions Board, Daniel Williams had moved even further into the hills, roughly halfway between his pastorates at South Fork and Red River on a watercourse known both then and now as Caney Creek. Frequently he would conduct worship services at his own home in addition to the one-weekend-a-month meetings of his pastoral charges, and tradition has it that he kept an old hunter's horn which he would blow from the top of a nearby hill to summon his neighbors to worship much as a Jewish *Baal Tekiyah* might sound a *shofar*, or a *muezzin* might climb a minaret to call observant Muslims to prayer at a mosque. But the most poignant story associated with the aging preacher is that of perhaps the next-to-last cabin that he ever constructed. On upper Caney Creek he and his younger sons found enormous quantities of a shiny black rock jutting from outcroppings on the hillsides, completely unfamiliar to them but light, easy to carry and extremely easily worked with a hammer and chisel. And so Daniel Williams built himself a fine, elegant chimney from the exotic rock as an adornment to his new cabin on Caney, but no sooner had Violet attempted to cook a meal over the fire (stoves didn't exist at that early date, at least anywhere near Big Sandy) than the chimney itself ignited and burned the entire house to the ground. So far as is known there were no casualties, and of course neighbors would have helped the family get back on its feet from the blaze. But of course the "new rock" was cannel coal, most readily inflammable of all coals and for which the mining town of Cannel City at the head of Caney Creek would be named nearly a hundred years later. Until Daniel Williams learned the hard way, few if any of the early settlers quite knew what to do with it. One wonders if Williams might have tried to draw a spiritual lesson from his experience, and perhaps preached about it: don't put too much faith or confidence in a worldly thing like that shiny black rock, because it may look pretty but one day it'll burn your house down right over you… and if only the men and women of the country around and about him on Big Sandy and its neighboring watercourses had taken such a message to heart, how different might our environment be now…

But we will never know. Daniel Williams died on July 3,

1820, at the age of fifty-seven years and four months. His mother survived him for at least eight years, tradition holding that she moved back to the Bluegrass for a time with her younger son Caleb, a Lexington cobbler, before he left Kentucky for Missouri, and that she then returned to the hills to spend her last days with the family of one of Daniel's daughters and sons-in-law. Violet Williams survived her husband by perhaps a decade as well, and his preaching partners Ambrose Jones until 1833 and Samuel Hannah 'til 1839, after homesteading with his sons first in Illinois and then in Arkansas. Daniel Williams' ministry was one of the principal historical conduits through which a great many of the religious expressions of the Big Sandy Valley entered from the larger, more "civilized" world, and after which they developed a life, and a character, all their own in Big Sandy soil. Blessed are the people that know the joyful sound, the old patriarch was wont to preach, and we might still learn from his example to try to be content with the joy of the hunt rather than the finding — because the discovery, after all, is always over the next hill.

George W. Gallup

COL. GEORGE W. GALLUP

By John David Preston

George W. Gallup was born October 28, 1828, in Albany, New York. His ancestors on his father's side came to America on the *Mayflower*. His father, Gideon Gallup, was a contractor and builder. His mother came from Belgian ancestors. Colonel Gallup was educated at the Aurora Academy and Central College. He taught school from 1845 to 1849. In 1849, he also began the study of law at Burlington, Ohio. He continued his study with Laban T. Moore, at Louisa, Kentucky, and was admitted to the bar. He engaged in merchandising for two years and then began a law practice with Moore, which continued until the beginning of the Civil War.

In 1851, Gallup, a member of the Methodist Episcopal Church, South, married Rebecca A. Moore, daughter of Permelia VanHorn Moore and Frederick Moore, who was a pioneer settler of Lawrence County. George and Rebecca had three children: Mary died in infancy; Harry died at the age of twelve; and Gideon Frederick Gallup became involved in the railway business and also served as postmaster at Catlettsburg. By virtue of his marriage, Gallup became a brother-in-law to his mentor Laban T. Moore, who served in the United States Congress from 1859 through 1861.

Gallup became involved in the great national conflict early on. In a request for leave written on August 14, 1864, he said that he had been engaged in the service of the state or federal government service since April 1861, when he began recruiting a group of Kentucky Home Guards. At that time, he became responsible for 300 stands of arms used by his regiment while they served as Home Guards. In August 1861, he applied to Major General Robert Anderson, of Fort Sumter fame, then the commander of the military district of Kentucky, for permission to raise a regiment for military service. Gallup personally signed a receipt for all the clothing, camp and garrison equipment, quartermaster and subsistence stores for a regiment of 980 men.

As a result of the efforts of Gallup and others, the Fourteenth Kentucky Infantry, U.S.A. was organized on November 19, 1861, at Louisa. Several hundred men were enrolled on that date and mustered into United States service on December 10, 1861, at Louisa. The thirty-one year old Gallup joined for three years or the duration of the war. His initial rank was that of quartermaster and first lieutenant. His brother in law, Laban T. Moore, was named colonel of the regiment. Military service evidently did not suit Moore, as he resigned his commission only a few days later, on January 1, 1862. He was succeeded by John C. Cochran, a resident of Lexington, Kentucky.

The Fourteenth Kentucky Infantry was assigned to Colonel James A. Garfield's Eighteenth Brigade, which was involved in the eastern Kentucky campaign of December 1861-January 1862. A portion of the Fourteenth Kentucky was involved in the Battle of Middle Creek, fought in Floyd County on January 10, 1862. One soldier of the Fourteenth, Sergeant Nelson Boggs, of Blaine, was killed in action in that battle.

In March 1862, the Fourteenth Kentucky was ordered to accompany Brigadier General Garfield to central Kentucky for service there. On April 5, 1862, the regiment left Louisville for Lexington. On April 12, 1862, he wrote to his wife Rebecca that he and his regiment were going to Cumberland Ford, in Bell County, to drill, and that they would be assigned to General George W. Morgan's Seventh Division. The regiment was assigned to the Twenty-sixth Brigade on April 14, 1862, under the command of Colonel John F. De Courcy. Morgan's division was assigned the task of defending the Cumberland Gap, deemed to be of vital importance in preventing a Confederate invasion of Kentucky. On May 9, 1862, Joseph R. Brown, of Boyd County, lieutenant colonel of the Fourteenth, died at Lexington. Two days later, Gallup was appointed lieutenant colonel to replace Brown. In receiving the promotion, he was promoted over a major and ten captains.

Gallup soon received another promotion. On June 21, 1862, he was appointed provost marshal for the Seventh Division. In a letter dated June 30, 1862, he told Rebecca that he had an office, five clerks, eighteen officers to assist him and 200 soldiers as guards. His job consisted of dealing with infractions by soldiers and trying them for those offenses. He was also in charge of issuing passes and dealing with restoring property to civilians. Undoubtedly, his legal experience was a major factor in his being chosen for the post.

Morgan's division occupied Cumberland Gap until September 1862. The poor condition of the roads from central Kentucky, and the lack of railroads, made supplying the Gap difficult, and the division ultimately withdrew and made an arduous 180 mile march to Greenup. Immediately prior to the army's withdrawal from the Gap, Gallup, who had clearly earned the trust and confidence of General Morgan, was assigned a special task. Before evacuating, the army needed to dispose of a large quantity of firearms, lead, ammunition, cannon balls and other paraphernalia of war to keep them from falling into the hands of the Confederates, the Union troops being unable to transport the material. Troops dug a large pit for the equipment and engineers set explosive devices to detonate the supplies. Gallup assigned men to destroy the material, when, on September 17, a group of Confederates approached under a flag of truce. The Confederates said they wanted to talk about surrender by the Union troops, but they really wanted to observe Union preparations for evacuation. Gallup led a small detail of soldiers and officers to meet with the Confederates, which occurred at dusk on the south side of the Gap. The parties engaged in some discussions for about an hour, when a glare of smoke and fire appeared from the Gap itself. The Confederate officer asked what it meant. The quick-witted Gallup replied that Morgan had cut timber obstructing the range of his cannon, and was burning the brush. The explanation satisfied the Confederates, and Gallup and Morgan were able to evacuate the Gap and destroy the supplies without tipping their hand to the Confederates.

On September 20, 1862, Gallup rejoined his regiment. On October 11, 1862, the Fourteenth Kentucky was ordered to report to Covington, Kentucky, and report to Major General Gordon Granger. The Fourteenth Kentucky spent the remainder of the year in the central part of the state. On January 12, 1863, Colonel John C. Cochran resigned, and Gallup was promoted to colonel the next day. On January 30, 1863, the regiment was ordered to proceed to Louisa and report to Brigadier General Julius White. On August 6, 1863, White was ordered from the state and with him went several out of state units. The only regiments left in eastern Kentucky were the Fourteenth and Thirty-ninth Kentucky Infantry units, and they were placed under Colonel Gallup's command on July 30, 1863. Gallup was the commander of the Military District of Eastern Kentucky from that time until May 1864.

On April 15, 1863, a skirmish took place at Pikeville. Gallup learned that Major James M. French had set up a camp there. He directed Colonel John Dils with 200 mounted men of the Thirty-ninth Kentucky Mounted Infantry to attack the Confederates. The Union troops attacked at dawn on April 15 and completely surprised the Confederates. Gallup reported that the troops captured eighty-seven men, including Major French, as well as their equipment.

Gallup's troops were active during his command. Units engaged Confederates on October 10, 1863 and November 30, 1863, at Salyersville. On January 9, 1864, Confederates surprised Union troops at Turman's Ferry, in Boyd County, which resulted in one death, eight prisoners, and numerous frost-bitten Union troops. Gallup was determined not to let the attack go unavenged. On February 15, 1864, he led Union troops on a raid in Wayne County, West Virginia, at a place named Murder Hollow, in which the Union troops surrounded the Confederates and routed them. Gallup's men killed ten Confederates and captured about forty more, including Colonel Milton J. Ferguson.

Gallup's finest hour as commander in eastern Kentucky occurred in April 1864. On March 28, 1864, Confederate Colonel Ezekiel F. Clay led 560 mounted men on a raid into Kentucky. Gallup mobilized his troops and dispersed them to various parts of eastern Kentucky. They skirmished with the Confederates at the forks of Beaver in Floyd County, on Quicksand Creek in Breathitt County and on Brushy Creek in Pike County. Gallup surmised that the Confederates intended to raid Paintsville and concentrated his 900 man contingent there by April 12. The Confederates attacked the next day, part of the fight taking place around the courthouse and more fighting taking place on a hill behind the town. Stung by the stiff Union resistance, the Confederates retreated from the town. Union casualties, killed, wounded and captured, numbered ten; Confederate losses were eleven.

Unlike more passive commanders, Gallup was not content with having driven off the Confederates. Shortly after their departure, he gathered his troops together and pursued them. He learned they were probably headed for a place in Magoffin County called "the Meadows," so named because of its good grazing for horses. Gallup's troops traveled through the night, and came upon the unsuspecting Confederates the next day,

April 14. They launched into them, and a fierce four and a half battle ensued. At the end of the day, the Confederates were completely routed. Gallup reported that sixty Confederates were killed or wounded, that sixty prisoners were taken and 200 horses, 400 saddles and 300 small arms were captured. One of the prisoners was Colonel Clay, who had an eye shot out in the battle.

On May 12, 1864, Gallup was relieved as commander for the Eastern District of Kentucky, and he and the Fourteenth Kentucky were sent south to join the Army of the Ohio under the overall command of General William T. Sherman. Although the move was a good one militarily, for the Fourteenth was an excellent regiment, Gallup called into the question the motives of those who had orchestrated the move. In a letter of August 1, 1864, Gallup told his wife that he believed that the removal of him and his regiment from eastern Kentucky was designed to prevent his being named brigadier general. He squarely placed the blame on Major General Stephen G. Burbridge, military commander of Kentucky, attributing it to Burbridge's mercenary motives and desire to save his friends. Gallup had complained to his wife about the state of affairs in Eastern Kentucky in his absence in a letter written two days earlier. He wrote: "The rebels are having everything their own way up in Ky. now. Burbridge, Brown & Co. engineered me out once, now find the Eastern District helpless and really the Pandora's box from which issues troubles they cannot control." The Brown of whom Gallup spoke was most likely John Mason Brown, colonel of the Forty-fifth Kentucky Infantry. William Ely, in his essay on Gallup, stated that Gallup would doubtless have attained a general's rank, had not red tape and jealousy prevented it.

Gallup's regiment faced hard fighting in Georgia. On June 22, 1864, he wrote his wife about heavy fighting near Marietta, Georgia. He told her his regiment was ordered to advance toward the Confederate line of battle about noon. They marched about a mile and captured forty-five enemy pickets. Confederates under General Patrick Cleburne attacked with two brigades, forcing Gallup's men to retreat a half mile. In the battle, Gallup claimed his men killed 104 rebels, wounded 250 and captured forty-five men. Unfortunately, his regiment suffered seventy-seven men killed and wounded, of 700 engaged, by far the worst day his regiment endured during the entire war. The next day, Brigadier General Milo S. Hascall formally commended Gallup and his regiment for their courage and bravery in the fighting.

Conditions at the front were miserable. For example, on July 9, he told Rebecca that his men had bathed for the first time in forty-two days. He kept her abreast of the continuing toll of war on his ranks. On July 21, 1864, he had two men killed and nine wounded. The next day, he reported the loss of six men. On August 3, he lost seven men; the next day, he had five men killed. On August 5, he sustained the loss of five more men. The loss of men had its effect on Gallup. In his diary entry of August 10, 1864, he wrote, "Sergt. George, Co. K, a brave and noble soldier has fallen today. A martyr offered up on the altar of his country. I feel deeply his loss. I am not fit to command men I love so well. None falls without causing me a pang of sorrow. May God preserve our men and restore them to their families."

On August 17, he was pleased to report that he had lost no men since August 10. He also observed the savage effects of war on the civilian population. Upon seeing the burned out remains of a once-fine residence near Decatur, Georgia, he wrote to Rebecca on September 8, as follows: "What a picture I am called to witness today. It does seem that God has cursed this people for their secession and no one with a heart can go by and see their suffering unmoved." After the fall of Atlanta, Gallup was placed in command of the First Brigade, Second Division, Twenty-third Army Corps, which he commanded until November 1864.

In November 1864, Governor Thomas Bramlette requested the return of the Fourteenth Kentucky to the state, and, on November 15, the unit was ordered to join the First Division of the Military District of Kentucky and to report to Louisa. By an order issued the next day, Colonel Gallup was placed in command of all troops at Louisa, which included the Fourteenth and the Thirty-ninth. The regiment remained there in relative peace until being mustered out there on January 31, 1865. Gallup was mustered out with his regiment. A total of 1,325 men had been mustered into the unit over time. Of that number, thirty-nine had been killed, 138 had died and 107 had been discharged. Factoring in transfers and desertions, 521 men were mustered out on their last day of service.

George W. Gallup thus returned to civilian life. One more military honor was yet to be bestowed on him. On July 16, 1867, by General Order No. 67 signed by President Andrew Johnson, Gallup was appointed to the honorary rank of brigadier general by brevet. The order recited Gallup's gallant and meritorious service during the war. Gallup was the only person from eastern Kentucky on either side to achieve that rank.

After the war, Gallup returned to Louisa, where he did not practice law, but was engaged in the milling and lumbering business. He moved to Catlettsburg and became a contractor for the C & O Railroad. He became involved in the Key's Creek Mining Railroad, but suffered financial losses on that venture. Gallup ran for state senator on the Democrat ticket in 1866, but was defeated in that venture. He then joined the Republican Party. He was appointed Postmaster at Catlettsburg and held that position until his death on December 31, 1880 at Catlettsburg. He was buried in the Ashland Cemetery.

George W. Gallup's contribution to eastern Kentucky lay in his military service during the Civil War. His brave leadership of his regiment as part of Sherman's army in Georgia contributed to Union victories in that theater. His bold and aggressive leadership of Union troops in eastern Kentucky helped to maintain Union control of that region. For these reasons, Gallup is one of the unsung heroes of the Big Sandy Valley.

JOHN C.C. MAYO

By Harry M. Caudill

John Caldwell Calhoun Mayo was born on September 16, 1864 on an exhausted mountain farm in Pike County. In that

John C.C. Mayo

time, rural hill people drew most of their sustenance from the soil — corn, vegetables, milk, sweetening, meat, and the flax and wool that composed the rough fabric that covered their backs. The Mayo family lived in this hard and simple fashion when their son was born near the end of the Civil War. In 1879, when Mayo was fifteen, his father sent him to the home of a sick neighbor to cut firewood. The barefoot boy, dressed in a simple garment, chopped the wood into suitable pieces. The ailing neighbor bore the old English name of Buckingham, and his five year old son watched the wood-chopper at work. He and young Mayo liked each other from that first meeting. They rose in the world together; Mayo became Kentucky's wealthiest man, and Buckingham, his student and business associate, became his banker and a co-executor of his will.

Young Mayo acquired an education that became the base for a hugely successful life. Untold thousands of Appalachian youths have grown up illiterate due to lack of opportunities. Mayo was different. His father moved to a more promising farm down the Big Sandy in Johnson County, and the boy got up in the frosty mornings and made his way to the rough, log schoolhouse nearby. The heat came from a cavernous fireplace; the floor was made of puncheons, and the seats were split-log benches. Like Abraham Lincoln, Mayo began life with an ax in his hand and learned his letters in a boisterous blab school presided over by a teacher who never attended a college.

Mayo was a voracious learner. He read all the books that were available to him in Johnson County and, in due time, did something almost unheard of in the hills in that era: he attended college. In better clothing purchased with borrowed money, he rode a mule to the nearest railhead and caught a train to Kentucky Wesleyan College at Millersburg, where his intense application to his studies soon paid off. At sixteen, Mayo qualified to teach a term in one of the old-field districts. He had learned enough to recognize his immense need for further learning, and he resolved to obtain a decent education. Mayo worked much of the time to raise funds. Still, he required help from home and, at great hazard to themselves, his parents provided a few hundred dollars to supplement their son's meager resources. Money was so scarce and times were so hard that John's father, Thomas Jefferson Mayo, had to mortgage his hard-won farm to raise money for his son's venture into higher education.

At Kentucky Wesleyan College, Mayo was quiet but brilliant. His mathematical skills led to a job as part-time instructor assisting fellow students. Upon graduation in 1886, he had a Bachelor's degree and a First Class certificate to teach public school. Mayo had not limited his studies to spelling, composition, history, grammar, and arithmetic; he heard lectures in geology by Professor A. C. Sherwood and learned for the first time about the extensive mineral resources of his native hills. The college library contained copies of voluminous geological surveys, and he spent hours poring over them, filling notebooks with data and comments.

After graduating, Mayo returned home to pay off the mortgage on his father's farm. Hill society had been so divided by the Civil War that the schools in Johnson County were segregated — not by race, but by politics. Mayo taught at the Democratic school in Paintsville for several years, earning a monthly salary of forty dollars. He kept his humble classroom meticulously clean. The blackboard was regularly washed and adorned with poetry, which he required his students to memorize and repeat on demand. He loaded his students with homework and insisted that they do it. He brought fresh flowers to brighten the drab place, and managed to inspire many of his charges with a vision of the vast and beckoning world beyond the hilltops. Even forty dollars a month was a considerable sum, and Mayo saved enough to pay off his parents' troublesome mortgage.

Mayo continued teaching for over a decade before he met Alice Meeks. The graceful young woman was one of his students and impressed him as precisely the kind of wife an ambitious man required. He judged well, for she became his sturdy right arm for the remaining seventeen years of his life. At the time of their marriage in 1897, she was sixteen — half the age of the groom. At his marriage, Mayo had come a long way from the country boy chopping firewood. He had studied law and gained admittance to the bar; while he never practiced extensively his law studies enabled him to draft one of eastern Kentucky's most important legal documents — the mineral conveyance, widely known as the Mayo deed or the broad-form deed.

In 1890, at the age of twenty-six, Mayo engineered a tremendously important change in the state's basic law. In that year, a convention assembled at Frankfort to write a new consti- tution. Mayo was not a member of the convention, but his friend and kinsman, attorney A. J. Auxier, was. He and Mayo had often discussed the ancient Virginia grants that complicated the land titles and the very future of Kentucky. The state's previous con- stitutions had contained an express sanction of the Virginia Compact that rendered the grants inviolable.

While teaching, Mayo managed to save 150 dollars. With that modest capital, he set out to transform the Kentucky hills and their people. In 1892, he found partners who were willing to risk a few of their hard-earned dollars — John W. Castle and Dr. I. R. Turner — and they formed the trading firm of Castle, Turner & Mayo, Inc. Each partner contributed 150 dollars, and with 450 dollars, Mayo began building his empire. His methods were simple: he combed through the deed books in the county court houses, identified the landowners with the best semblance of title, and compared the lands against his notes made in the college library at Millersburg. Where titles to valuable minerals appeared worth the risk, he approached the landowner and offered him fifty cents or one dollar to buy the minerals underlying his land. The agreement lasted several years and provided for ultimate payments of fifty cents to six dollars per acre. In almost all instances, the farmers were eager to execute the options, signing their names and praying that Mayo could raise the purchase money within the time specified. Eventually, Mayo bought out his partners, retained the options in his own name, and continued buying with the small sums saved from his teacher's salary. In 1893, he contacted the Merritt brothers of Duluth, Minnesota, known in the world of steel as "the iron brothers." Mayo persuaded the brothers that a gigantic steel industry could be built in the area of Ironton, Ohio and Ashland, Kentucky, for Mayo testified that is where coal and iron meet.

Mayo became "land poor," the owner of tens of thousands of acres of valuable minerals but no money. To combat this, Mayo went back to his friend John Buckingham and borrowed a few dollars for printing and postage. He prepared a letter describing his mineral lands and mailed them to dozens of industrialists in major U.S. cities. One of the letters fell into the receptive hands of Peter L. Kimberly, the president of the Sharon Steel and Hoop Company. Kimberly sent Mayo a telegram inviting him to come to Chicago for a conference, and the faithful Buckingham financed the trip. The wire from Kimberly came in the nick of time;

options for thousands of acres had expired or were about to, and imploring mountaineers were hounding his tracks. They begged him to find the promised funds for the purchase of their minerals and threatened to sell them to other bidders. Mayo urged them to be patient and promised them more than any of the late-comers would pay. He kept his word; he paid little for his acquisitions, but he routinely paid more than his competitors in the land market.

When Mayo returned from meeting his new partner in Chicago, he was a different man. He wore a new suit and with it an air of brash confidence. He had signed a contract under which Kimberly's company would pay him five dollars per acre for mineral lands in Letcher, Pike, and Floyd counties, but this was not all; Mayo retained a twenty-five percent interest in all such lands including participation in such royalties as they might produce when mining began. He had a check for 10,000 dollars and authority to draw on Kimberly's account for additional funds as needed for his operations.

The word that the woodchopper-teacher-lawyer was about to become wealthy spread. John C.C. brought in a new roll-top desk and other impressive office furniture, the first of their kind ever seen in the Big Sandy. He opened the huge cartons on the street so that everyone could see the splendid items while his rented offices were being refurbished. He took Kimberly's check for 10,000 dollars — an enormous sum for that time and place — and showed it to all. He brought in large bundles of cash and bags of shiny gold coins, flashing them before his visitors. When his office had been painted and furnished, he conducted scores of people through it so they could see his desk, conference tables, upholstered chairs, rugs, typewriters, and shelves of new law books. He told his amazed guests about his contract with Kimberly's Sharon Steel and Hoop Company and the magnitude of the company's operations. His flamboyance and bravado paid off, as many people were selling to him. Sometimes Mayo bought land outright but only rarely. He preferred to buy the underlying coal, oil, gas, salt and salt water, stone, shale, and other mineral and metallic substances together with the right to mine and remove them by all means "deemed necessary or convenient."

With his newfound wealth, Mayo paid off Buckingham, bought himself a fine horse and an impressive buck-board, laid in a supply of good cigars and mellow whiskey, and stocked up on printed blank option and deed forms. With crisp new paper currency and freshly minted gold coins, he headed into a land of eroded farms, atrocious creek-bottom roads, and stands of towering oak and tulip trees. Sometimes, he was rebuffed by an adamant landowner, but most of the time when he returned, dusty and trail-worn, to his office, he had stacks of options and deeds for recording. He operated in Johnson, Floyd, Pike, Perry, Leslie, and Letcher counties, and people vied with one another to keep him in their homes overnight and to sign his documents. His generosity was legendary because after the conclusion of a successful trade, he generally handed the wife a five dollar gold piece as a gift.

Sometimes, the coins were preserved for half a century and shown proudly to heirs and visitors as "John Mayo money." Legends grew up around his success story, turning him into a towering folk hero. Mayo murmured that he desired only to "develop the hills" and provide jobs and economic opportunities. Sometimes, Alice accompanied him on his buying forays. She sewed stacks of twenty dollar gold coins into long narrow leather bags which she carried under her voluminous skirts. Men were duly impressed when she brought out those glittering discs, and women thought she was the "purtiest" woman they had ever seen and named their daughters after her. As the new century emerged, Mayo was a wealthy man by Kentucky standards; his net worth was approximately 250,000 dollars. His successes simply encouraged him to look for other ways to swell his fortune on a larger scale.

By 1902, Mayo had become eastern Kentucky's first millionaire. In 1907, Mayo negotiated a stupendous deal with the officers of Consolidation Coal. Around the conference table sat some of the most able businessmen in the United States, including the President, Clarence Wayland Watson, A. B. Fleming, A. T. Watson, George W. Fleming, Frank Haas, Jonathan Jenkins, and John Gordon Smyth. In return for 20,000 acres, he had a check for 50,000 dollars plus enough stock in Consol to give him a respectable voice in its management. The check, by far the largest ever seen in the Big Sandy Valley, set off new tremors of admiration and envy, and the number of mountain boys named John Calhoun Mayo multiplied mightily. But Mayo came out of the Miller's Creek negotiations with something infinitely more valuable than the check and stock certificate. Coal lands were valueless without railroads to haul the fuel to mills and factories. Kentucky's ineffectual politicians and underfinanced business interests had struggled for decades to get railroads into the heart of the state's hill country, but their accomplishments had been meager and slow. Consol, with ties to the Rockefeller colossus, assured the building of the lines from the terminus at Stafford, Kentucky to the company's new holdings. Camden and his associates financed the Miller's Creek Railroad, a four mile stretch from the Consol's new holdings to the Chesapeake & Ohio. The tycoons moved so expeditiously that the first carload of coal left the Miller's Creek mine in 1910.

By January 2, 1911, when other deeds from Northern vested additional lands in Consol, the Camden-Watson, Fleming-Haymond ring had control of what their engineers and chemists believed to contain 1,000,000,000 tons of the finest coal in North America. When Northern Coal & Coke was organized, Mayo had been granted a quarter of the stock, so the conveyance to Consol made him an even wealthier man. Part of his profits from that transaction were set aside to draw interest and the rest was invested in mineral options in eastern Pike County and along the Kentucky River in Letcher, Knott, Perry, and Breathitt counties. While the townspeople lined up outside his office to sell some of the planet's most important fuel beds, the railroads commenced building the extensions that would increase the value of those minerals a hundred times over.

Mayo took an initiative that settled for all time the rights of the competing railroads in his immense coalfield. For wealthy investors, he arranged a tour, or rather a strenuous overland journey, across the corrugation of steep ridges and twisting valleys. The moguls were eastern bankers, financiers, the presidents of the Baltimore & Ohio, the Western Maryland, and the Chesapeake & Ohio, and representative of the Louisville &

Nashville. The C & O had opposed the opening of the field on the ground that it would glut the markets. Mayo wanted the cooperation of all the railmen in devising a lasting and dependable transportation system that would serve all parts of the field, so he created a winning plan involving hiring a famous chef.

In a letter to George C. Jenkins dated October 25, 1909, Jere Wheelwright described the quality of the gigantic mineral treasure Mayo had pinned down: "... the coals of Eastern Kentucky are of a character which are essential in the arts of metallurgy, in processes where modern practice demands pure products... The coals of the Northern Coal and Coke Company property belong to the highest coking class. This places it at once in the manufacture of pig-iron, in copper, smelters, and numerous other industries of less magnitude where coke is essential in the manufacture." In 1913, at his urging, the Fairmont Ring organized the Elk Horn Fuel Company, soon to be re-named the Elk Horn Coal Corporation. To this new West Virginia corporation, the Northern Coal and Coke Company conveyed most of the remainder of Mayo's huge acquisitions in the Elk Horn mineral field — the superlative deposits of steam and metallurgical coal, and oil and gas under 265,000 acres, the equivalent of a Kentucky county. This transfer made him a substantial stockholder in the new entity. He also remained the owner in his own name and right of approximately 20,000 acres in Johnson and Pike counties, plus a controlling interest in 10,000 acres owned by the Tom's Creek Coal Company. His holdings in other corporations — Montrose Coal Company and Hamilton Realty — were merged into Elk Horn.

With railroads converging on these companies from the

north, east, south, and west, a juggernaut suddenly struck the primitive counties, which took on a new image almost overnight. The region became an Eldorado and men arrived from many parts of the globe. They trooped in from the exhausted valley of the Tennessee River, from the farmed-out cotton country of the deep south, from the cities of the east coast, and from the older coalfields of Maryland and Pennsylvania. They were joined by multitudes in immigrant ships — Italians, Croats, Serbs, Russians, Syrians, Swedes, Swiss, Albanians, and Jews. Entire valleys were drained of young men as the Kentucky hill people turned from subsistence farming to new lives as coal miners. Work on the new towns began long before the rails could reach the sites. Nicola Construction Company was the largest of the contractors and the builders worked at an almost frenzied pace.

Mayo brought off another tremendous accomplishment in 1906. With funding from Kimberly and the Fairmont Ring, he persuaded the state's legislature to tackle the problem of those vexatious Virginia land grants. He advocated a bill, and it passed so quickly and quietly that the heirs of those long-dead revolutionaries suspected nothing until the law had been passed and signed by the governor. The Revenue Law of 1906 made it the duty of a claimant of land to pay all taxes which had been, or should have been, assessed against it for the years 1901-1905 inclusively, made failure to pay such taxes for any three of those years grounds for a mandatory forfeiture of the title to the Commonwealth, or to any adverse claimant in actual possession of all or part of the land, who had paid such taxes. The Virginians had neglected to pay taxes on their ancestral claims and, with this law on the books, Mayo's companies computed the delinquent levies and paid them on behalf of their grantors and themselves. Some of the Virginians promptly sued to invalidate the act but hundreds of heavily armed mountaineers came to the trial and scowled at the judge until he perceived that the law was sound and entered judgment upholding it. On appeal it was sustained by the state's highest court on December 20, 1907.

By 1911, Mayo's dream of riches and power had been realized. He had emerged as a power broker in two states and was Kentucky's member of the Democratic National Committee. He had been offered a U.S. Senate seat and his party's nomination for governor but had rejected both. He had begun the promotional work that would send Johnson Camden, Jr., to the senate from his adopted state in 1914. He was rich in lands, in corporate stocks, in money, and in public esteem. Poverty was safely behind him but not the memory of poverty. He once showed a friend 200,000 dollars worth of bonds which, he said, represented cigar money. When he was younger, he could not afford the luxury of tobacco but those bonds and their coupons guaranteed that he would never again be without the cheering influence of fine Havanas.

Mayo vowed to build a great mansion for himself and his wife. He bought a swamp on the fringe of Paintsville and filled it with dirt to make well-drained lawns. He housed a hundred Italian masons in temporary shacks and set them to work with bricks and roof tiles imported from their sunny homeland. They quarried from the hills the blocks of stone for the foundations and the wall that enclosed the grounds and hauled them suspended from a groaning cable to the swarming site. They carved eight gigantic stone pillars and conveyed them on six, specially built ox-drawn wagons to their places in front of the edifice. The house rose in dark red brick, roofed with indestructible tiles and fronted with those breath-taking pillars — a home suitable for a coal king at home amid his retainers, vassals, and allies. The rafters and roof sheathing were sawed from Kentucky white oak and yellow poplar, and the interior was panelled and balustraded with yellow oak and exotic mahogany from Honduras. It stood sixty-six feet wide and seventy-eight feet long. There were porches and balconies, parlors, reception chambers, a ballroom, conference rooms, a library, a music chamber, a sewing room, bedrooms, kitchens, dining rooms, quarters for servants, and, of course, suites for visiting moguls. The walls were of solid brick laid course upon course and many courses thick, built to endure for centuries. In scope and grandeur it exceeded the habitations of his fellow moguls at Fairmont and Baltimore. In brick and stone, it proclaimed him successful, secure, powerful, and rich. The architect laid off wall spaces for canvases and sent to Rome for proper allegorical paintings. In due time they came, gleaming with paint fresh from the artist's brush. They were glued to the walls of the ballroom — eight of them depicting Mayo's vision of the past and future.

Mayo did not release his workmen when his mansion stood complete, its huge and numerous rooms carpeted and furnished. He set them to building a new Methodist church a short walk from his mighty door, a suitable place in which a mogul could serve his God. At Mayo's request, the steel tycoon Andrew Carnegie paid for the organ. Then, a block beyond, he had them build the new First National Bank of Paintsville. Church and bank bear the imprint of those master masons — staunch, enduring, and singular. Finally, at a corner of his grounds, they built an office where Mayo could manage his empire. All of them — mansion, office, church, and bank — stand close together, convenient to the master spirit that created them. Then, he laid a railroad track to a short brick-paved street by the side of his home, where private railroad cars could be parked when business or pleasure brought important people to his door.

In February 1914, he became ill at his immense gleaming home. Clarence Watson sent his palatial railroad car to carry John C. C. to New York and the nation's finest specialists. He fought hard as for his life as he had fought for his fortune, but this time he lost. Despite a remarkable new procedure — a blood transfusion from the veins of his brother Washington — he died of pericarditis in a princely suite at the Waldorf-Astoria on May 11, 1914. Clarence Watson's special car, draped in black and smelling of flowers, brought him home. All of Kentucky's state-level elected officials went to Paintsville in a chartered train loaded with mourners. Watson arrived with sixty bankers and officials of his companies. Mayo's honorary pallbearers included the state's governor and a former governor, a United States senator from Kentucky, Congressman Slemp, both senators from West Virginia, the president of the nation's biggest coal company, the president of the Louisville & Nashville Railroad, and his faithful and beloved friend John Buckingham. There were so many moguls that the huge, solemn special trains with their luxurious private cars could find no parking space. The railroad tycoons stopped coal shipments for several hours and the gleaming locomotives and coaches of the visitors stood in line on the main track. No greater tribute could have been paid to a coal king than to bring the rumbling coal cars to a halt in his honor. An eloquent minister was imported from Louisville, and the church was so crowded that even the standing room was taken and an immense somber crowd filled the streets. The poor, too, paid their respects — including many made much poorer by the sale of their mineral riches. On the day before the funeral, they passed the body in silent hundreds, staring at the immobile features and looking around with startled, uncomprehending gazes at the splendid rooms. In a funeral tribute, Clarence Watson and Jere Wheelwright summed up the feeling of an age about this strange, compelling man: His abilities were such that he made the skeptics see, as he saw, the inexhaustible riches sealed in those remote hills.

Practically every newspaper in Kentucky and many in other states reported his death and editorialized about his accomplishments. *The Big Sandy News* devoted its entire front page and half of another to him and his works. *The New York Times* said he was the wealthiest man in his state with a net worth of 20,000,000 dollars. Mayo was buried on a hilltop above the valley of Levisa Fork. A huge stone patterned after the tomb of Napoleon bears the word "Mayo," and a flat slab tells his name and the days of his years. The rains of many autumns have watered his grave and the man, so honored and respected in his lifetime, now lies almost forgotten.

Effie Waller Smith

EFFIE WALLER SMITH

THE RUSTIC SCENE IN BLACK AND WHITE

By Edwina Pendarvis

A few years ago, shortly after my aunt died, while I was looking through the books on her shelf, I came across a small red book titled *Rhymes from the Cumberland*. The inscription in the book showed it was a gift to my aunt, Juanita, whose friends all called her "Johnnie."

> Johnnie,
> May this little book help recall memories of the happy and carefree days we spent in our little town. I wonder if we fully realized what a great world we had. ...
> Love,
> Danny

A torn piece of newspaper marked the page with a poem about Elkhorn City, where my aunt and her friend Danny went to high school. As I read the poems in the book, I realized that even though its author, Effie Waller, later to become Effie Waller Smith, had been born half a century earlier than my aunt and even though Effie Waller was African American, or as some scholars might say now, *Affrilachian*, her life in Pike County, Kentucky, shared many similarities with life there as my aunt's generation knew it, and as many people still know it today.

Effie Waller was born at Chloe Creek, a rural, racially mixed community a few miles from Pikeville, the county seat. Her father, Frank Waller, came to eastern Kentucky after the Civil War. He was an aide to General Stonewall Jackson and is said to have served the famous general's last meal. Before the war, Frank had been enslaved on a plantation called "Cedar Point" in Spotsylvania County, Virginia. Her mother, Alvindia "Sibbie" Ratliff, also a former slave, was born and raised in eastern Kentucky. Frank Waller, a blacksmith, bought and sold land to increase the family's income. Effie, born on January 6, 1879, was their third child.

Like many children of the time, the Waller children had to travel a long way to get to school, but their parents insisted that all of them get the education that slaves had been denied. As the youngest girl in the family, Effie was kept at home for a good portion of every term, however, because the closest school for Black children was in Pikeville. When the weather was too bad to permit Effie to walk to school, she studied at home under her mother's watchful eye and in the company of her little brother, Marvin, born in 1882. It is uncertain when she first started writing poems and stories. Maybe it was on those long winter days at home. The earliest date noted on one of her poems is 1895, when she was sixteen.

In 1901, when Effie was twenty-two, the family moved to Division Street in Pikeville. In 1902, a local newspaper, probably the Pikeville or Williamson newspaper, published some of her poems. Like her older brother and sister, Effie taught school and saved money toward her tuition at Kentucky State Normal School for Colored Persons (Kentucky State University) in Frankfort. In 1903, not long after she completed her schooling in Frankfort, the first of several tragedies struck, her brother Marvin died. Though Effie's poetry often expressed her feelings about events in her life, Marvin's death isn't mentioned in her first poetry book, *Songs of the Months* (a publication arranged and paid for by local admirers of her work). The book, published in 1904, may have already been sent to the publishers when her brother died, or she needed more time to grieve before she could write about him.

Songs of the Months testifies to the intelligence, imagination, and high spirits of this young poet. Her thoughts range far beyond the mountains of eastern Kentucky. In addition to poems about the landscape and happenings around her, are poems about patriotism, African American soldiers in the Spanish American War, about what culture means, the tragedy of alcoholism, and, of course, (she's Appalachian, after all), about graveyards and the loved ones buried there. Her time spent at the Normal School probably inspired poems set in Frankfort, one about the Daniel Boone monument and another about the locks on the Kentucky River near the state capital. Several poems reflect her light-heartedness, such as "Possum Hunting: A True Incident."

Six little boys gathered
In a group at school one day,
Were talking very earnestly,
And I overheard them say:

"Now wouldn't it be funny,
And it wouldn't be impolite,
If we could get our teacher
To 'possum hunt to-night?"

The boys and their teacher try to lure a possum with pawpaws, instead of taking a dog along to tree it with.

Her teenage interest in romance comes through in another poem that depicts fun-loving youngsters. In this poem, Effie and her sister Rosa give four of their friends, probably visiting from Pikeville, a ride back home.

Humpty, bumpty, o'er stones we drove,
And anon through a shady grove
Then up the mountain's steep ascent,
Past farm-houses old and quaint.

Thus we merrily jogged along,
Eating apples, and full of songs;
Guessing what our sweethearts would say
If they should meet us upon the way.
(from "The Wagon Ride: A Real Happening")

The same year that *Songs of the Months* was published, Effie married Lyss Cockrell; but the marriage didn't last long. She divorced him in 1905. About three years later, she tried again, marrying former classmate Charles Smith in 1908; but that marriage, too, was doomed. It precipitated the second tragedy of her life — her and Charley's baby died in infancy. Not much later, Effie filed for divorce from her second husband.

Published in 1909, *Rhymes from the Cumberland*, the collection my aunt's friend gave to her, includes several poems recalling happy times with Charles, though the Cumberland Mountains and their natural beauty are the main subject of the book. Her poem, "On Receiving a Souvenir Postcard," written during her second marriage, describes a postcard sent to her from eastern Kentucky. In its "rustic scene in black and white" depicting places in the Big Sandy Valley, she takes great pleasure, remembering her and Charles' courting days.

The light-heartedness of her earlier collection is tempered in *Rhymes from the Cumberland* by a more melancholy tone. In "At Pool Point," she hints at suicidal thoughts and then expresses regret at having such thoughts in so lovely a place. Like many other poems in this collection, "At Pool Point" is set in the Breaks, which Effie describes as "a picturesque gorge about five miles long in the Cumberland Mountains, through which the Big Sandy river flows." The lush, wild landscape fascinated her as it has fascinated many, before and since.

Despite the more melancholy tone of some of the poems, a spirit of adventure is strong in *Rhymes from the Cumberland*, and in "The Lake on the Mountain," she describes some of the pleasures she enjoyed on her treks through the Breaks. Despite the hardships she'd endured, she fully realized what a unique world the eons of geological change had created there, and she wanted to share that realization with readers of her poems.

> We stopped and plucked some wintergreen
>   We gathered pine cones brown,
> We paused awhile where chestnut trees
>   Had dropped their harvest down.

Her third and final poetry collection, *Rosemary and Pansies*, also copyrighted in 1909, was published by Gorham Press, a commercial press in Boston. Her reputation had grown through the publication of her poems and three of her short stories by the popular and respected periodicals, *Putnam's Monthly* and the *Independent*. *Rosemary and Pansies* is dedicated to her younger brother Marvin, and in this volume, she responds to his death and to the death of her baby. Not surprisingly, religious thoughts imbue many of the poems in this collection. The ebullience of *Songs of the Months,* the adventurousness of *Rhymes from the Cumberland*, and the playful wit of her short stories is replaced by a chastened hopefulness.

> If no man died till his long life should leave
> All hopes and aims fulfilled, until his feet
> Had trod all paths where men rejoice or grieve,
> I might have doubt of future life more sweet;
> But as I look on you, I must believe

There is a heaven that makes this life on earth complete.
(from "To a Dead Baby")

Only a couple of years later, in 1911, Charles Smith was killed. Smith, a Pike County deputy sheriff, was shot by the sister of a moonshiner, while serving a warrant on the man during a raid on his still. In 1916, Effie's father died, and the following year, her writing career ended. "Autumn Winds," the last poem she ever published appeared in *Harper's Monthly* in 1917. In 1918, Effie's life took a sudden turn. She and her mother joined the Metropolitan Holiness Church Association, which was proselytizing in eastern Kentucky at that time. Effie cashed in her assets, and the two women moved to the church's headquarters, a commune in Waukesha, Wisconsin. They lived there three or four years, but decided to leave the commune and get their own home. Effie sued to get her money back; and she and her mother bought a house in Waukesha, and lived together until Sibbie's death in 1927. Alfred, Effie's older brother, came to live with her after he retired and remained until his death in 1934. After Alfred's death, Effie traveled to Kentucky to visit Ruth Ratliff, the orphan daughter of a good friend and former student, Polly Ratliff. She adopted Polly's daughter and raised her as her own. Like Effie, Ruth became a teacher.

Effie Waller Smith's work was virtually forgotten for years; but in 1991, thanks to the dedication and scholarship of another eastern Kentuckian, David Deskins, *The Collected Works of Effie Waller Smith* was published by Oxford University. It includes her three books of poetry and three short stories. Though her poems have gotten more attention than her prose, her witty tale of redemption and backsliding, "The Temptation of Peter Stiles," puts her in a class with the best local color writers.

Today, we know more about her literature than we do about her life. Why she stopped publishing is a mystery, as she lived to be eighty. Personal tragedies may have caused her to give up writing and seek solace in religion. Surely being an African American woman from eastern Kentucky offered a barrier to her success in a publishing world dominated by white men in urban centers. In the yard of her home in Wisconsin, she created a rock garden that was visited by thousands of people. Maybe she got more pleasure out of creating a land-scape of her own than of writing about landscapes she'd seen. Deskins' introduction to *The Collected Works of Effie Waller Smith*, mentions that Vicey Stewart, a white woman who lived in Elkhorn City in the late 1800s and early 1900s, told her son that not many white people would talk to Effie when she visited the town and that Effie earned her board at a rooming house near the Breaks by cooking meals for the loggers who stayed there. This and many elements of Effie's biography, along with her prose and poetry, show her to have been a strikingly inde-pendent woman who was keenly aware of the intense racial prejudice of the time, but who nevertheless went her own way, pursuing her interests boldly. Whatever the reasons she stopped publishing, the kaleidoscope of poems and stories by the exuberant young Effie Waller and the sadder, wiser Effie

Smith is an original and artful reminder of the geography that shapes our lives and helps us define what we find meaningful and memorable, whatever our race and time.

Right: Jean Bell Thomas. Photo courtesy of the Highlands Museum and Discovery Center.

Below: American Folk Song Festival

JEAN THOMAS

THE TRAIPSIN' WOMAN

By James M. Gifford

Jean Bell Thomas was a significant yet nearly forgotten figure in the dramatically interesting history of Appalachian music. Born Jeanette Mary Francis de Assisi Aloysius Narcissus Garfield Bell in Ashland, Kentucky, in 1881, she graduated from Holy Family School of Business in 1899 and later achieved fame as an author of eight books by national publishing houses, and as a photographer, lecturer, folklorist, and founder and promoter of the American Folk Song Festival. As a young, unmarried woman, she defied many of the conservative conventions of her culture by attending business school and learning stenography. After becoming a court reporter, she traveled by jolt wagon with a circuit judge to courts in the county seat towns in the mountains of eastern Kentucky and earned the sobriquet, "The Traipsin' Woman." Thomas said her family had opposed her taking the job, because they "thought it was shocking for a young girl to go traipsin' around the country with a passel of law-men." But she had to have a job and her "heart was set on it."

Thomas saved her court reporter wages and moved to New York, where she spent a decade living a bohemian life in Greenwich Village. In New York, she took writing classes and continued to work as a stenographer. A feminist long before the term was coined, she then held a variety of unconventional jobs, including work as a script girl for Cecil B. de Mille's film *The Ten Commandments*, as secretary to the owner of a professional baseball team, and as press agent for socialite Gloria Gould Bishop and later for Ruby "Texas" Guinan, a notorious entertainer and owner of prohibition-era speakeasies.

During her early travels in eastern Kentucky, and on subsequent visits, Thomas often carried her camera and photographed musicians and other mountain people she encountered. With her portable typewriter, she documented lyrics and tunes to ballads. In 1926, Jean Thomas heard James William Day, a blind fiddler, playing and singing in front of the Rowan County Courthouse in Morehead, Kentucky. Thomas signed him to a management contract, changed his name to Jilson Setters, secured a recording contract for Day in 1928 with RCA Victor, and booked him as the "Singin' Fiddler from Lost Hope Hollow" in theaters in America and Europe. Setters eventually played at the Festival of the English Folk Song and Dance Society in London's Royal Albert Hall.

Thomas' most enduring contribution to Appalachian music was the American Folk Song Festival, which she established in 1930. With the exception of years 1943-1947, Thomas' old fashioned Singin' Gatherin' was held at various sites in and around her hometown of Ashland until ill health forced her resignation in 1972. During those four decades, Thomas was the moving force behind the annual music festival. She planned, publicized, and financed it. She collected costumes and musical instruments, and booked participants. She even painted directions on roadside boulders to guide motorists to the event that became the primary passion of her life.

In accordance with long-established mountain traditions, Thomas' festival was held the second Sunday of June under an open sky on a homemade platform. The event attracted tens of thousands of spectators who sat on fences, the tops of automobiles, and in buggies to hear the old mountain songs and see the old dances. Thomas wanted to showcase traditional music that had originated in the British Isles and crystalized over more than a century of Appalachian influences into her notion of mountain music. Part concert and part stage drama, the American Folk Song Festival followed a similar script each year. A fox horn that had once belonged to Devil Anse Hatfield announced the beginning of the performance. Then a mountain couple with two children arrived on stage in a covered wagon where they were greeted by a Cherokee woman singing the Cherokee Song of Welcome. Dialog conveying the settlement of Appalachia was followed by children performing an English country dance. Old songs like "Barbara Allen" were followed by "Old Sally Gooden" played on the mouth harp and "Billy In the Low Ground" played on the fiddle. Musical performances featuring home- made dulcimer, banjo, fiddle, guitar, accordion, harmonica, and recorder were interspersed with more dramatic action like an enactment of an olden marriage ceremony or an interpretation of an eighteen-century murder legend, often featuring Thomas as the narrator. Characters dressed in mountain garb with a historical backdrop that included cultural props like churns, egg baskets, brooms, drinking gourds and other manifestations of practical Appalachian art presented thousands of visitors with Thomas' view of Appalachian history and culture. The American Folk Song Festival went through five distinct phases of development.

Phase one began in September of 1930 when Miss Thomas staged a private musical presentation at her home featuring the blind fiddler, Jilson Setters. Special guests included future radio personality Dorothy Gordon, Mrs. Susan Steele Sampson, the first lady of Kentucky, and the editor of the *Ashland Daily Independent*. The success of this presentation prompted Thomas to reflect:

> If seventy-five or a hundred people from my home town will turn out on a cold September day to see and hear an old mountain minstrel...perhaps, if I selected a warm June day and a place "nigher the county seat," more people would come. Why not try it then on the next second Sunday in June?

> Then, too, I reasoned that these old minstrels were fast passing. There would be no one to take their place. The children in the valleys, in the foothills, and in the moun tains should be given the opportunity of hearing the ballads of their forebears, as the old minstrels, like Jilson

Setters, sing them; the jig and frolic tunes of Elizabeth's time, as he plays them on his ancient fiddle.

It was high time that our nation had an organization to preserve our folk music and songs, and folklorists every where agreed. England had had a similar organization since 1878. Of course, there was the American Folklore Society, founded in 1888, the outgrowth of the work of Professor Child of Harvard; but I felt that research and printed journals were not sufficient in themselves. There should be a living, a vital presentation of the song of our fathers. I believed, too, that in an annual American Folk Song Festival only those mountain minstrels to whom the ballads had been handed down by word of mouth should participate. Only those untrained fiddlers and musicians who had learned their art from their forebears should take part.

In August of 1931, nearly a year later, Thomas formally presented her plan to the governor's wife. Mrs. Sampson enthusiastically approved it and the American Folk Song Society was incorporated by Susan Steele Sampson, Helen C. Sampson, and Jean Thomas. The second American Folk Song Festival, open to the public at large, took place on June 12, 1932. The Festival was repeated on June 11, 1933. The local newspaper provided little coverage and expressed doubts in Thomas' claim that Governor Laffoon would attend. However, the Governor came and "stayed to the very end."

In 1934, Thomas' landlord refused "to permit the festival to be held on his ground" and she had to find a site somewhere on Mayo Trail. Fortunately, a local farmer offered a large meadow. But she needed immediate financing to move the trademark windowless log cabin and the heavy stage properties and sound equipment to the new site and build a new outdoor theatre. Then came a saving answer to one of her urgent telegrams: "Find the site, and if there isn't a windowless log cabin on the place, get one and put it there." Thus, the 1934 Festival was rescued in the nick of time by Captain B. Franklin Cross. The 1935 Festival, held on June 9, and all the succeeding festivals through 1949, took place on this site, about eighteen miles south of Ashland, just off Route 23 then called the Mayo Trail.

Those first few years, from 1930 to 1935, represent the first of five phases in the history of the Festival. The main accomplishment of this first period was the acquisition of a festival site off the Mayo Trail. There was little overhead, since the artists performed for free and the physical setup was handled by Miss Thomas and a number of volunteers. Financial support came from private donations and from Thomas' publication royalties.

The second phase, from 1936 to 1942, saw the festival gain prominence through national press coverage. The festival's success was even more remarkable in light of the fact that America was mired in the Great Depression. Among the folk music programs recognized by the New Deal's Federal Music Project was Thomas' American Folk Song Festival. This federal program provided employment for people to assist in setting up the Festival and striking the set. But the national recognition was more important than the assistance provided by New Deal workers. A grant from the Rockefeller Foundation financed the recording of some of the early festivals. This material now resides in the Library of Congress along with six scrapbooks of clippings and memorabilia pertaining to the festivals.

By 1940, Thomas' success prompted community leaders to seek a closer affiliation with the music festival. On January 5, 1941, the *St. Louis Post-Dispatch* carried a major article noting that Ashland had "never taken the Singin' Gatherin' to its bosom and has joined only grudgingly in annual big doin's out in the hills." The same article reported that Thomas had rejected a proposal from the editor of the *Ashland Daily Independent* to transform the festival into a two-day event sponsored by local merchants. Thomas' leadership and artistic vision were the strengths of the festival, but they also proved to be the major weaknesses. I will "carry on alone, as long as I live" had been Thomas' reply. On June 15, 1942, she presided over the last Festival to take place for six years. The inactivity brought about by World War II created this third phase.

The years 1948-52 constituted the fourth phase of the Festival. Five years of inactivity had caused the Festival to lose its pre-war national prominence.

Finally, in 1950, Thomas agreed to move the Festival to Ashland. At this point, local newspaper coverage increased in the *Ashland Daily Independent* and in the West Virginia newspapers, particularly the *Huntington Herald Dispatch*. The new site for the Festival was the lot adjoining Thomas' residence at 3201 Cogan Street in Ashland. The attractive site featured a stage in front of a one room school and an elevated platform for television equipment. In 1952, the Festival was professionally recorded for the first time.

The fifth and final phase in the history of the festival lasted from 1955 to 1972 and was often promoted in national travel magazines. The June/July 1959 issue of *Buick Magazine* observed the American Folk Song Festival was "easily reached on U.S. 53, 60, and 23" and noted the availability of several local motels "with accomodations costing $7.00 and up for a single." During these years, the names of the performers changed, as many of the "old-timers" who had participated since the thirties had died or become too old or sick to continue performing. Because of her advancing age, Jean Thomas often talked of finding a successor but no one was ever chosen. In 1966, the festival was moved from the woodland adjoining Thomas' Ashland home to Carter Caves State Resort Park, where it became the Sunday afternoon segment of a much broader arts and crafts weekend.

Thomas and her festival were the subjects of both local and national scrutiny for many years. Some scholars, including her Eastern Kentucky contemporary Cratis D. Williams, questioned the authenticity of her productions. Although Thomas had a national support base that included some of the leading literary talents of the mid-twentieth century, she did not cultivate local support for her music festival. "She cared little for local opinion," observed her hometown newspaper, "but sought the light of a distant star." Her egocentric approach to promoting her singing gatherings included the creation of a china doll wearing a black dress which had been designed for her by a professional costume design company. She called it "The Traipsin' Woman-Jean Thomas." According to noted folklore scholar Lynwood Montell, many of the leaders of her hometown of Ashland opposed her efforts because they felt her emphasis on the old mountain culture was inconsistent with the progressive ambitions of a community that boasted major corporate headquarters and significant business enterprises. "Jean saw roads, radio, and industry as destructive," Montell observed during a public lecture in Ashland in 1980. "In my subjective evaluation, she was not in favor of Ashland's rapid growth." The publisher of the local newspaper, Col. B. F. Forgy, was a particularly vocal detractor of Thomas's efforts. Not surprisingly she received little local publicity until 1958 when James T. Norris became the editor and publisher of the *Ashland Daily Independent*. Norris, who had a farsighted vision of cultural tourism, recognized the economic potential in Thomas' music festivals.

Thomas died on December 7, 1982, at age 101 and was buried in her hometown. She had outlived her fame and died, not as a local heroine, but as an unpopular eccentric. George Wolfford, a highly respected local journalist, observed that some of the negative opinions about Jean Thomas "were so deep-seated they live on in the second and third generation."

Prior to her death, Thomas formalized a plan to donate her extensive collection of folklore to the Jean Thomas Museum, opened in her home in 1979, but this project suffered from a lack of local support. Later her museum was moved to the American Heritage Park, west of Ashland, and became part of an unusual effort called "Jesse Stuart Land," a bizarre and poorly conceived plan to "strengthen and coordinate" a number of facilities—the Jesse Stuart Nature Preserve, the (non-existent) Jesse Stuart State Literary Park, the American Heritage Park, the Jean Thomas Museum, the Gatherin' Place, the Negro Baseball Hall of History, and the John C. C. Mayo Amphitheater. These disparate facilities existed an hour away from one another in two separate counties. In retrospect, the plan of action seemed like a Saturday Night Live comedy skit. Not surprisingly, it was a miserable failure.

Today, Thomas is an obscure footnote on the pages of history, known to few people outside the scholarly community yet memorialized in several significant ways. Her accomplishments merited detailed recognition by the great scholar Charles K. Wolfe in his book *Kentucky Country*. A fascinating exhibit in Ashland's Kentucky Highlands Museum and Discovery Center includes photographs and memorabilia that relate to Thomas's life and accomplishments. The University of Louisville's Dwight Anderson Memorial Music Library maintains about 60 boxes of material on Jean Thomas which includes thousands of letters, newspaper clippings, programs, diaries, manuscripts, notes and photographs. According to archivist James Procell, the Jean Thomas collection is currently being digitized, with the "hope that it can be made available online within the next couple of years." Today, Shirley Boyd, a retired educator who is editing Thomas' unpublished, romanticized story of the Hatfields and McCoys, is also writing a much-needed biography of Jean Thomas.

Thomas' amazingly full, and often controversial, life truly merits a new biography, but her life merits examination on other levels, too. Her broad range of efforts to preserve the music, dance, and culture of the people of eastern Kentucky and central Appalachia was a precursor to popular regional outdoor dramas in southern Appalachia and an informal jump-start to the Appalachian Studies Movement that began in the 1970s. Thomas' life also cries out to be examined within the context of feminist scholarship. In rhetoric, Thomas did not serve as spokesperson for women's rights and opportunities. Although she didn't overtly talk the talk, she clearly walked the walk. Her life was a testament to seizing opportunities that were normally not available to her female contemporaries. Although Thomas normally stopped short of advocating equal rights and opportunities for the women of Appalachia, she often articulated the problems that Appalachian women regularly encountered.

"We have a saying down there that's mighty true," Thomas told a New York reporter, "The mountain's all right for men and horses, but Hell on women and mules." Thomas observed that the women of Appalachia often "do most of the work and look old at thirty," because their problems and responsibilities were overwhelming. They had large families in the days before the pill and their duties included child care, home care, gardening, caring for the cow, and carrying water from a nearby body of water.

In a verse in one of her songs, Thomas sang

"Don't never let your woman have her way
Kase (because) if you do bad luck'll come to stay."

Another song that seemed to encourage mountain women

to accept their traditional roles intoned

>"Geese in the pond and fish in the ocean,
>Devils in the women
>When they take a notion.

None of those songs affected or defined Thomas whose life followed another traditional Appalachian verse:

>"If hard times don't kill me,
>I'll live till I die."

MARTIN M. HIMLER
FOUNDER OF HIMLERVILLE

By Cathy Corbin

Eighteen year-old Hungarian immigrant Martin M. Himler sailed to America aboard the *SS Carpathia* in the Spring of 1907. When Mr. Himler stepped onto American soil on May 9, 1907, he had nine cents in his pocket and two goals in his mind. One goal was to serve America, the country of freedom, democracy, and free enterprise. Himler's father had dreamed of immigrating to America, and to the young and determined Martin Himler, "America was the answer for everything." Himler's second goal was to become an entrepreneur and a participant in America's free enterprise system. He was eager to escape the Hungarian caste system, eager to seek his fortune in America for, as Himler said, "Anyone willing to work can make it in America."

Martin Himler worked his way across the Atlantic Ocean as an *SS Carpathia* steward, but the steward's pay was a meager sum. For his first job in America, he worked as a coal miner in the Thacker Mines in Thacker, West Virginia, and he continued his career as a coal miner in Gleason, West Virginia, and in Iselin, Pennsylvania. Himler's entrepreneurial spirit then led him away from coal mining and into a job as a peddler to the residents of coal mining camps. While working with customers at the Holden (West Virginia) Mine Camp in the winter of 1913, he decided that the miners needed a newspaper published "for miners by miners", so Himler penned the first issue of a weekly newspaper that became an international success- *Magyar Bányászlap (Hungarian Miners' Journal)*[hereafter referenced as *Hungarian Miners' Journal*]. The newspaper contained news from both America and Hungary, along with notices of available coal mining jobs in America and information about becoming an American citizen. Within five months, *Hungarian Miners' Journal* was self-supporting, and soon Himler's voice was heard by 60,000 Hungarian and American coal miners. Many of the issues of *Hungarian Miners' Journal* were published in both Hungarian and English; the success of this newspaper inspired Himler's life-long career in journalism.

Martin Himler's entrepreneurial spirit guided him again in 1919 when he and several other Hungarian-American coal miners founded the Himler Coal Company in Ajax, West Virginia. The Ajax mine was successful, but the Himler Coal Company wanted and needed a larger mine, and Himler was ready to test his idea for a unique, co-operative business model for Himler Coal Company. The Ajax mine sold for a good sum, and on June 24, 1919, the Himler Coal Company leased from Buck Creek Coal Company two thousand acres of coal-rich land across the Tug River in Martin County, Kentucky. Himler then announced his plan for the Kentucky coal mine and mining town owned by Hungarian coal miners and advertised the sale of Himler Coal Company stock in the *Hungarian Miners' Journal.*

Himler Coal Company soon had 1,700 stockholders and a capital stock of $2,000,000.00. The Company then constructed a five-span, 465 foot concrete and steel railroad bridge across the Tug River to enable Himler Coal Company to easily transport coal to West Virginia. The Company also laid two miles of railroad tracks, the first tracks in Martin County. Himler Coal Company then constructed a powerhouse and steel coal tipple, along with power poles, a water reservoir, and water and sewage lines to provide Himlerville residents with electricity and indoor plumbing. At this time, only five Martin County homes outside Himlerville contained bathrooms. The Himler State Bank opened for business on March 1, 1920, and construction at Himlerville was soon booming. Himler's theory that a coal mine and mining town owned by the Hungarian miners would instill pride, a sense of accomplishment, and dedication to hard work by the miners proved to be true. In a *Saward's Journal* August 24, 1921, article, Eugene J. Lang, Secretary-Treasurer of Himler Coal Company, observed: "We know that Mr. Himler's experiment is being watched with a great deal of interest by all those who know of it...laborers can realize that all the profits made by their employers can be made by themselves, for themselves, in a free county like ours if they only get together and are willing."

By 1922, the coal miners had built one hundred homes in Himlerville, and one thousand people were living in Himlerville. Native Martin Countians also worked at the Himler Coal Company

Mine, which had the capacity to produce three thousand tons of coal per day, but only Hungarians could own stock in Himler Coal Company. Himlerville soon contained an elementary school which was designated as the best elementary school in Kentucky in 1923 by the state Board of Education, as well as a general store, a community building, a theatre/opera house, St. Stephen's Catholic Church, a bakery, an ice cream parlor, a round house for locomotive maintenance, a cemetery, a baseball field, an office for the Himler Coal Company and the *Hungarian Miners' Journal*, the homes of Martin Himler and Eugene Lang, and a community park in the center of town. White picket fences and an abundance of beautiful flower gardens made Himlerville an idyllic little town.

Martin Himler's publishing and coal mining successes in America were well known in Hungary, and Hungarians were proud of their native son. Many Hungarians viewed Himler as somewhat of a celebrity, and Hungarians who did not know Himler were eager to meet him. For example, when Himler visited his mother and siblings in Hungary in 1922, he was traveling via train and was approached by a gentleman passenger who extended his hand and said, "I beg your pardon; I could not help hearing your name. Do I have the privilege to meet Mr. Himler of Himlerville?"

The Himler Coal Company eventually faced financial difficulties caused by decreasing coal prices following World War I and the enormous $450,000.00 cost of the railroad bridge. The original bridge cost estimate was $125,000.00, but when contractors sank the pillars for the railroad bridge, they found quicksand at a depth of fourteen feet. So the pillars then had to extend to a depth of forty-two feet with an accompanying increase in bridge cost and time for bridge construction. Also, an inch of slate suddenly appeared in the middle of the five feet of Himlerville coal. The thickness of the slate grew until it reached nine feet. Mining coal became impossible unless the miners mined nine feet of slate with five feet of coal. The excellent sandstone roof of the Himlerville mine disappeared about the same time that the slate appeared, but the miners remained optimistic. According to Himler, "Hoping that we would leave the slate behind and at the same time regain our good roof, we carried on for two years."

Too much debt and too little profit forced The Himler Coal Company into receivership with the Harrigan National Bank of Columbus, Ohio, on May 22, 1925, and the Company declared bankruptcy in 1928. The $1,250,000.00 assets of Himler Coal Company were sold to another coal mining corporation for $50,000.00. Martin Himler lost all of his personal property, except for the *Hungarian Miners' Journal* which was a separate corporation. During the Himler Coal Company's final bankruptcy hearing, the Judge of the Federal Court of Columbus stated, "Himler Coal Company is one of the cleanest bankruptcy cases in this court, and Martin Himler, the worst-hit victim of the circumstances, reached his end with clean hands."

The final blow to Himlerville came when the raging flood waters of the usually dry Buck Creek washed away twelve miners' homes and much of Himlerville on June 28, 1928. Martin Himler, deeply discouraged and saddened, declared, "I took this to be a notice from God Himself that Himlerville was wiped out."

Fifteen years later, after Martin Himler's successful careers as a newspaper publisher and as the Agriculture Consultant for the Chicago, Milwaukee, St. Paul, and Pacific Railroad, he began to fulfill his goal of serving America. Himler received a telephone call from the Office of Strategic Services, the precursor to the Central Intelligence Agency, in September, 1943, and the caller told Himler to arrange his affairs because he soon would be called to serve America. Although Himler was then fifty-five years old, he excelled in three military training schools.

The Office of Strategic Services had plans for Martin Himler. Within two years, Colonel Martin Himler was on duty in Salzburg, Austria. High-ranking United States military officials listened to the intelligence that Colonel Himler and his team gathered and discussed the intelligence with Colonel Himler. Based on these intelligence reports, the officials ordered Colonel Himler to locate, arrest, and hold more than three hundred Hungarian Nazi war criminals. Duncan Bare, Ph.D. Candidate and specialist in Hungarian-American Intelligence Studies at the University of Graz, Austria, suggests that "Martin was a pre- networker who had an absolutely amazing network of friends, acquaintances, and contacts in Hungary, especially among the 'good guys' or those members of the Hungarian Independence Movement, the Smallholders Party, and other liberal-democratic groups." Colonel Martin Himler, "good guy" and ardent American patriot, then served America and the world as he interrogated the worst of the Hungarian Nazi criminals. Many of the criminals interrogated by Colonel Himler were hanged in Budapest.

When Martin Himler's work for the Office of Strategic Services was finished, he moved to California and continued his journalism and publishing career. Himler's editorials were published in foreign and American newspapers, including the *Washington Post*. Pancreatic and liver cancer took Himler's life on July 8, 1961.

For many years, Kentuckians and Americans have known little about Martin Himler and his life after Himlerville. Now, the Martin County Historical and Genealogical Society and its Himler Project are working to bring Himler's story to the public eye with the publication of his compelling autobiography, *The Making Of An American (The Autobiography Of A "Hunky")*, and the restoration of Himler's home at Himlerville, renamed Beauty, Kentucky. The Himler home is currently listed on the National Register of Historic Places. The Mountain Missions Development Corporation gifted the home and surrounding land to the Martin County Historical and Genealogical Society on November 7, 2014. The Kentucky Heritage Council advised the Society that a quality restoration of Martin Himler's home could result in the home's designation as a national landmark and as a center for Hungarian immigrant culture and Appalachian coal mining history. Please visit www.himlerhouse.org for more information on the Himler Project. Additional Himler Project information can be seen on the Save The Himler House Facebook page and the @himlerhouse Twitter address.

* Sources for this essay include: public documents housed in the Martin County Court House, Inez, Kentucky, "Himlerville Revisited", a series of articles written by Himlerville citizen Mary Domosley Koblass and published in The Martin Countian from August 20, 1975, to July 28, 1976, and Martin Himler's autobiography, The Making Of An American (The Autobiography Of A "Hunky").

Fred M. Vinson. Collection of the Supreme Court of the United States.

FRED M. VINSON

PUBLIC SERVANT

By Kevin Coots

No native of the Big Sandy Valley was so widely influential in his day or as unjustly forgotten in ours as Fred Vinson, who served with distinction in all three branches of government. He represented his eastern Kentucky district in the U.S. House of Representatives for 12 years and served as Secretary of the Treasury under President Harry S. Truman before being appointed the 13th Chief Justice of the Supreme Court. At the end of President Truman's tenure in office, many Democrats urged Vinson to resign from the court and run for President, encouraged by polls showing him a leading candidate. Vinson refused, thinking such partisan interests inconsistent with his duties as a member of the nation's highest court. During his long career in public office, Vinson's willingness to take on difficult jobs at the request of Presidents Roosevelt and Truman earned him the nickname "Available Vinson" and underscored his commitment to the high calling of public service.

Frederick Moore Vinson was born January 22, 1890, in the small eastern Kentucky town of Louisa. His paternal forbearers came to the Big Sandy Valley from South Carolina, while his great-grandfather James was part of the great westward migration which came over the Appalachian Mountains in the early part of the nineteenth century. On the maternal side, his ancestry extended to Samuel Ferguson, Sr., who migrated from southwestern Virginia in the early 1800s and established himself in farming, timber and mercantile interests.

Despite Vinson's later claim to have been born in jail, he actually was born in the new jailor's house in front of the jail on the courthouse square in Louisa. He lived there with his parents, Jim and Virginia Vinson, as well as his three siblings, sisters Lourissa and Georgia, and brother Robert. Growing up around the jail, Vinson made friends from an early age with people associated with the legal process, from prisoners to law enforcement officials to judges and officers of the court. In the years ahead many proved to be of real help to the young lawyer and politician. Occasionally Circuit Judge Gerard Kinner, a friend of the family, would even let Fred, still a child, sit beside him on the bench while court was in session.

Reflecting on his early family life for Bela Kornitzer's *American Fathers and Sons* (Hermitage House, 1952), Vinson recalled

> Mother read a great deal. She believed in duty and service. I was raised in a rather disciplinarian household—just but discipline[d]. In the first place, Mother's deep love and confidence in me are known to everyone

in our community. She believed in me, and fought my battles and helped me to desire to secure an education. I loved baseball, but I did not continue in that field. I loved her more, and I had confidence in her judgment that I ought not to get side-tracked from the legal profession. She was an omnivorous reader and well-informed. She was firm and determined, tempered by a deep religious piety. She planted in me a deep regard for religion, respect for law, and faith in a good cause. She taught her family to do the proper thing without expecting any reward save the knowledge that we had done right.

From an early age, Vinson exhibited two talents which were to stand him in good stead well beyond his schooling: a prodigious memory which would later allow him to remember the names of so many of his constituents when he was a member of the U.S. House of Representatives and a facility with mathematics and numbers which would later allow him to master the detailed tax data as a member of the Ways and Means Committee. In addition to being an avid student — valedictorian at both his high school and Kentucky Normal, the teacher's school in Louisa — Vinson was also a talented and determined athlete, quarterbacking his high school football team to an undefeated season in 1906, and playing a superb shortstop on the baseball team, too. In fact, Vinson made some money during his college days by playing semi-pro baseball.

With the financial help of a local doctor and the support of some of his teachers at Kentucky Normal School, Vinson entered

Centre College as a student with advanced standing. He completed his Bachelor's degree in 1910 and his law degree the following year, while achieving the highest grade standing since Centre opened and winning the prize for top student.

After graduation, Vinson returned to Louisa to set up a law practice and pursue various business opportunities, such as silent partner in a wholesale grocery operation. Vinson volunteered for service during World War I which ended before he could complete officer training. Based upon a reputation for integrity and legal skill, Vinson began his political career in 1921 by being elected commonwealth attorney for Lawrence, Elliott and Carter counties. In 1923 Vinson married Roberta Dixon, daughter of a Louisa businessman and member of a rival faction of the local Democratic party, further proof of lawyer Vinson's advocacy skills.

William J. Fields was elected governor of Kentucky in 1923; this left vacant Field's former seat representing the Ninth District in the U.S. House of Representatives. Vinson had been recognized by many politically minded people in the region as a rising star in the Democratic party, and he was chosen unanimously by a district committee to be the party's candidate in the special election called to fill the remainder of Fields's term. He won over 70% of the vote against Republican W.S. Yazell of Maysville.

Vinson ably represented Kentucky in the House of Representatives 1924-1929, losing his bid for re-election in 1928 primarily because of his principled support for his party's candidate for the presidency, New York Governor Al Smith. Smith was very unpopular in eastern Kentucky because of his ties to the Tammany Hall political machine, his opposition to Prohibition, and his Catholicism. Vinson caught the eye of powerful John Nance Garner, Democratic Representative from Texas, in an early speech criticizing Treasury Secretary Andrew Mellon's tax reduction plan for the wealthy and supporting Garner's plan for saving money for taxpayers making under $50,000 a year. Later, when Garner would become floor leader, he would include Vinson among a small group of allies and friends, such as Sam Rayburn and John McCormack, who worked together on significant legislation. Garner, Rayburn and McCormack all would later become Speaker of the House.

As a good Kentuckian, Vinson supported coal and tobacco interests consistently throughout his years in the House, while also developing quite a reputation as an expert on tax issues. As a good patriotic American, Vinson supported various attempts to get bonus money paid to veterans of World War I, at times breaking with President Roosevelt and other leaders of his own party. Vinson was especially helpful in getting federal assistance to his home district after the floods of 1927 devastated large portions of eastern Kentucky. Ultimately, Congress authorized $2 million for Kentucky, an amount which the state matched, for flood relief.

Chastened by his defeat in the Republican landslide of 1928, Vinson determined to reconnect with his constituents and return to Congress, which he did in 1930, overcoming stiff primary opposition from former Governor William J. Fields ("Honest Bill from Olive Hill") before defeating Republican Elva R. Kendall, the man who had unseated him two years earlier. The Democrats had taken control of the House for the first time since 1919, and Vinson's old ally and friend John Nance Garner became Speaker of the House, insuring that Vinson would play a substantially greater role in Congress.

The Hoover administration proved unable to deal with the horrible effects of the stock market crash and nation-wide depression. Not surprisingly the Democrats swept into power behind President Franklin D. Roosevelt in the 1932 election. During the one hundred days after Roosevelt's inauguration on March 4, 1933, the country remade itself as Roosevelt proposed and congress enacted historic legislation at lightning speed. Except for disagreeing with President Roosevelt about the veteran's bonus — which passed the house but not the Senate — Vinson proved a loyal New Dealer, playing a key role in the Social Security bill in 1935. He also supported two of Roosevelt's most controversial proposals: to pack the Supreme Court with supporters of the New Deal to overcome the opposition of the sitting justices and to reorganize the executive branch. Even with Vinson's assistance — he actually introduced the measure in the House — Roosevelt suffered his worst defeat on the court-packing measure.

Vinson delayed assuming his position on the U.S. Court of Appeals for the District of Columbia Circuit, where he served 1938-1943, until final passage of the Revenue Act of 1938 which was his final major effort as a legislator. Roosevelt put Vinson forward for the Court of Appeals as part of his broader strategy of dealing with the Supreme Court's invalidation of numerous New Deal policies. His court-packing plan had been a misstep but time afforded Roosevelt opportunities to appoint replacements to the highest court, and the makeup of that body changed markedly to one more receptive to the President's ideas. However, less attention was paid to his moving younger and more sympathetic individuals into district courts and especially circuit courts of appeals.

Having neither graduated from nor taught at a prestigious law school, nor having served as a district judge, Vinson may have been viewed by some as a political appointment. With hard work and a pleasing personality, however, Vinson overcame these prejudices and earned the respect of the other members of the court, such as Chief Justice Lawrence Groner, who had served ten years as a district judge before being promoted to the Court of Appeals. During his time on the court Vinson consistently deferred to legislative intent, as he understood it applied to each case, and relied on precedent, avoiding any hint of judicial activism.

In March of 1942 Chief Justice Harlan Stone appointed Vinson as chief judge of the Emergency Court of Appeals, which was established to hear complaints about price controls on commodities and rents. He served on this court for fourteen months simultaneously with his service on the court of appeals. This experience well prepared him to serve as Director of the Office of Economic Stabilization, beginning in May 1943. In this position and his later ones as Federal Loan Administrator, Director of War Mobilization and Reconversion, and Secretary of the Treasury 1945-1946, Vinson had significant responsibility, along with Presidents Roosevelt and Truman, for managing the war economy and then guiding the nation through the transition to a Cold War economy.

Vinson has been judged unfairly as one of the least successful Chief Justices of the twentieth century, largely overshadowed by the accomplishments of his successor, Earl Warren. Vinson's accomplishments as Chief Justice can be better appreciated by considering his relatively short term — just over seven years, compared to the 21 years of his predecessor Harlan Stone and the 15 years of his successor Earl Warren — and the challenges he faced when he took the oath of office as the nation's 13th Chief Justice on June 24th, 1946.

When Chief Justice Harlan Stone died in mid-1946 the court was so divided by back-biting and personal animosity among several judges that it was widely known among the public that certain members of the court were not even on speaking terms with one another. In fact, Associate Justice Robert H. Jackson, to whom President Roosevelt had supposedly promised the Chief Justiceship, assumed President Truman would appoint him to that position, while Justices William O. Douglas and Hugo Black reportedly leaked to newspapers that they would resign should Jackson receive the appointment. When the feud between Jackson and Black became public, the dysfunction of the nation's highest court became a matter of national concern.

Vinson's affability and formidable conciliatory skills undoubtedly marked him as a viable option to heal some of the divisions among the justices and return the nation's highest court to good working order. However, the suggestion that Truman appointed a card-playing crony who had no background or training to head the highest court in the land is patently false. Vinson had served three years as either a county or district attorney, as well as 15 years in private legal practice. Not only had Vinson served on the U.S. Court of Appeals for the District of Columbia from 1938-1943, but he also had served as Chief Justice of the Emergency Court of Appeals.

Additionally, Vinson, like Truman's other Supreme Court appointees, Harold Burton, Tom Clark, and Sherman Minton, had held public office, were political allies and personal friends, and held the president's trust and confidence. Truman was consistent in his appointments to the highest court, choosing men who held moderate, pragmatic views and whose decisions reflected that philosophy. Once Clark and Minton joined the court in 1949, it was as much a Truman court as it was a Vinson court.

An unbiased assessment of Vinson's achievements as Chief Justice would acknowledge that while not a truly first-rate legal thinker, his opinions, though generally conservative, except in the area of civil rights, were not poorly reasoned. He was a pragmatic man guided by a few major convictions: participatory democracy was the best form of government, a strong central government was the best guarantor of individual rights and freedoms, and the president should have as much freedom as the Constitution could allow to lead that government, especially in the fight against communism. In other words, Vinson was a product of his times. That he came to these conclusions based on his own experience makes perfect sense for someone who had come of age during the World War I, had a hand in crafting much of the New Deal legislation, and then had the responsibility for steering the economy from a wartime footing toward the postwar period.

The Vinson Court represented an important transitional phase between the preceding "Lochner Era," when the interests of business dominated the docket and the decisions, and the succeeding Warren Court, which played such an important role in shifting the focus to the arena of individual rights and liberties, often at the expense of the state. Vinson did not develop any overarching legal theory or philosophy, nor did he assign many important cases to himself, two decisions that probably hurt his reputation.

In two of the most important cases of his Chief Justiceship, Vinson supported the state's powers to act decisively against inflationary wage demands in a time of crisis, first in *United Mine Workers v. United States in 1947* and then again in Y*oungstown Sheet and Tube v. Sawyer* in 1952. Vinson helped craft a 7-2 decision that upheld a contempt of court conviction against UMW leader John L. Lewis and the union and ended their strike. Vinson was not on the winning side in the latter case, dissenting from the 6-3 decision to disallow President Truman's seizure of steel production facilities to prevent what he felt would be inflationary wage hikes during the sensitive time of the Korean War. Both votes stemmed from Vinson's strong belief in the powers of the state and the President, particularly in a times of crisis such as the Cold War or the Korean War.

As for *Brown*, it appears likely that Vinson would have achieved similar results to Warren in the case, though perhaps in quite a different manner, once relevant prior cases before the Vinson court are examined. Although none of the trio of cases that paved the way to *Brown v. Board of Education of Topeka* — *Sweatt v. Painter, McLaurin v. Oklahoma* and *Henderson v. U.S.* — overturned *Plessy v. Ferguson* and its "separate but equal" doctrine, it is difficult to imagine *Brown* occurring as and when it did had these cases gone the other way. The lack of dissent from these decisions indicated that the justices were well aware of the historic nature of their rulings and the need to speak with one voice when possible.

The results of these cases chipped away at the "separate but equal" argument which undergirded so much of the legal scaffolding on which segregation in the South depended, *Sweatt* ruling against it in regards to legal education in the state of Texas, *McLaurin* ruling against it in regards to graduate education in Oklahoma and *Henderson* ruling against it in regards to dining services offered in rail cars. Writing for the court in *Sweatt*, Vinson identified intangible factors, such as what would be referred to today as networking opportunities, not just quantitative elements such as the number of volumes in the law library, as crucial to achieving "substantive equality". There could be no comparison of the potential access afforded a University of Texas law school graduate to the legal power structure of the state to that provided a graduate of the ersatz law school created by the state of Texas for its African-American residents. The consideration of intangible as well as tangible factors would come to play an important role in *Brown*.

Also, the Vinson Court had ruled against racially restrictive covenants in real estate in the 1948 case *Shelley v. Kraemer*. The court determined that any state action to enforce such a covenant would be discriminatory and was therefore prohibited by the Equal Protection Clause of the Fourteenth Amendment.

Given these factors, it is likely that Vinson would have been able to craft a unanimous *Brown* verdict as Warren did, by limiting the scope to the facts of public school segregation rather than a broad finding that would attempt to mandate immediate and full desegregation. As a practical-minded jurist with broad experience in both the executive branch and congress, Vinson may have understood far better than some of his more intellectual and academically minded colleagues the importance of the judiciary not outpacing society's desire and ability for change on the controversial subject of desegregation.

Much of the consensus that Vinson would have not been up to the challenge of *Brown* stems from rather self-serving comments by Felix Frankfurter and his allies, such as his infamous quip upon Vinson's death that "this is the first solid piece of evidence I've ever had that there really is a God." Ironically, much of the delay in the process of reaching a verdict in Brown was due to Frankfurter's conflicted position. On one hand, he wanted to find against segregation but he also wanted to be on firm legal footing in the decision, and not to appear to take other factors, such as sociological or political ones, into consideration. As was typical of Vinson's desire to seek consensus, he set *Brown* for reargument the following session to give everyone more time but then died unexpectedly before being able to hear the case again.

Although Vinson did not unify the court as he and Truman had hoped, he at least was able to get the personal bickering among the justices out of the newspapers and return the court's proceedings to a more decorous and professional tone. The occasional criticism of Vinson not being independent enough from President Truman or of having somehow colluded with him is unfair. They were close friends and political allies because they saw the world in very similar terms. No collusion was needed for them to agree on basic issues such as the need for the president to have a relatively free and strong hand, especially in times of crisis, or for deference to be shown congress as the maker of laws by courts whenever possible. Vinson held these positions consistently throughout his career, even before he entered the judiciary.

Had Vinson not died before bringing the Brown case to a decision, he might have been remembered as one of the greatest Chief Justices of the twentieth century. Despite having wielded significant power in Washington, D.C., Vinson never lost touch with his constituents back home or with their concerns, which informed his work in the House, as Treasury Secretary and as Chief Justice of the Supreme Court. Fred Vinson had one of the most distinguished careers in public service in our nation's history and deserves to be remembered as one of the greatest political figures in the history of the Big Sandy Valley.

Russell Williamson

RUSSELL WILLIAMSON

By Linda Scott DeRosier

In the 1940s and 1950s, before the wave of school consolidation permanently changed the culture of eastern Kentucky, county high schools were the center of community life. School activities provided a place for people to socialize and share a common purpose. High school basketball programs, in particular, inspired intense loyalty across generations, and they provided a reason for many young men to stay in school past their sixteenth birthday. Even when young people left the hills for work or further education, it was not uncommon for them to come back home for district or regional tournaments to support their teams. Coaches were local stars and one of the brightest stars was Russell Williamson, former principal and coach of the basketball team at Inez High School.

Russell Williamson lived to be ninety years old. On the surface, he appeared to live a very conventional life—a life spent as a teacher, coach, school administrator, banker and businessman in Martin County Kentucky—but his accomplishments were anything but conventional. Born March 4, 1903 at Tomahawk, a small farming community about six miles west of Inez, Russell was the fourth son of James A. and Eliza Williamson's nine children. Williamson's father was a farmer who also operated a delivery service for merchants in Inez. In the community, the Williamsons were known for their work ethic and ambition. They were "nobody's fool and cussedly independent," said Nealy Porter, who raised 10 children on a nearby farm. As further evidence of their independence, the family was well known for being Democrats in a county that was, at the time, about 90 percent Republican. "Martin County had about as many Democrats then as it had good roads," said Porter.

Roads, as much as basketball, were threads that coursed through Russell Williamson's life, lacing it up like one of his early out-seam basketballs. In a 1978 interview, Williamson said, "When I was a boy people from Inez would sometimes walk through Tomahawk on their way to Whitehouse in Johnson County to catch a train," a distance of about 10 miles. "Sometimes I could make a little money by taking them to Whitehouse on a mule."

"I was just a barefoot boy from Tomahawk," he said. "I hunted crows, dug 'sang, hoed corn, fished and killed snakes." Williamson's description of himself growing up as a little barefoot farm boy was not an exaggeration, said his sister, Dixie Marcum. "He was skinny as a rail," and a quiet-natured boy who said little "unless he had something to say." His wife Nolda offered, "Whenever Russell set himself to do something, he would do it."

Mrs. Marcum, four years younger than her brother, remembered Russell said when they were young: "Dixie, when I grow up, I'm not going to be poor." Of course, then, Mrs. Marcum said, "We didn't know we were poor. We had a happy family. We had everything—except money."

While still a boy, Williamson met a teacher at the old Mayo College in Paintsville. "They also had a high school there," he said. "This fellow got interested in me, so I wound up going to high school at Mayo. We didn't have a real high school in Martin County yet. Earl Cassady, a lawyer in Inez, taught some, but the school wasn't accredited or anything."

After graduating from high school, Williamson took a few college courses at Mayo before enrolling at the new state college in Morehead in 1922. "When I went to Morehead, there wasn't but one brick building on the campus and all the sidewalks were wood," he remembered. "We had classes in an old building that was heated by coal." He paused and grinned. "We used to say it was heated by smoke."

As many other eastern Kentucky educators would do later, Williamson worked his way through school by coal mining and teaching.

Another part of the Russell Williamson basketball legend is that the lowest grade he made in college was in coaching basketball, a game he had never played. "It's true," he said. "I took the class under Hunter Downing and he nearly failed me. I got out there on the court—we were playing rough—and got a rib broken." Young Williamson did not tell his basketball instructor that he was injured.

He began his teaching career at the Head of Stafford in a one-room school which, he said, "my dad and uncle built...I went from there to Tomahawk School." In 1926, "when I just about had my degree," Williamson said he took his basketball goals and moved to the county seat at Inez. The high school, variously called Martin County or Inez, was just beginning. Mr. Williamson became its third faculty member under B.E. Hickerson, whose wife also was a teacher. Although he was never official hired and therefore unpaid, he also undertook to teach basketball to the 15 boys enrolled in the school.

By teaching school, and by coaching basketball, Williamson first put Inez, and himself, on the map. According to local lore and legend, Russell Williamson came home from college at Morehead in 1927 with a basketball and two goals and nailed the two backboards together and built a dynasty.

"Nobody here knew much about the game," he said. "At the time, I didn't, either." The turning point, he said, came in about 1927 or 1928 when he took his first team to participate in the district tournament playoffs. "I don't recall the year, exactly," he said, "but I know where it was. It was at Pikeville." Roads out of Martin County were just old rutted country roads. Williamson remembers, "Many times, we rode in wagons over to Whitehouse in Johnson County where we would take a train to wherever we were going. Anyway, when we got to Pikeville, they had canceled our game. They said we didn't get there on time. Well, finally, they hustled up somebody to play us and then they threw us into a pretty bad hotel and so on…they just kind of made fun of us, you know? Well, I determined right there that I'd live to beat every team in that tournament."

Family members and friends say that when Russell Williamson set his mind to do something, he did it—and he always took considerable satisfaction in having done it. "He compiled the most impressive record of any coach in the history of Kentucky high school basketball," said John McGill of Lexington, whose 1978 book, *Kentucky Sports*, contained the most comprehensive statistics available on high school coaching records at the time. According to McGill, Inez teams won 892 games while losing only 108 during the 27 years Williamson played an active coaching role. Williamson's teams won two state championships, finished runner-up once and made it to the semifinals six times in nine state tournament appearances. When Inez won the state title for the last time in 1954, there were still only about 100 boys enrolled in the high school.

McGill, a novelist and sports editor, cited some of Williamson's accomplishments:

> • Seven regional championships in an eight-year span; four in succession.
> • A winning percentage of .720 in state tournament competition.
> • Twice went undefeated in regular-season play; compiled season records (against statewide competition) such as 36-2, 39-1, 40-1 and 44-4.
> • Placed all five starters on the Kentucky-Indiana All-Star team in 1941 after Inez won its first state tournament after four of these players made the all-tournament team.
> • Ran up a 13-2 margin against 16th Region power, Ashland.

"All things considered," McGill concluded, "it was an era

unmatched in the annals of Kentucky schoolboy basketball."

Colleagues offered praise, too. "In my estimation, Russell Williamson has to be classified as one of the greatest coaches in Kentucky basketball history, high school or college," said a former coach and all-state player at Ashland. "I've known them all—Rupp and Diddle included—and Russ rates right up there with any of them." In 1978, Ernie Chattin, a respected civic leader and former basketball referee, claimed to have seen or partici- pated in every state tournament for the previous 57 years. "Governors, congressmen, outstanding people all over the state know [Williamson]" he said, "and they all have the same high regard for Russ Williamson that I have." Earl Ruby, former sports editor of *The Courier-Journal* in Louisville, observed that Williamson's "mark as a coach and leader of boys has been fabulous. No man in Kentucky ever matched his achievements at Inez."

Inez became an accredited school for the first time during Williamson's first semester there as principal in 1930. He also began to develop a basketball program with one basketball, two goals and a relatively flat school yard.

"We used to rake the snow off and then carry sand from the creek bank to dry up the mud holes," said Bob Allen, a guard on the Inez team that won the school's first 15th Regional tour- nament in 1934. "We became pretty used to practicing outside with earmuffs and gloves."

No one on the team, which included Tom Williamson, the coach's brother, complained about conditions, Allen said, chuckling. "It wasn't all that bad; you see, if you didn't know anything else, it was alright."

In particularly severe weather, Williamson would load his team into a wagon or a couple of cars and go over to Himlerville (Beauty) and play inside the coal camp's commissary where someone had erected a backboard and goal. Dress was informal, Allen said, grinning. "We had one player who always played with his hat on."

Despite winning four straight trips to the state tournament, Inez did not have a gymnasium until 1937—after it had lost in the championship game to Midway. That gym, however, lasted only one season before it burned. Another larger gymnasium and classroom building was erected in 1941, after the Inez team won its first state tournament title.

"We played some games outdoors here," Mr. Williamson said, "but mostly we played away from home. It might have been a good thing that we played away so much. We never developed any feeling about home-court advantage, so almost anyplace was home to us."

When roads were dry enough to drive on, Mr. Williamson and his father-in-law would take the team to games in their cars. "We used to have to stay all night when we went to Paintsville," he said, a 27-mile trip now that takes less than 30 minutes. Lexington was an all-day drive and sometimes more. "It seemed like the worst weather we would have would be in March, at about state tournament time," he said. "Snow, rain and floods—but we always got there."

When Williamson first began coaching basketball, he read all he could find about the sport, attended coaching clinics and, particularly, watched other games. "Mr. Williamson was an astute watcher," said Bob Allen, who also praised Williamson as an amateur psychologist. "For certain, he knew how to get everything out of you. He taught all day (math and physics), practiced in the afternoons, and we would play at night. That was one of his secrets. He really knew his players. He knew how to get everything out of you. He figured you out and I think he did it in class more than during basketball practice. He knew what made you tick. He knew how you thought. Some, he would pat on the back and some he would kick in the pants, but he got the same thing out of you. And he could put it together."

From the first, there was a uniformity about his Inez teams. "We didn't have any individual stars," Williamson said. "The boys played as a team." The keys, he said, were "conditioning, teamwork and discipline...without discipline, you can't have anything." No smoking was allowed on school property and there was a tacit understanding about neat dress.

Discussions with those who were close to Russell Williamson suggest that he expected nothing but the best efforts from everyone around him and that he valued academic performance more highly than athletic performance. He believed that there was plenty of time in the day to achieve excellence in both. Moreover, he cared about students living up to their potential and he spent a good deal of his time seeing to it that they did precisely that. For example, he handed out report cards individually to every student at Inez High School, a practice inconceivable to those who have seen education evolve over the past five decades. More than two decades after his death, Mary Jo Hallaway, Williamson's only surviving child remembered sitting apprehensively in the high school auditorium along with her fellow classmates, waiting for her father to share not only her grades but also his judgment of those grades with all her contemporaries. She recalls the time she received a B and her father not only sharply criticized her in front of her peers but was even more critical when they went home that evening. "I told myself that was never going to happen again," she said, "and it didn't."

And Williamson's baby sister, Rowena—now in her nineties—still recalls how nervous she was in the math class she took from her brother because he had such high standards. According to Rowena, "Russell expected every student to take his/her work seriously and being a family member did not mean any special treatment." That sentiment was repeated by his niece Lisa, a successful Washington, DC artist and graduate of Inez High School. Indeed, apparently everybody respected, admired, and was more than a little afraid of Russell Williamson, especially his basketball players. A woman who, as a teenage girl, dated one of Coach Williamson's basketball players recalled sitting with that young man in the Inez Sweet Shop—a place to drink Cokes, jitterbug, and socialize—one Sunday after church. She, her boyfriend, and perhaps a dozen others were enjoying themselves when the coach walked in and the noise level dropped considerably. He did not acknowledge them but walked directly to the counter, bought something and left. Shortly after he left, he was followed by the four boys on his team. There was no rule about being in the Sweet Shop on Sunday afternoon but the players knew they would be held accountable for not using that time more wisely. Just as he set the same high standards for himself, the coach simply expected every young person to approach life with passion and give their very best to every endeavor.

Coach Williamson's teams never sat down during timeouts or between periods. They never drank water during practice or games. Candy and soda pop were prohibited for players and the townspeople knew it. "You couldn't buy a piece of candy in town if you played ball," Bob Allen said. "The merchants wouldn't sell it to you." Inez students, proud of their team, also helped enforce training rules. "Our students just would not stand for a player to break training," Williamson said. "They knew, the whole school knew, what it took to win."

From the beginning, Williamson placed heavy emphasis on sportsmanship, said John Williams, a former Warfield coach and school system administrator. No student ever booed an opposing team or its players while Russell Williamson was coach and principal of Inez High School. He did not allow students to so much as yell, "Miss it!" while an opponent was shooting a free throw.

Inez and Ashland began playing each other in 1936 after Ernie Chattin became the Ashland Tomcats' coach. "Russ was always a great technician," he said. Inez teams were always well coached on defense and rebounding and they were always in condition. "If you didn't get them down in the first half, they'd run you right out of the gym in the second."

For years, many in Martin County likened their famous coach to Adolph Rupp. Like Rupp, Williamson wore a brown suit to most of his team's games. He sat on the bench, knees apart, with one hand on his knee and the other on his tie. About the only emotion he showed, observed his nephew, former school superintendent Shelly Hardin, was to say, "dad-lem!" and chew on the end of his tie.

Billy Ray Cassady, an all-state player who helped lead Inez to its 1954 state title, also was a member of Rupp's 1958 national championship team at UK. "They knew each other and were pretty good friends," said Cassady, who later became a success-ful coach himself. "There were quite a few similarities between them, especially where discipline was concerned. They did about the same things in practice, which were very organized, all seri-ousness, and they would go full speed, trying to create game conditions. Both devoted part of every practice to work on a close man-to-man defense and they believed in a kind of set offense off the fast break." Both believed that "the way you play in practice is the way you perform in a game."

Williamson retired in 1966 after 40 years as principal at Inez High School. In retirement, Russell Williamson spent his days in relative tranquility, following a routine he approached with customary discipline. He would leave his two-story brick home in downtown Inez and walk three doors up Main Street to the Inez Deposit Bank, where he was president. There, he attended to bank business and, sometimes, to his business as chairman of the Big Sandy Area Development District. He was also chairman of the Area Development District board's transportation committee; a member of Governor Julian Carroll's legislative committee; on the advisory board of former Governor Harry Lee Waterfield's insurance company; on the board of trustees of Highlands Regional Hospital in Floyd County; and a deacon in the Inez First Baptist Church, located next door to his home. In the afternoon, he would often climb into his 4-wheel drive pickup and visit various real estate, mineral and mining interests—all of which he had been cultivating since he was 22 years old. "It's a funny thing about Russ," the late U.S. Rep. Carl D. Perkins told an ADD Board meeting. "The millionaire was always teaching school!"

In retirement, Williamson was quiet with a wry sense of humor. He was a popular after-dinner speaker whose repertoire of stories was made more effective by the fact that he apparently never forgot names. When the Ashland Kiwanis Club honored Ernie Chattin at a banquet after he retired, dignitaries from all over the state were invited. Williamson was asked to say a few words. "Ernie," he said, "used to play for Ashland; he used to coach for Ashland; and later on…he used to referee for Ashland." Chattin laughed. "We had big names on that program, but Russ stole the show."

Williamson's success in business was the continuation of his boyhood goal of "not being poor." Before he graduated from Morehead in 1927, Williamson decided to "get into business." "Russell got started by buying and selling cattle for our father," said Tom Williamson, his youngest brother who became a prominent Martin County businessman himself. "Then, when he was about 22, he began to buy natural gas and mineral titles. Back then, gas was the thing; nobody even thought about coal here, so a lot of times, the coal was just thrown into the deal." After purchasing mineral rights, his older brother began drilling for gas and oil himself, Tom Williamson said. "Herbert (an older brother) ran the drilling operations and the more Russell would make off the drilling, the more gas and mineral he would buy. That's one thing about Russell: He never bought anything that wouldn't pay for itself." Russ Williamson's investments continued to pay off.

For many years, Williamson was an avid foxhunter, a nighttime variation of the English ride-to-the-hounds sport which, in eastern Kentucky, was practiced by men around campfires on hilltops, releasing their dogs and listening to them bark while chasing a fox. Owners would argue over whose dog was running closest to the fox. This hobby doubtlessly contributed to Williamson's abilities as a raconteur, but it also affirmed the competitive side to his personality, remembered Harvey Preece, a former deputy sheriff and a legendary figure in Martin County foxhunting society. "He liked to run his dogs, but he wanted his dogs on the front end," Preece said. "Russell never fooled with a plug dog. I remember he didn't sleep much; he'd stay up all night and listen…he was a good sport a 'hunting, but if he outran a feller, he'd rub him a little bit."

Late in his life, Mr. Williamson took great pride in a new four-lane highway that connected Inez to U.S. 23 in Lawrence

Russell Williamson, bottom row right, with friends.

County. He had worked as hard for it as he had worked for everything else he accomplished. "Every time any mention was made of roads at a Big Sandy ADD meeting, or wherever they were talking about industry or anything, I would say we couldn't do anything in Martin County until we get a road. It got to be almost a joke," he said.

"The time we have to get ready for is when the coal is gone, when we'll have all these people and nothing for them to do," Williamson said in 1978. "If we can get roads in here, why, it'll be an ideal situation for bringing industry in to use a lot of our labor that we've had for coal production."

Russell Williamson died April 7, 1993, before seeing Inez wind up with two highways connecting it to U.S. 23 at junctions in Lawrence and Floyd counties. A third four-lane road, under construction today, will run past a proposed new high school to the West Virginia border.

By 2016, all three of Martin County's new highways will merge at a four-lane bypass in Inez. Years ago, state Transportation Cabinet officials christened it the Russell Williamson Bypass, a worthy tribute to a great coach, a far-sighted businessman, and a devoted educator.

AUTHORS NOTE

In addition to personal research and interviews, the author credits information from a 1978 newspaper article by Lee Mueller.

Loretta Thompson in the Philippines.

Loretta Thompson c. 1945.

Loretta and Ova L. Thompson.

LORETTA PRESTON SPEARS THOMPSON

By Clyde Roy Pack

In November, 2002, 92-year-old Loretta Thompson sat on her sofa and slowly thumbed through a tattered box of yellowed, dog-eared photos. She paused briefly to study a picture taken nearly 60 years ago, then patted the head of her dog Abby, an American Eskimo, who had parked herself next to her master and refused to be ignored.

"This is a picture of me and another nurse taken in the Philippines," Loretta said. Then, almost as an afterthought, she added, "Write what you want about me, just don't say I'm a hero or anything. I didn't do anything anyone else didn't do. I just did what I was told."

Sitting in the comfort of her Offutt, Kentucky home, this tiny woman, a World War II veteran, recounted incidents of an exciting life that reads like a novel; a life in which — despite her denials — she had indeed done things that had elevated her to hero status. Her life changed dramatically when at age 27,

Loretta Preston Spears found herself a widow with a 5-year-old son. In the early 1920s, like so many Appalachian women, she had dropped out of school, married and "set up housekeeping" with husband Ellis Spears in the rural Offutt community, about 10 miles northeast of Paintsville, the Johnson County seat. But Ellis' death in an automobile accident in 1937 left her with few options so she and son Wendell moved in with her parents.

Her top priority was to educate her son. However, the mines had closed, reducing the once-busy coal camp to just a dusty little Appalachian community with a few abandoned company buildings, two or three dozen residences, and a railroad.

"Daddy was too old to go someplace else," Loretta said. "He wanted to stay here and farm."

So, realizing that she was lacking in formal education, she decided to enroll at Caney Creek (which years later became Alice Lloyd College) to finish high school. The school was not more than 50 miles away — in the Knott County community of Pippa Passes — but it was a daunting trip for a woman who had never been away from home.

She packed her and her son's clothes in an old pasteboard suitcase, and her father took them to the Offutt depot and bought their tickets.

"He had three dollars left over and he gave it to me. That's all the money I had," she said.

She persevered and three years later, at age 30, she returned to Offutt with a high school diploma. Within a few months, still feeling the need to better herself, she enrolled in a nurses program in Charleston, West Virginia.

"Since I was the oldest girl, Daddy felt that my place was at home with the family, but I went anyway," she said.

She spent three years at Charleston General. She got out of nursing school during World War II.

"They made you feel about this high if you didn't go and help out," Loretta said, holding her palm a few feet from the floor. "So, I left Wendell in the care of my parents and joined the Army Nurse Corps. That was in 1943."

Her parents were opposed to that, because, as Stephen Ambrose notes in *Citizen Soldier*, women in uniform were targets for mean-spirited and sexist jokes of a male dominated society. Because they were so widely told, recruitment slowed to a trickle. A questionnaire taken at the time showed 41 percent of the nurse volunteers had to overcome the opposition of close relatives.

But nurses were needed badly. In one of President Roosevelt's State of the Union addresses, he responded to the critical shortage of nurses in Western Europe by proposing that they be drafted. A bill to do so passed the House and came within one vote of passing the Senate.

By volunteering when she did, however, Loretta's timing couldn't have been better. In June 1944 the Army granted officers' commissions and full retirement benefits to its nurses. From July 1943 until September 1945, approximately 27,000 newly inducted nurses graduated from 15 Army training centers. Loretta was among those completing the orientation program at Fort Breckinridge, Kentucky.

Thus began a ten-year sojourn that would find this young Appalachian woman moving into the role of "world traveler" and practicing nursing skills (many times while ducking for cover) in places that heretofore had been mere names in a geography book to her.

"I was in the Nurse Corps, but I was in the Army first," she said. Living conditions were anything but delicate and the women wore helmets, fatigues and boots. They lived in tents, used latrines and had to guard their privacy constantly. On top of all that, they were often targets for air raids.

"They first shipped us to Oran in North Africa, where they exercised us in everything they thought we would need. We did all the drills just like the regular Army did. Then they shipped us to Naples, Italy, where we hooked up with the 182nd station hospital," she said.

Station hospitals were the third of four steps in treating battle causalities (after field hospitals and evacuation hospitals). There patients often needed surgery and specialized treatments. Field hospitals were the closest to the action and were the first to see a wounded soldier. Doctors there performed triage on patients and, depending upon the severity of their wounds, either recommended they be taken by ambulance to evacuation hospitals, the second step, or they treated them right on the battlefield. After station hospitals, the last stop was the general hospital. Patients needing diagnosis, specialized lab tests, or long periods of recuperation and therapy were sent there. When patients were released, they were either sent back to duty or to the states for further treatment.

Loretta had been in Italy only a short time before she got her first taste of war. Her group had been dropped off in front of an old theater and told that this would be their home for a while. "There were eight of us nurses staying there and as night fell, they sent a little guard over to our area," Loretta remembered.

"He was a very young, handsome-looking soldier. As the days went on, he learned all our names. He was just down-town with us and we all liked him. Every night he would come and walk up and down in front of the theater while we slept. Then one night about three o'clock in the morning, we heard gunfire … like 'pingggg.' Every one of us flew to the windows. A sniper had killed our guard."

For the next year and a half, the 182nd station hospital, evading sniper fire and bombing raids as best they could, followed the troops of the newly-formed 5th Army — which had battled ashore at Salerno on September 9, 1943, and fought continuously for 602 days. Those days of battle cost America 109,642 casualties.

Despite being clearly marked with large white crosses, the Germans could have cared less that the 182nd was a hospital unit, and before her tenure in Italy was over, Loretta had survived seven major bombing raids.

"One in particular, I thought we were all going to be killed," she said. There had been a lull as far as patients were concerned, so when the alert was sounded that night hospital personnel had ample time to get everyone to a shelter. Loretta, several soldiers and a few other nurses had gathered in an area below the basement of the building they were occupying.

"You could hear the bomb coming … 'zingggg,'"she said. "Somebody hit me on the shoulder and said, 'Down nurse, it's going to hit.' It hit all right and raised us up and slammed us down. I think we were all out for a little while. The first thing I remember was being in total darkness and some little boy (a soldier) in the far corner of the room yelling, 'Wake up, wake up every body, we're alive!' As far as I was concerned, that was the worst raid I was in."

Farther into Italy, barracks for the 182nd were set up close to a grove of nut trees. The nurses dug holes at the base of those trees and when German planes would strafe, they would take shelter in those holes.

"We'd make ourselves as small as we could, hold our helmets as tight as we could on our heads, and wait," Loretta remembered. "Each wave of planes would last about a minute and a half and sometimes would go on all night long ... wave after wave. There were plenty of times as I hugged the base of that tree while those Germans were strafing, that I sure wished I had been back in dear old Offutt, Kentucky. Memories like these live forever."

On another occasion when there was a lull and only a few patients needed immediate care, several of the nurses went into a nearby town and visited a place of entertainment called Garden of Oranges.

"There was this band and the tuba player was a very small man," Loretta remembered. "While we were enjoying the enter-tainment, quite unexpectedly, we got bombed. The last I saw of the tuba player were his feet sticking out from his tuba. He had crawled as far as he could back into it to escape the bombing. Thankfully, no one was seriously hurt that night but the bombing did stop the show."

More often than not, however, after a raid the nurses faced every kind of wound imaginable and sometimes worked up to 24 hours straight.

When most patients came back to consciousness, they were in a field or evacuation hospital. They were groggy from morphine. The first sight many of them saw was a nurse from the Army Nurse Corps. She was wearing fatigues, exhausted and busy. But she was an American girl, and she had a marvelous smile, a reassuring attitude, and gentle hands. To the wounded soldier, they looked heaven-sent.

"By the time those wounded boys got to us at the station hospital, they had the greatest respect for Army nurses. They were always on their best behavior when we were around," Loretta said.

Working under often primitive conditions and constant, sometimes deadly, attacks from the enemy, Loretta and the other members of the 182nd tended the wounded soldiers as best they could, sometimes operating all night with just light from flash-lights. Patients with heart wounds and frostbite were especially troubling for Loretta, as were those men in the amputation ward.

"No one there had all four limbs. The boys who had already been fitted would hang their artificial arms and legs on the sides of their beds at night. It was a pitiful sight," she said.

Loretta also served briefly as a flight nurse. Although it was dangerous just working in a war zone, fight nurses assumed much greater risks than their on-land counterparts because the C-46, C-47 and C-54 transport planes used in patient evacuation were also used as cargo planes. Therefore, they could not display the markings of the Geneva Red Cross to protect them from enemy fire. If that wasn't bad enough, pilots nicknamed the C-46 the "flying coffin" because heater problems sometimes caused the coffin-shaped planes to explode during flight. Some pilots refused to turn on the heaters, even when they were carrying patients. This complicated nursing care because critically ill patients cannot tolerate low temperatures. Nurses improvised and tried to keep their patients warm with blankets and hot drinks.

"I had made only one trip with an experienced flight nurse before they sent me by myself," Loretta said. "I was absolutely terrified but a captain came up and gave me this advice: First, do what you know about nursing; second, follow your normal instincts and do what your mother taught you. The worst thing you can do is wring your hands and do nothing."

When the shooting in Italy finally stopped, Nurse Loretta Preston Spears was sent stateside for a short time, then to the Philippines. Her memories of experiences there, although not as harrowing as those in Italy, were no less memorable.

One Philippine incident had its roots years before when she was in high school at Caney Creek.

Although she had been a student, since she was older and had a child, she had been asked to serve as a housemother for nine elementary school-aged boys. One summer Kevin, one of the older children, decided that he didn't need to bathe every day as was required by school rules. Even after hearing several fiery lectures on the virtues of cleanliness, Kevin still balked. So one night the argument ended with "Mama Spears" (as she was known by her charges) tossing him, clothes and all, into a tub of soapy water where she proceeded to scrub his neck and ears. She then left the room after telling him that if he didn't finish the job, she would return and finish it for him. From then on, he was a regular bather.

"When I was in the Philippines, I had gone to the PX looking for some cards," she said. "I noticed that when I went in, three or four soldiers sitting over in the corner were watching me. Within a few minutes, one walked over, tapped me on the shoulder and said, 'Mama Spears?' I said 'yes' and he said, 'Look, I washed behind my ears.' It was Kevin. He made a fine looking soldier."

Loretta was discharged in 1953 with the rank of Captain and a souvenir from the Philippine Islands that she still carried on her left leg between her ankle and knee. "Despite being shot at, bombed and strafed by German planes, I never got a scratch from enemy fire, but I got this," she said as she displayed her calf, covered with faint, red splotches. "They call it 'Monsoon Itch.' It doesn't bother me unless it rains, then it itches like the devil."

Soon after her discharge, at age 43, she married Ova L. Thompson, also a war veteran and childhood friend from Offutt. He died on Loretta's 82nd birthday — August 25, 1992. Former Army Nurse Corps Captain Loretta Preston Spears Thompson lived the rest of her life in the house that once belonged to her parents — the house she and her young son Wendell moved into in 1927.

As for Wendell, he received his education, served as a

radioman in the Korean War and later operated an airport in the Dayton, Ohio, area. He lives on a farm in Tennessee.

Even though clouded by a half century of life away from the military, she admitted that her bloody wartime experiences sometimes did play over and over in her memory. Yet, Loretta Thompson never, even for a moment, considered herself a hero. Perhaps that's why others did.

Loretta died on December 27, 2004, at age 94, and was buried, with full military honors in the Preston family cemetery at River, Kentucky.

Author's note: I found valuable information for this essay in Tom Brokaw's *The Greatest Generation*; a brochure by Judith A. Bellaire entitled *The U.S Army Center of Military History*; a brochure prepared by the Fifth U. S. Army, Ft. Sam Houston, Texas; and *Citizen Soldier* by Stephen E. Ambrose.

CRATIS WILLIAMS

APPALACHIAN EDUCATOR

By James M. Gifford

This essay highlights the educational career of Cratis Williams, America's preeminent scholar in the field of Appalachian Studies who died May 11, 1985 at age 74. The first two sections are autobiographical statements and the concluding section is a memorial to Dr. Williams.

A HUMANIST REVIEWS HIS LIFE

This is a statement about myself and my odyssey from the happy innocence of a secure childhood in the cultural and social context of an Appalachian valley through troubling adventures of doubt, challenges to selfhood, denial, shame, and rejection, to understanding. acceptance, and affirmation of self as an Appalachian person who embraces his culture, searches out its history, and is proud of his identity as an Appalachian without feeling that he is therefore something less of an American for being an Appalachian.

That I found again something of the security I enjoyed as an Appalachian before I left the community in which I grew up

Mr. Appalachia delivering an animated lecture at Morehead State University.

while advancing through the humanities to a Ph.D. in an eastern university and in my profession from one room school teacher in the mountains of Kentucky to university president without compromising my integrity as a humanist and obscuring my identity as an Appalachian means, it seems to me, that there is sustenance in the culture of the hills "from whence cometh my strength." As a humanistic interpreter of my culture and as a teacher, speaker, entertainer, and writer, I feel that I have helped hundreds of other Appalachians toward self-acceptance and pride in who they are. I am most gratified that my sustained effort over many years helped to mount burgeoning Appalachian studies in school and college curricula throughout the region and inspired sincere scholarly reevaluation of America's most easily identified and possibly most significant subculture. It pleases me that nearly 400 doctoral dissertations have been written about Appalachia since 1965, for it is beginning to seem to me that 15 million Appalachians might soon lift their heads proudly in self-acceptance as they embrace their heritage.

In my childhood in a remote mountain valley relatively untouched by outside influences I played in my grandfather's distillery; heard my mother and my grandmother sing ballads and tell tales in the old prototypical dialect of the mountains, essentially the same that had been brought from Lowland Scotland to Ulster in the early 1600's and on into Appalachia immediately following the American Revolution; went to a hardshell church where hymns were sung in Gregorian fashion and sermons were chanted; played traditional singing games at school and Sunday gatherings; danced for my grandfather when he played his banjo; went to annual funeralizings at family graveyards; attended family reunions; helped my father gather herbs for family medicine; gathered chestnuts and hickory nuts with cousins; hunted and trapped; listened to patriarchs tell of family kinship ties; followed Civil War soldiers about on Sunday afternoons to hear them swap tales about the war; and worked in the fields, beginning at age six, with my father.

It was a comfortable but at the same time an exciting world in which I lived as a child. I saw women riding on side saddles and carrying baskets of eggs to country stores; mules loaded with great bags of wool being taken to a carding mill, horseback riders, buggies and surreys on the dusty trails. I saw grooms and their brides riding to their "in-fares" (the "in-fare" was a wedding dinner and party in the home of the groom). Peddlers of all kinds came, including basket makers and housewives selling salves and patent medicines. Travelers who stopped to spend the night with us talked far into the night. We went to workings, bean-string-ings, corn-shellings, where sometimes we could square dance ("run the sets" or have "play parties"); and during the hog-killing time we swapped work with neighbors. The schoolmasters, none of whom had gone to high school, spoke the Appalachian speech along with the rest of us, but many of them were excellent teachers.

There was also violence in the community. I witnessed many family fights and saw bloody encounters on the "church grounds." I saw bleeding men dying after gun battles. My teacher during the third grade was shot and killed at church one Sunday. But for all the violence and display of mean temper, it never occurred to me that I was living in a "dangerous" place, even though an average of two a year in the community during the decade of the 1920's were involved in killings.

At the age of 12 I rode on my father's farm wagon out of my valley to school in Louisa, the county seat town, 25 miles from my home and psychologically as far away as San Francisco is from Frankfort today. What I found at school was a jolt to me. I was shamed by my English teacher and laughed at by my fellow students. Obviously, I was to reject my culture and deny my identity, which I was able to do within a few months, but I felt unreal. The real me stood within the shadows to monitor as I asked myself from time to time, "How am I doing?" For the long Christmas holiday seasons and the summers I returned to my valley, where people were real but where it was important that I prove to everybody that going away to school had not changed me in any way. Returning for a few months each year into the culture in which I had grown up led in time to my reevaluating it. By the time I was a senior in high school I was beginning to speak positively for the Appalachian culture, to collect ballads and songs, and to read what I could find about Appalachia.

In college I picked up from professors and students from outside the Appalachian region the negative attitudes toward us Appalachians that fictional stereotypes had created. It was a shame to be Appalachian. An Appalachian person's first obligation to himself was to identify and correct or reject everything about himself that betrayed his identity. As I considered and tried alternatives, I found many of them superficial, unreal, often pretentious, and sometimes hypocritical. I had to pretend, for example, that young middle class women were innocent little girls who played at life as if they were still in doll houses. I had to substitute shallow euphemisms for the colorful and vigorous language in my dialect. People played religion in middle class churches and few seemed to take it very seriously. In time I was pleased to discover that my advancement in liberal studies had taken me beyond middle class concerns, which I felt no need to reject or attack or criticize, for they had never been vital to me anyway.

As a teacher, principal, university professor, administrator, I found that I could honestly tolerate, without feeling compelled to attack, social agencies and institutions and that I could work with students, fellow teachers, and administrators with backgrounds much different from my own without "putting anybody down." My good will and spirit of tolerance were the foundation stones of my "educational statesmanship." My acceptance of people as they saw themselves stood me in good stead.

My ability to listen, consider, ask questions without condemning or rejecting appealed to those whose fate it was to work with me. It has seemed to me that such success as I might have enjoyed as a "public person" is owing largely to my having accepted myself with confidence, and without significant loss of self-esteem, as an Appalachian. I never feel the need to apologize for who I am or try to obscure my identity. I find it enormously comfortable to be myself.

THE BOY FROM CAINES CREEK

I was now a teacher. I recall the cool, dank stretches of the sandy road beside Blaine Creek and the dust on the tall weeds and the leaves on the sycamores, willows, and water birches as I strolled along. Occasionally, I would be blinded by the dust kicked up by a car, but after I turned up the Caines Creek road I saw no more cars. The afternoon was hot. Poison ivy along the fence rows and the trumpet flowers that dipped from the Virginia Creeper growing on posts were still and dark in the hot sun. I thought of my trip up the creek in the wagon a year and a half before when I held proudly on my knee the loving cup I had received at the high school commencement and how pleased I had been to find on the front page of the *Big Sandy News* a week later my picture and a writeup that Earl Kinner had prepared. I remembered the trip in the wagon less than a year before when my father brought me to Blaine to find a ride to Louisa when I left by train for Cumberland College. That had been a hard but pleasant year, for all of that. I had made good grades, earned extra credits, and felt confident that I would teach a good school. I had also felt more keenly the pinch of poverty and recognized more deeply than ever before that I was depressed much of the time. The running sore on my thigh had never healed. My left leg tired easily. But I also knew that I felt irrepressible joy, especially with other people, and that I would go on to the University of Kentucky where I would have the money I had earned as a teacher to support me without my having to try to work and to go college at the same time.

My shirt was wet with sweat and soiled from the dust and my pants were heavy on my hips and dusty to the knees when I reached home about 4 o'clock. I changed to a hickory shirt and overalls and went to the schoolhouse to tidy it up for the beginning of the school the following morning. I threw up the windows, tore away nests of wasps and dirtdaubers, swept the floor, dusted the desks and the cottage organ that the school had bought the previous year with money raised at a pie mite. I pumped water from the well and found it clean and cool. The schoolyard had not been fenced off from the pasture in the edge of which the school had been built. The farmer pumped water from the well for his cattle. The cattle had kept the grass grazed down and the weeds away.

I fetched the coal bucket and fire shovel from one of the cloakrooms and shoveled up and carried away the fresher piles of manure left around the school house by the cattle. Then I cut away the taller weeds and bushes that had grown up around and through the steps of the style over the pasture fence by which one gained access to the schoolyard. The two-holer toilets, each with a box of old papers and catalogs children had contributed the year before, lay on the floor beside the door. There was a stench rising from the pits, so I dug sand from the bed of the branch behind them and covered the decaying excretion in each pit.

Everything in order at the school, I returned home in time to do my share of the chores. After supper I sat at the dining room table and I wrote out on theme paper a plan for the first day of school.

Thirty-three children and two parents, one the local trustee, reported. Four were beginners and eight were in the eighth grade. Among my pupils were my brother and sister, my aunt, four years younger than I, four of my first cousins, and many, only a year or two younger than myself, with whom I had been in school and played on weekends before I left to go to high school. Several of them, both boys and girls, were taller and heavier than I. At eighteen, I weighed only 118 pounds and was five feet four inches tall.

I had dressed myself in my quilted pants and a clean blue shirt with an open collar. The boys dressed in overalls and hickory shirts, the girls in clean gingham and calico. All were barefoot.

One of my "innovations," which we all liked, was to seat grades in sections so I could have all of those in the same grade together for convenience in supervising written exercises. I would not always call them to the recitation bench but would, instead, come to their section to conduct discussion. Always they had sat boys on one side of the room and girls on the other and gone to the recitation bench for "reciting." The idea of sitting two at a desk, boys at one and girls at another, appealed to them. But I told them that this arrangement was an experiment and that if I learned it did not work well we could return to the seating arrangement with which they were familiar and use the recitation bench as they had always done.

Another of my innovations was to march the entire student body into the schoolyard after lessons for the first grades in the afternoon for ten minutes of breathing, bending, and stretching exercises to tone them up and help them overcome the drowsiness from which students suffer after lunch. They liked this and become competitive in acquiring skill in touching their toes with their fingertips in the bending exercise.

Not all of the pupils owned books, but those who had books were placed to share them with seat mates. I did not have a complete set of books for all grades myself. It was necessary for me to borrow books from students to use in making lesson plans. Except for an ancient unabridged dictionary and two or three old hymnals at the organ, there were no books in the school building at all.

Four of the eight in the eighth grade had taken eighth grade before. It soon became apparent to me that they should be encouraged to consider enrolling at the high school scheduled to open at the beginning of September in Blaine. The other four, though not excellent students, were old enough to be in high school and ought to be encouraged, it seemed to me, to go. I had not completed eighth grade myself, I reminded them, and I had graduated from high school second in my class of 41. They could succeed if they were willing to try.

Two experiences that first year made deep and lasting impressions on me. One bright little boy, the youngest in his family and the favorite of his father, had a speech impediment. He talked so fast that it was difficult to understand what he was saying. Other children mimicked him playfully, and asked him to say again for their amusement things that sounded funny to them. Everybody stopped studying to listen to him read aloud and laughed when he mispronounced words. I observed that the boy was having difficulty with palatals. He said "sty" and "tloud" for "sky" and "cloud," "drampa" for "grandpa," and his "l" and "r" did not come out for certain vowels, especially when they were related to nasals. He said "borne" for "barn," "forme" for "farm." One day I asked him at recess when no one was close by to pro-nounce words after me. He was unable to pronounce them correctly. I then asked if he would let me look at his mouth. He opened his mouth widely and I squatted in front of him to look into it. He had the steepest highest palate I had ever seen. It was so high that the boy's tongue simply did not make contact with it when he tried to say "cloud."

I worked with him carefully for a few minutes a day for a week or two and taught him how to slow down and take the time to lift his tongue to his palate to be sure the sounds were formed correctly. He was so proud of his achievements that his speech became almost normal within a few weeks, although a hissing sound continued with certain sounds until he was grown. It occurred to me that his grandfather, then an old man with a white beard, and his uncle, then approaching middle age, had similar speech impediments. No doubt the steep palate was an inherited trait, but apparently nobody had ever attempted to help the grandfather and the uncle to overcome the difficulty.

Paul Alexander, the teacher at Upper Caines Creek School, married Christine Ison, one of the young women in the district who had tired of repeating eighth grade but had not cared to go to the new high school at Blaine. I attended the wedding, to which Christine's nieces, whose fathers were coal miners in Pike County, came. One of the nieces, tall, slender, black haired, and with almost violet eyes in a beautiful face, attracted my attention. I sat with her in the porch swing for a time after the wedding. We liked each other. She would return to Pike County the following day with her parents, but they would come back for a visit in a few weeks. She would be glad to have me come to see her when she came back. I got her name, Irene Miller, and her address, McVeigh, Kentucky. We exchanged letters.

When she came back to visit her grandmother, I had dates with her in the evening. Following a long date from which I returned about two o'clock in the morning, I was tired and sleepy the next day. Everything went wrong at school. I was irritable. The children had little interest in what they were doing. The school almost deteriorated into a pandemonium while I fussed and scowled. My temper was bad. The one day when they should have been especially good were particularly trying on my nerves. My speaking sharply to them had seemed to make them worse. On my way home that afternoon I recognized that that day had been the only day all year that I had not enjoyed. It occurred to me that the trouble was mine, not the children's. My own feelings, the state of my irritability, my private problems, must not in any way affect my attitude and behavior as a teacher. A teacher, when before the class, is a public person. A public person does not betray in attitude or behavior his private feelings. That was one of the soundest principles I ever learned in my life. I have been amazed at the numbers of teachers, secretaries, and administrators I have known, many of them with years of experience, who never learned that lesson.

CRATIS WILLIAMS'S IMPACT ON EASTERN KENTUCKY

In 1929, Cratis Williams began his teaching career at a one-room school on Caines Creek in Lawrence County. Over the next fifty-five years, he contributed to secondary and post-secondary education in Eastern Kentucky and throughout Southern Appalachia.

His approach to one-room school discipline was unique. He assumed "that all thirty-three children were capable, eager, and industrious." Proceeding on that assumption, he laid down no rules, as one-room school teachers before him had always done. Rather, he referred to "the desire of everyone to be thoughtful and considerate of others and to have others return thoughtfulness and consideration." With this as a guide, he observed, "we would most certainly get along well and enjoy school." Cratis was so successful in presenting his basic guidelines for conduct that it was not necessary all year to whip a child with a switch, the "traditional terminal punishment" for misbehavior in one-room schools.

Cratis's keen sensitivity to other people's feelings and his compassion and appreciation for others became personal trademarks. As a one-room school teacher, he had "three little tow-headed girls" who could not buy tooth brushes for their oral hygiene class, and so Cratis asked parental permission to buy the brushes as presents. "The father and mother looked at each other for a moment. Tears came to the mother's eyes as she nodded her head slightly."

The father said that he would like "for the girls to be able to do what the other children did," and he told Cratis that the children quoted him as the "pure Gospel." The father offered to repay him, but Cratis told him that he had not come to urge him to go into debt for the brushes, that he liked his little girls and they were doing so well in school that he wanted to give them the brushes ... but did not want to run the risk of hurting (the parents') feelings, and so he sought and received their approval. On his way-back home, Cratis stopped at the country store and post office and bought three toothbrushes.

Throughout his career, Cratis extended this kind of loving help. He was the star attraction at Berea College's workshops in Appalachian history and literature in the 1970s. Unlike many living legends, he equaled his advanced billings and exceeded his reputation. He enthralled audiences with his knowledge, and he captivated individuals with his charm. Not surprisingly, his work at Berea was a springboard to developing an Appalachian Studies Program at Morehead State University – and other regional schools – in the 1970s and 1980s.

In November, 1979 Cratis served a consultancy at MSU's Appalachian Development Center. As always, he kept a hectic schedule. He met with the Appalachian Studies Advisory Committee, delivered a public lecture one evening, addressed several classes, and met informally with interested students and faculty. Afterwards, he submitted a detailed and extremely beneficial set of guidelines that provided intellectual, curricular, programmatic, and developmental cornerstones for our emerging program. His greatest effect, however, was on the individuals he encountered. One faculty member wrote to him: "words have not the power to convey either my Joy from or the positive effect of your three-day visit to our campus...I am delighted to have met a person with your knowledge of our cultural heritage and zest for sharing it with others. I eagerly await your next visit to Morehead." Another wrote that his lecture to her literature class "provided one of the finest academic experiences that our students could ever have."

In June of 1980 and 1981 and again in 1984, Dr. Williams served as Scholar in Residence for MSU's Annual Appalachian Celebration, impressing hundreds of people with his wide-ranging knowledge and with his enormous personal charisma. Again, his contributions were great and far-reaching and the positive effects of his visits reverberated across the campus long after he returned to his home in Boone, North Carolina, where he remained actively "retired" as a special assistant to the chancellor of Appalachian State University. On September 17, 1981, Cratis made the first presentation in MSU's "Our Mountain Heritage" lecture series. Until his death, he maintained a regular interest in and support of Morehead State's Appalachian Studies Program.

Cratis's contributions to Morehead State University's Appalachian Studies Program exemplify the type of assistance he gave throughout Eastern Kentucky. He worked closely with Ron Dailey and Mike Mullins at Alice Lloyd College and with Leonard Roberts at Pikeville College. He regularly worked with Loyal Jones in Berea College's highly regarded summer workshops. He served on the Board of Directors of the Hindman Settlement School and as Chairman of the Alumni Board of Cumberland College. His contributions to Eastern Kentucky institutions illustrate the service he provided throughout Southern Appalachia. Teachers and counselors who are searching for a role model would find much value in studying Williams's life and educational philosophy.

Like Tennyson's Ulysses, Cratis become a part of all that he met. Although he received many honors and awards (including honorary doctorates from Morehead State University and Marshall University), his most significant awards are not inscribed on plaques or printed handsomely on diplomas or books. They are written with love and admiration on the hearts of hundreds of people who are forever grateful for his friendship, advice, and good company. Cratis made his mark upon the immortal mind! He set fires of love and learning that will burn and brighten to all eternity.

Leonard Roberts.
Courtesy of the
University of Kentucky
Libraries. These photos
originally appeared in the
Lexington Herald-Leader.

LEONARD WARD ROBERTS

By Loyal Jones

When Leonard Roberts told a story, you could see that he enjoyed it as much as his audience. Every now and then, he would be overcome by the humor or absurdity of his tale and pause to laugh out loud and slap his leg. Roberts was a master storyteller but beyond that, he was a noted scholar of the Old World folktales that had been brought to the new world by his ancestors and passed down through generations in Kentucky. He collected and published several volumes of these tales, and through them he showed the world that these wonderful old tales were still being told in the Cumberland Mountains.

Leonard Roberts was born in a weatherboarded log house at the head of Toler Creek in Floyd County, Kentucky, on January 28, 1912. His parents were Lewis Jackson and Rhoda Jane Osborn Roberts. Leonard was the seventh of eleven children and the sixth son. His siblings were William Vernon, Edward Virgil, Mary Bayard, Samuel Jesse, Teddy Adrian, Alonzo Dale, Elmer Wall, Arminta Helen, and Faustina Fern. The Roberts, Osborn/Osborne, Sturgell/Sturgill families began intermarrying in

Virginia in the late 1700s, and they moved to Floyd County, Kentucky before the turn of the nineteenth century. There they intermarried with the Barnettes, Kings, Monroes, Rices, Comptons, Ratliffs, Keatherleys, Martins, Iricks, and others.

Lewis Roberts, Leonard's father was a farmer who also floated log-rafts on the Big Sandy to sawmills at Catlettsburg and later operated his own sawmills. Around 1920, he also became a preacher in the Church of Christ that outnumbered the Baptist churches seven to one on Toler Creek. Leonard's mother, Rhoda Jane Osborn, was hard pressed to feed and clothe her large family, but she also ran the Osborn Post Office that had been established and named by her brother, Edward Leonard "Dick" Osborn, for whom Leonard was named, and Dick was married to Anna Laura Roberts, Leonard's aunt. In addition, with the help from her children, she grew a large garden and sold vegetables to her neighbors on Toler.

Leonard, already able to read at six, walked the mile-and-a-half to the one-room log school on Toler, where his brother Sam was the teacher. For parts of three years, he lived with and did chores for his grandmother Arminta Sturgill Osborn, a widow. From 1921 to 1926, he lived back with his family and helped to work the farm and garden and care for livestock while finishing the sixth grade in a new white-framed school, still only with one room.

Lewis's sawmills, the farm, and his preaching brought in enough money for him to put some aside, and in 1926, he moved the family to Pikeville, where he had bought two houses, one for the family and one to rent. He also purchased one of the first automobiles in the town but demolished the shed he was using for a garage while learning to drive it. The children were enrolled in the Pikeville schools, but they were all set back a year because of poor schooling on Toler. Lewis wanted all of his children to get an education, and so he set up an account for their books and school supplies and encouraged them in their learning.

According to a biographical account that Leonard wrote years later, after 18 months Lewis bought a boundary of timber that was nearer to Toler than Pikeville, and he moved his family back to Toler. Another family version is that when Rhoda learned that Lewis had begun an affair with a woman in Pikeville, she moved the family back to the farm. Later, the story goes, when Rhoda found out that Lewis had bought a hotel in Pikeville and set the woman and her blind husband and child up in it to manage, she mounted their mule, Old Stafford, and rode the twelve miles to Pikeville, dragged the woman into the street by the hair of her head, denounced her, slapped her enthusiastically, then re-mounted Old Stafford and rode back to Toler.

Lewis wanted Leonard to continue his education, and so he arranged for him to board with a family living in one of the houses he had bought in Pikeville until he finished the 8th grade in 1929. Leonard later wrote that the Pikeville years changed him, introduced him to poetry and literary stories, and he greatly enjoyed the mostly Western picture shows at the movie theater, as well as other forms of entertainment. He was converted and baptized there in a tent revival run by a Church of Christ preacher. He confessed that thereafter, he had a conflict over his desire to be both a cowboy *and* a Christian.

The summer after Leonard graduated from the 8th grade, he and two cousins got jobs in a coal mine. In the meantime, Lewis declared bankruptcy, owing some $8.000, and ran off with his mistress. Rhoda struggled with the help of the children to keep the farm and household going.

That fall, Leonard was invited by his aunt, Columbia Roberts, to live with her in Harold where he could enroll in the Betsy Layne High School. In return, he was required to help her run and maintain the telephone system that she and her sister Olga owned. He maintained forty miles of wire, run on trees, houses, fence posts, and poles. He figured out how the boxes for each house and business were wired so that he could install and repair them, and he sometimes worked the switchboard. In addition, he fed the cattle and chickens, milked the cows, split stove wood, and carried in coal to heat the house. He had to get up early to do his chores and then walk the two miles to Betsy Layne High School, taking his pole-climbing spikes and tools with him. He frequently had to skip classes to make repairs to the telephone system.

Leonard praised his teachers, especially Jesse Elliott, the director of the band, who taught him to play the trombone and found an old one for him to buy. Leonard was known to tell funny stories, and one about bathing a dirty tomcat earned him the nickname of "Old Souser." Even with his missed classes, he earned seven A's and a B+ that year, while also playing in the band and on the basketball team.

He went home the following summer and helped put out a crop, but he had rambling on his mind. He yearned to see the big cities, so he went to Lexington and then on to Ashland and Huntington, apparently hoboing on freight trains. In Ashland, he visited an Army recruiting station and found that he could join up and be sent to Hawaii. He passed the entrance exam, but he needed a parent's signature because of his age. He returned home with his papers, but his mother refused to sign them because she needed him at home. However, he was adamant and remembered a day he worked in the cornfield. "I stepped along behind the mule, watching the dusty ground slide away from the plow point. But all the time, I was thinking of cities and their million lights and of the sea. I was going down to the sea in ships." His mother eventually signed the papers, and he was sworn into the Army in Columbus, Ohio, and shipped to Scofield Barracks in Hawaii. Because he knew how to play the trombone, he was sent to Army music schools and learned to play all the band instruments. He served three years as a member of the 21st Infantry Regiment band.

Leonard came home to Kentucky in 1933 and went back to Pikeville to finish high school. He also joined a dance band that played for dances on weekends. The high school was a joint venture between Pike County and the city of Pikeville, but Pikeville College, financed by Presbyterian churches, allowed students from remote areas to live in its dormitory to attend the school. Leonard's sister Arminta was a dorm student, and her roommate was Edith Reynolds from Grapevine Creek, and she and Leonard began dating off and on. They graduated in the spring of 1933.

Leonard found out about Berea College through an adver-

tisement in a Montgomery Ward Catalogue. Apparently, appli-
cants were encouraged to recommend other students who might
apply. He decided to go to Berea, and he took along five others,
his brother and sister, Carl and Faustina, his cousins Rell and
Lydia Roberts, and Frank Akers. Leonard was accepted to the
college, and the others entered the college's Foundation School,
a junior high school and high school.

A story was passed around that Leonard showed up at
Berea's athletic field where they were having low-hurdle races
and asked, "What are those fellers in their underwear doing?"
After inquiring about the rules, he entered the next event in his
regular clothing and set a new record! This is probably an early
example of his trickster nature. Actually, Leonard who was tall
and muscular succeeded in most of the field sports at Berea —
javelin throw, shot-put, pole vault, and broad jump. He majored
in both English and music at Berea, and he gained attention by
winning a music competition demonstrating on the stage of the
college auditorium that that he could play all 15 instruments in
the college band.

In the meantime, Edith Reynolds, whom Leonard had
dated in Pikeville, had transferred from Pikeville College to
Eastern Kentucky State Teachers College in Richmond, just 12
miles from Berea. Her roommate was Myrtle Mae Dotson, a
relative who had a crush on Leonard's Berea roommate, Gether
Irick, his distant cousin also from Floyd County. Myrtle talked
Edith into a double date with Leonard and Gether. Thus Edith
and Leonard resumed their courtship and were married in 1939,
the summer after he graduated from Berea.

For two years he taught English and organized and directed a band at the Jackson, Kentucky, City School. A daughter, Sue, was born to Leonard and Edith in 1940.

During this time, he and Lawrence Bowling, a fellow Berea graduate who had earned an M.A. in English at Vanderbilt, got together at a Berea reunion. Since they both admired Jesse Stuart, the celebrated Kentucky novelist, poet, and educator, they made plans to visit him at his remodeled log home in W-Hollow in Greenup County. They arrived unannounced, but Jesse and Naomi Deane received them graciously, fed them dinner, and they spent an exciting evening talking with Stuart about his writing. Stuart offered them a cigar and a glass of wine but, heavily influenced by Berea's abstemious values, both refused. Jesse called to Naomi Deane and said, "Here are two young men, graduates of Berea, who neither drink or smoke, Isn't that wonderful!" (It was rumored that Jesse's brother James had been kicked out of Berea for smoking.) Bowling took along a couple of his unpublished manuscripts to show to Stuart, but Leonard said that he never mentioned his own desire to become a writer at this meeting. However, he was so inspired that he wrote in the guest book, "Time of my life!" He later published an a fictional account of this visit, "A Night With Jesse Stuart" (Wind, Vol. 6, 1956, pp. 75-81), and he and Stuart corresponded for several years. Stuart was complimentary of Leonard's writing and wrote letters to publishers promoting Roberts's unpublished novel, *Home in the Rock: A Novel of Eastern Kentucky*.

In 1942, he taught English at Brevard Junior College in North Carolina. He had harbored a strong desire to be a writer and felt that he ought to do further study toward that end. No doubt, he was influenced by his friend Lawrence Bowling to apply for admission at the premier creative writing program at the University of Iowa, where Bowling was studying in the English department. He was accepted and as a part of his studies, he wrote *A Personal History of Eastern Kentucky* and a novel, *Home in the Rock*, the latter his masters thesis, and earned a Master of Arts degree. In the summer of 1943, Professor Hardin Craig, a native Kentuckian and distinguished Shakespearean scholar, came to the university to lecture, and both Bowling and Leonard attended. Craig, who was a visiting professor at the University of North Carolina at Chapel Hill, offered Bowling a fellowship at U.N.C. for further study in Shakespeare, but Bowling needed to complete his work at Iowa. Therefore, he recommended Leonard, who received the fellowship. Enrolled as a doctoral student at U.N.C., Leonard moved his family to Chapel Hill, and his second daughter, Margaret, was born in December of 1943. During 1944-1945, Leonard taught for the U.S. military: the Navy V-12 program for future Naval officers at Chapel Hill and a similar program for future Army officers at North Carolina State College in Raleigh. He took graduate courses on the side.

From 1945 to 1948, Roberts taught English at the Berea College Foundation School. Rita, a third daughter, was born in 1946. His students were mostly from eastern Kentucky and elsewhere in Appalachia, and they were homesick for their own people. Leonard had acquired a copy of Richard Chase's *The Jack Tales* (Houghton Mifflin, 1943), a collection of tales that Chase and others had collected in North Carolina and Virginia, and he read them to his students. These tales were about a boy named Jack, living in the same kind of place students had grown up in, who triumphed over all sorts of troubles through cunning or magic. The students let him know that they had heard similar tales back home. He asked them to write them down, and thus he discovered that these Old World folktales with characters like Jack, and Nippy, and Merrywise were still being told in the mountains of eastern Kentucky. This led him to go home with students on weekends to begin recording tales, jokes, riddles, songs, and ballads from their kinfolk and neighbors on cumbersome reel-to-reel recording machines. He also inquired about such lore in his own family and found that his aunt Columbia Roberts, with whom he had lived and helped to maintain the telephone company, knew a tale about a magic horse and girl. However, by the time Leonard got to her with his tape recorder, her memory was shaky, but her daughters to whom she had told the tale to as children, were there to prompt her. Thus, it was from his aunt that Leonard learned his favorite tale, "Raglif Jaglif Tetartlif Pole."

After he had recorded numerous tales, Leonard felt the need to begin classifying them, and he went to the Indiana University department of folklore during the summer of 1948 to study with Professors Stith Thompson and William Hugh Jansen, authorities on folktales and their classification. He had probably already met Thompson and Jansen while he was a graduate student at U.N.C. through his association with another distinguished folklorist, Arthur Palmer Hudson, who taught folklore there.

While teaching at Berea, Leonard called on President

Francis S. Hutchins who had succeeded his father William J. Hutchins as president of the college. He stated his desire to pursue a doctorate in English and folklore and to return to Berea to teach in the English Department of the College. Both Hutchinses were educated at Oberlin and Yale, and the younger was director of Yale in China when he was called to Berea. Leonard commented on this memory, "[President Hutchins] studied me for a moment and said, 'I don't believe there would be a place for you there.'" Berea was already famous for educating "poor but bright" Appalachian young people, and although there had been other teachers, such as James Watt Raine, John F. Smith, and Gladys Jameson, who were interested in aspects of Appalachian culture, folklore was not seen as a plausible vehicle for intellectual uplift in Berea's curriculum. This rejection was a hard blow to Leonard's self-esteem, but he went on to become one of the most-published graduates of the college, and his papers and recordings are now among Berea's huge research collections on Appalachia.

Nevertheless, he applied and was accepted to the doctoral program in English at the University of Kentucky. There, he studied under William Hugh Jansen who had moved from Bloomington to Lexington to establish a curriculum in folklore at the university. Leonard moved his family to Pine Mountain Settlement School in 1950 where he and Edith taught and he continued his collecting trips and worked on his dissertation, a collection of folktales from Eastern Kentucky that was accepted for his doctorate in English.. This collection of 105 folktales is meticulously annotated to show parallel variants in other cultures, predominantly from the British Isles and Germany.

Their last child, Lynneda, was born in 1952. In 1953, Leonard served as head of the English Department at Piedmont College, Demorest, Georgia from 1954 to 1958. He was Chair of the Division of Languages and Head of the English Department at Union College in Barbourville, Kentucky. From 1958-61, he held the same positions at Morehead State College, and from 1961-68 at West Virginia Wesleyan College. At the latter he started and edited a magazine, *The Laurel Review*. From 1961-83, he chaired the Languages and English Department at Pikeville College. There, he developed an Appalachian Studies Program and edited a magazine, *Twigs*, later re-titled *Cumberlands*, and established the Pikeville College Press to publish historical and literary works of regional writers. He also worked with the Pike County Historical Society to publish numerous books and articles on Pike County history and the Hatfield and McCoy families.

Roberts was involved in the Kentucky Place Name Survey initiated in 1971 and personally interviewed, and enlisted his Pikeville College students in interviewing residents of obscure places to be added to the survey. This material was included in the late Robert M. Rennick's monumental work, *Kentucky Place Names* (University Press of Kentucky, 1984).

Leonard published over 50 articles and folktales and 42 book reviews in such magazines as the *Journal of American Folklore*, *Kentucky Folklore Record*, the *Tennessee Folklore Bulletin*, *Midwest Folklore*, *Mountain Life & Work*, and other folklore, state, and regional journals. He also contributed to 14 books by other writers and editors, and he edited and published numerous books on regional subjects under the imprint of the Pikeville College Press.

Leonard's greatest achievement was the discovery, interviews, and publication of the vast lore of the Couch family of Eastern Kentucky. He describes his discovery:

> [A]cross the long ridge of Pine Mountain to the northeast lie the most isolated acres of the state — on the headwaters of the Kentucky River. Here are such picturesque branches and valleys as Cutshin, Greasy, and Big Leatherwood. Here I have explored for a decade, discovering many strange and lingering folkways, primitive farming and folk handicrafts, lumbering and hunting, funeralizing and moonshining. The most valuable treasure, however, has been an old-fashioned family tradition of Old World folktale telling and ancient ballad singing. On a small branch of Cutshin Creek I met Mandy Couch Hendrix, who directed me back across Pine ridge to Putney on the Cumberland, a stringtown lumber camp some eight miles above Harlan, to her brothers Jim and Dave Couch, who recorded for me the family store of folklore — sixty old tales and one hundred folksongs and hymns.
>
> (From the Preface of *Up Cutshin & Down Greasy: Folkways Of A Kentucky Mountain Family*).

Most of the tales and songs, riddles and jokes came from Jim and Dave Couch, who had learned them from their father,

Tom, and mother, Mary Ann Couch; additional material came from other members of the family. The content was collected in 10 lengthy sessions from 1951 to 1955 while Leonard taught at Pine Mountain Settlement School, Wallins High School, Piedmont College, and Union College. After he had filled 30 reels of tape, Leonard commented, "I left the lore of the family still unexhausted." He transcribed the material into a 700-page manuscript containing 100 folksongs and 16l folktales, riddles and jokes, with copious notes and annotation. The entire body of the collection was too large for a single book, but the University of Kentucky Press released it on Microcard in 1959. Leonard then decided to break the material into two parts, family narrative and family story and song. The first part was published as *Up Cutshin & Down Greasy: Folkways of A Kentucky Mountain Family* by the University of Kentucky Press in 1959, with a few illustrative stories and songs included. Then in 1974, the University of Texas Press published the entire collection for the American Folklore Society's Memoir Series as *The Sang Branch Settlers: Folksongs and Tale of a Kentucky Mountain Family*. In this way the Society paid homage to one of its most distinguished members.

In his interviewing and arrangement of this material, Leonard had little interest in the new trend in folklore of theoretical analysis, but he was in the vanguard of another trend, that of placing the performance of folklore in the context of the lives of the performers.

By the time Leonard found Jim Couch, his father, Tom, was 92, living in a nearby house. His mother, Mary Ann, the primary teller of the old folktales, had died in 1921. Jim had served in the

Army in France in World War I, and was wounded four times. He signed up for a second hitch to disinter and ship remains of casualties back to the States. Back home, he cut and logged timber and did some moonshining ("I have made whiskey, enough to float all those sawlogs out of here"). He admitted to doing some witch-doctoring, and he worked in the mines where he lost a leg in an accident and later became an expert lumber grader. Finally, he bought a farm and ran it while still working in the lumber business. Roberts got detailed information about all the jobs he had done. However, he found out that Jim could be elusive on his days off from work. As his son said, "We don't know when he's going to come back in the door when he takes off. He goes down there in that town [Harlan] and stands around joking with ever'body, and he shoots pool, and he might wind up in the picture show and not come in until the bus runs at seven o'clock, or somebody brings him in."

Jim's brother Dave was the banjo picker and singer and had the best memory for the material folk culture about how things used to be and how they made a living while he was growing up. He thought that life and living was better then than now. He talked about the natural fruits and nuts and how they grew and how they preserved other things to eat, almost everything they needed. He told how he could stand in their garden and throw a fishing line into the Cumberland River to catch a mess of fish. During the winter they supplemented their table with wild game they killed on their frequent hunts. He said he never made moonshine while his mother, a good Christian woman, was alive, but when she died, he went to live with his brother Jim, and they made whiskey for several years. When he took a job with the C&O railroad near Hazard, he brought moonshine and sold it to the railroad workers. He later worked in the mines, and then took a job at Pine Mountain Settlement School where there was a considerable interest in the folklore of the mountains, especially in the songs and dances.

Each of the Couches had scant schooling in one-teacher schools, but both had terrific memories, and a vast store of ballads, hymns, lyric songs, folktales, riddles, and jokes, as did others of their kin. They may not have known much about the printed literature that was taught in other parts of the country, but they had a literature of their own, and they presented it clearly and colorfully in their native speech. *The Sang Branch Settlers* was reviewed widely and became a model for how folklore should be presented as part of the lives of those living in the culture.

During his life, Leonard was involved with the American Folklore Society and was president of both the Kentucky and West Virginia folklore societies. He also worked enthusiastically with fellow Kentuckian Sarah Gertrude Knott, who headed the National Folk Festival Association and founded its long-running festival, and he served as its vice president and president for four years. However, he was at odds with his board because he stressed folk authenticity over artistic excellence of their performers. He often was at odds with other folklorists over how folklore should be collected and presented.

A fatal traffic accident in 1983 silenced Leonard Roberts's story-telling voice and ended his monumental work in documenting the folklore of eastern Kentucky. Edith Roberts survived

Leonard by 27 years; she died in 2010. They are buried in the Davidson Memorial Gardens in Ivel, Kentucky.

All of the Roberts children survive. Sue Carolyn Roberts, a teacher, married William Walter Atkins in 1967, and they have three children, Grace Aletheia, Eduel Joshua, and Joy Stephanie. Margaret Anne Roberts, a librarian, married David Francis O'Connor in 1966, and they had a son, Kevin Leonard; she married Larry Neal Biller in 1975, with a step-daughter, Laura Lee. Rita Helen Roberts, a nurse, married Gerald Henry Phillips in 1969, with no children; she married Robert Arnold Kelly in 1972, and they have two children, Leonard Meriton Robert Aragorn, and a step-son, Jimmy. Lynneda Jane Roberts, an office worker, married William Dallas Bradley Denny in 1971, and they have no children. There are ten great-grandchildren.

In 1993, the Appalachian Center of Berea College issued a Cassette recording, *Leonard Roberts : Raglif Jaglif Tetartlif Pole*, with him telling several of his favorite tales and riddles and also his comments on storytelling. It is the only commercial recording of Roberts himself.

In the summer of 2003, Dr. Carl Lindahl, Professor of English and Folklore at the University of Houston, organized a workshop at Berea College where the Leonard Roberts papers are archived, for students, teachers, storytellers, and researchers. Lindahl, a long-time admirer of Roberts's work, declared that "The Roberts Collection is among the largest holdings of field collected, traditional English-language American narratives in the nation." Noting that Roberts had published many of these tales in his books, the purpose of the workshop was to work with the "many tales that remain unpublished." Lindahl and other specialists from Indiana University, the University of North Carolina, and Berea College led the workshop in analyzing and transcribing from sound recordings enough material for several projects of scholarly importance.

In 2008, Professor Lindahl organized two sessions on Roberts at the annual meeting of the American Folklore Society when it met in Louisville. Lindahl gave a splendid presentation on Roberts's work in showing that the Old World magic tales were still alive in the Cumberland Mountains and then presented Jane Muncy Fugate to tell "Merrywise," a full-blown narrative learned from her grandmother, as she had told it to Roberts in 1949 when she was an eleven-year-old schoolgirl. This writer followed her to do the best he could with Leonard's favorite tale, "Raglif Jaglif Tetartlif Pole." The second session was "Leonard Roberts and the Cumberland Mountains," with family members and others who had known Roberts contributing.

Leonard Roberts lived an interesting life and was one of the true scholars coming out of the Big Sandy area. While many other Appalachian scholars were looking at the big picture of the region — economics, educational advancement, social improvement, and above all change, he was visiting families in the coves and ridges and valleys and documenting their inner lives — what they thought and said, how they entertained themselves, what they thought funny, what was sacred, and what was worth remembering and passing on to the next generations. It is this legacy that Roberts passed on, much of it still unpublished.

Sources:

The Leonard Roberts Papers and Recordings at Special Collections in the Hutchins Library at Berea College.

The Leonard Roberts Memorial Issue of *Appalachian Heritage* (Vol. 15, No. 2, Spring 1987).

South from Hell-fer-Sartin: Kentucky Mountain Folk Tales. Lexington: University of Kentucky Press, 1955; rpt. Berea: Council of the Southern Mountains, 1964; rpt. Pikeville College Press, 1970.

The Sang Branch Settlers: Folkways of a Kentucky Mountain Family. Austin: University of Texas Press for the American Folklore Society, 1974; rpt. Pikeville College Press, 1980.

I am grateful also for advice and materials from Lynneda Roberts Denny and Dr. Carl Lindahl, folklorist at the University of Houston and author of a forthcoming book on Leonard Roberts.

VERNA MAE SLONE
GRANDMA MOSES OF THE MOUNTAINS

By Paula Kopacz

Mike Mullins, longtime director of the Hindman Settlement School, often referred to Verna Mae Slone as "Grandma Moses of the Mountains." It is a fitting moniker. Like the pictorial artist, writer Verna Mae Slone developed her craft later in life. Slone was 65 when she published her first and most famous book, *What My Heart Wants to Tell*. Like Grandma Moses, Slone identified most with the simple life of family and community in a rural setting. And like Grandma Moses, she was surprised by the unexpected fame that came from what some might call folk art.

But Slone should not be regarded merely in the shadow of someone else, for she was a strong and talented one-of-a-kind Appalachian woman, singular, yet still the kind of woman who has come to represent Appalachia in the twentieth century. Born on October 9, 1914, to Isom and Sarah Slone, their eleventh and last child, Slone grew up to be not only capable, strong, and efficient, but also talented, sensitive, and intelligent. She married

Verna Mae Slone. Photo courtesy of The Hindman Settlement School.

Willie Slone, not related despite the same last name, and gave birth to five sons. She went to school through the eighth grade, but ventured to the next level only when her oldest son, Milburn, was able to attend. Pregnancy with her fifth child ended her formal education. She never traveled far from her Pippa Passes home. But it is clear from her books that despite what we might think to be a narrow background, she had a strong mind, an excellent memory, an ear for language, and good writing skills. Slone's son believed his mother had a photographic memory. Clearly, however, the most important thing for the writer Slone was her fierce appreciation for Appalachia, its values and practices, and this is the memory she preserves in her writing.

In addition to writing, Slone is remembered locally for her quilts and doll-making. Her love for fabric arts is evidenced in the thousands of cloth dolls and quilts she gave away; some folks estimate the number of quilts to be as high as 1800. Quilting and doll-making are both conventional Appalachian women's crafts whose artistry has only relatively recently come to be recognized and appreciated. For Slone and many Appalachian women like her, such handwork was merely something useful that she enjoyed. These "conventional" Appalachian talents comprise the life she lived as wife and mother while her husband was away working on a bulldozer to clear roads throughout the region. As a housewife, Slone kept a garden and cooked and preserved and sewed and provided for the daily needs of her family. Like other Appalachian women in her generation, she was a hard worker, devoted to her family, and enjoyed keeping her hands busy. When later in life she began to write, she was as surprised as the fictional Gertie Nevels in Harriette Arnow's *The Dollmaker* to discover that others thought her work worthy of notice.

By the early nineties, when New Jersey photographer Barbara Beirne identified Slone for her "Women of Southern Appalachia" exhibit, Slone had published a number of books celebrating her beloved Appalachia and therefore was an appropriate subject for Beirne's study. The 1993 photograph of Slone became one of the centerpieces of the 1999 traveling exhibit entitled "Serving Home and Community: Women of Southern Appalachia." Beirne recalled Slone as "a gracious, dignified, intelligent woman." Slone died on January 5, 2009, at the age of 94. Alert until fifteen minutes before she died, she lived a full and rich life in her beloved small corner of Kentucky. By the time of her death she had become an icon of mountain life, the Grandma Moses of Appalachia

SLONE AS AN AUTHOR
What My Heart Wants to Tell

Slone's most famous book, *What My Heart Wants to Tell*, is primarily a memorial to Slone's father, Isom "Kitten Eye" Slone, Verna Mae Slone's mother having died when Verna Mae was only five weeks old. What makes the work more important and valuable than its function as a tribute piece is the fact that like most of Slone's writing, it describes with love and respect the values, customs, traditions, and practices that obtained in the first half of the twentieth century in Appalachia. Even though Slone wanted to honor her father in writing the book, she had a larger goal in mind. She was determined to set the story straight regarding Appalachia.

She came to the book almost accidentally. Mullins remembers that interviews his students conducted with Slone for an oral history project through Alice Lloyd College were always fascinating. Slone was rich with stories and anecdotes. When she saw transcriptions of these interviews, she became interested in the print medium. Using the transcripts of her interviews, Slone created that first book about her father. She had 100 copies printed and like her dolls and quilts, gave them away mostly to family members. Her Preface is addressed "Dear Grandchildren" (xi). Passed from person to person, the book made its way to National Public Radio, where segments were read aloud for the listening audience. New Republic Books picked it up in 1979 and gave it the title *What My Heart Wants to Tell*. It has been republished since then several times by the University Press of Kentucky.

In her opening Acknowledgments Slone announces her purpose for writing the book, "to honor my father" (vii). Immediately, however, she situates him as representative: "only one of many mountain people — proud, brave, sturdy, hard-working, god-fearing, and sensitive," in a distinct time and place — "a place and time so unique and different that its very simplicity is too profound to be fully understood and explained" (vii). While it is easy for us from this vantage point in the twenty-first century to look at descriptions of the past and identify their outstanding characteristics, it is not often that someone who has lived through that period can faithfully remember so much of the daily common activities that changed so gradually over the years, especially when that observer never lived outside the region. It is human nature for a child to believe that his experience is mainstream, and usually it isn't until he learns through formal education or travels elsewhere that he can identify the unique features of his own culture. Such is not the case of Slone, however. Her memory of the past contrasted with her own lived experience of the present and became the primary way in which she culls her recollections for the details of mountain life in her father's generation. No wonder her son so much respected the power of her memory.

There is one more motivator that propelled her throughout her entire writing career — her deep anger at the stereotypes that abounded about Appalachian life and her intense desire to refute them — not head on, but by showing what Appalachian life was really like from an insider's perspective. In the Acknowledgments to *What My Heart Wants to Tell* she writes that she hopes "to dispel some of the myths and misunderstandings" about mountain people. In the Preface addressed to her grandchildren, Slone is more urgent and more detailed: "So many lies and half-truths have been written about us, the mountain people, that folks from other states have formed an image of a gun-totin', 'backer-' spitting, whiskey-drinking, barefooted, foolish hillbilly, who never existed" (xii). She is angry not just because the stereotypes are unflattering to her people, but because she feels they have done real harm to the children growing up in Appalachia, "more damage than anything else":

> They have taken more from us than the large coal and gas companies did by cheating our forefathers out of their minerals, for that was just money. These writers have taken our pride and dignity and have disgraced us in the eyes of the outside world. When our children go into the cities for work or are drafted into the army, they are forced to deny their heritage, change their way of talking, and pretend to be someone else, or be made to feel ashamed, when they really have something to be proud of. (xii-xiii)

The memories of her father that she records in *What My Heart Wants to Tell* are intended to set the record straight. Even in the last chapter of the book Slone is still advocating for

Appalachia. She reports a question from an Oregonian as to why a person would want to live in a place where a quarter of the babies die in infancy. Like an investigative reporter, Slone questions the statistic and reports doing her own survey, which finds the rate much less, not only in her own family of Slones (8 percent) but among all the folks on Caney Ridge (10 percent). She also notes that even after telling her friend the results of her first-hand survey, he doesn't change his misconception (136). Despite the absence of formal records of births and deaths, Slone observes the power of Washington statistics, even when spurious, over the lived realities of mountain life.

Pride for mountain life and mountain people motivate Slone in her tribute to her father. The book is filled with accounts of the activities that made up the days and nights of his life. Slone writes, for example, about her father's job bringing the mail from Wayland to Pippa Passes, how he used the trip to serve as a bus for folks going to the dentist or doctor or catching a train elsewhere; another job was making chairs for Mrs. Lloyd, who opened the Community Center that eventually became Alice Lloyd College, and transporting extra chairs to the train station to be sent to the north. Another anecdote she tells about her father is how he pursued and finally retrieved his mule after it had been stolen by a cousin. And still another incident Slone recounts is what happened one day when he was courting her mother by taking her to church: in his best Sunday clothes he headed out to the pasture to catch the mule he hoped to use for transportation but remembered that his pants would be ruined if he walked through the weeds laden with damp yellow pollen.

Since no one was in sight, he took off his pants, hung them on the fence, and went after the mule. When he caught the mule and led it back to where he had hung his pants, they were no longer there, so he got on the mule and rode as quickly as possible past his waiting future wife. The embarrassing story was long remembered in family tales.

One might expect an inexperienced author writing about her deceased father might lapse into sentimentality or idealism. Slone does neither. Her father is sometimes the butt of the joke, as in the embarrassing incident above when he must pass by the woman he is courting without his pants. She writes, "I don't know how he ever explained it to her, but I guess they had many a good laugh about the time they did not go to church together" (38). The tone neither belittles nor aggrandizes him: we are drawn to such a man, for who has never been embarrassed over something that could be laughed at later? Like the love that pervades comic vision, we laugh and warm to the man. Like ancient comic vision, such incidents remind us of our common humanity.

Other anecdotes show that the man was not perfect, but the calm tone and absence of judgmental language mitigate the error of his ways. Although her father apparently fathered a child out of wedlock, we learn about it only as Slone recounts the odd circumstances that brought about her father's decision to marry the woman who became Verna Mae Slone's mother. All dressed up and on his way to marry the mother of his child, he stops at a neighbor's house. The neighbor asks if he really likes the woman "a whole lot"; when he says he intends the marriage mostly for his son's sake, she reminds him of her own daughter: "if ye want to wait a few more months, I believe everything will work itself out. Lay them [marriage] license there in the fire" (36). He did. Sarah Jane Owens and Isom B. (Kitteneye) Slone married on July 28, 1887. "And they loved each other until they were separated by death" (36). Did he act as a father to his first-born son by another woman? Did he financially or emotionally support him? Did he visit him? We hear nothing more of Cleveland or his mother. Instead, the modern reader's interest is directed at the seemingly serendipitous replacement of one woman for another. Slone neither condemns nor justifies her father's behavior; she merely reports it.

While the book is replete with anecdotes about her father, they are embedded in the broader view of Appalachian customs. In fact, the reader can easily forget that her father is at the center, for even the selected anecdotes reveal more about daily customs and social practices than about the individual. A "workin,'" for instance, was an occasion for socializing as everyone on the ridge was invited to come and help build a log cabin or barn or other structure, or clear land for someone. While the men worked, the women cooked; then the men ate first, followed by the women and children. The pattern was almost ceremonial. Another community event was the "molassie stir-off," at the end of which every visitor got a bucket or jarful to take home. It is this way of life, this sharing of bad times and good, that Slone celebrates in the book: "They worked together, ate together, and loved each other as neighbors were intended to do since time began. I think a lot was lost when these old ways were changed to so-called better ones," Slone concludes (40).

In this rhetorical strategy of generalizing about Appalachian customs and traditions from anecdotes from her father's life, Slone extends a practice seen most clearly in the American slave narrative tradition. In the classic slave narrative genre represented by Frederick Douglass's 1845 *Narrative*, the author writes not only about incidents in his own experience of slavery, but about those of others, and he shares the customs and practices of the time, even if he himself was not subjected to them. Perhaps Slone never read any slave narratives, and perhaps she was unaware of the rhetorical moves she was making in *What My Heart Wants to Tell*. Nevertheless, the strategy works for her as well as it worked for the anti-slavery advocates in providing a credible historical and social context for the central figure's life and in advocating for a larger cause than the individual. *What My Heart Wants to Tell* pays tribute to Kitteneye Slone, but more importantly, it pays loving tribute to the ways and values of mountain folk.

Common Folks

Slone's next work, *Common Folks*, picks up on her social advocacy for Appalachian ways. The book was written after her tribute to her father but before that work was brought out by a commercial press. Published by Alice Lloyd College in 1978, *Common Folks* begins as an autobiography but quickly evolves into a defense of shared Appalachian attitudes and customs and a righting of outsiders' misconceptions and judgments. In *Common Folks*, Slone shows awareness of the negative term "hillbillies" and seeks more aggressively than in *My Heart* to show the error of such negative views by describing some interactions with outsiders from her own point of view.

One that she reports at some length is her first interaction with outsiders. It occurred when she was a child, and her tone is unmistakably hostile. She begins the account saying she "bitterly learned" from the meeting that "we hillbillies had a status rating somewhere between the animals and plants" (227). Even as an adult reflecting on a past event, her anger is evident in her tone. She writes that when she didn't respond immediately to a stranger's request for water, "he slowly repeated what he had said, in a much louder voice, speaking as though I was deaf." When she said she would get the water and invited the couple to come in, she adds for our benefit: "I had been taught to always invite anyone into your home." When the stranger declined the invitation and told her instead to bring out the water, she writes, "It was not a request, but a demand. I did not understand, there was something about his voice that made me feel very uncom-fortable, as if I had done something wrong, and needed to be ashamed." She said the lady was smiling, "not a friendly smile, but more of a smirk" (228). She notes the woman's perfume was "more repellent to me than the odor of leather and horse" (228). According to Slone, the man declined her offer of water and turned to his companion and began talking "as if [Slone] was not present" (229). She quotes him as saying, "You never know about these people. The water may not be clean. Their toilets may be near their wells, some even use water from the creeks" (229). Slone says she knew this was not true, but had been taught never to contradict an adult. The passage goes on to report the stranger's objection to her family's using a worn out American flag to cover a chicken coop. "Folks who care anything about their country would not use a flag as you have." And she reports the man's summary judgment, "That's what you can expect from these backward people" (230). Slone's adult sister replied then to the man that she loved her country as much as anyone, but "I don't think any government's going to care if I raise chickens or not. [. . .] It's none of your business what I do, and I would take it kindly, sir, if you would go on and attend to your ownself" (230). But this is Slone's story now, decades later, and she finally gets to respond to the situation she remembers so vividly from childhood. To this end she writes, "Little did [my sister] know that day, that the little baby she was holding in her arms would serve over thirty-five years of his life defending the American flag, and that his son would one day pay the 'Supreme Price' while in the Armed Service" (230). Little did Slone herself know then, and little did the strangers know then. But now and for all time Slone has the last word about this incident and Appalachian patriotism, and now it is she who talks to us, her readers, as though that "stranger" is not present. The writer knows exactly what she is doing.

Another strategy from American slave narrative tradition is direct refutation of errors. In Chapter 2 of his 1845 *Narrative of the Life of Frederick Douglass, An American Slave*, Douglass writes about his surprise in discovering that white people interpreted slaves' singing as signs of their happiness. He writes bluntly, "It is impossible to conceive of a greater mistake." He then goes on to explain what the singing really means. Slone also engages in direct refutation, which in some instances seems to emerge from her interest in language. For example, in talking about the family's circadian rhythms she reports that "like all people who live 'up the hollers,'" family members went to bed "'with the chickens'" and got up with them. She explains that it means they would go to bed at about the same time that the chickens went to roost, and adds parenthetically, "maybe this is where a certain writer got the idea we let the chickens live in the house with us" (279). Thus, in an apparently casual and offhand way she directly refutes the untruth.

Her comment about the chickens suggests the stronger tone she uses in *Common Folks*. While she is still speaking from her heart, in *Common Folks* she addresses some of the most controversial issues of her time — issues such as unions and strip mining and government aid. No one living in eastern Kentucky in the twentieth century could be neutral on the position of unions, given the violence of union controversies and strikes in 1931 and again in 1973-74. "Bloody Harlan" gained national attention, and Slone, like everyone else in the area, was touched by the controversy. She reports that not only was a brother-in-law involved in the strike, but her sister "was one of the women to carry banners and join the picket lines" (275). She writes, "I am a very firm believer in all unions and would back them up with my life. I believe they are the best thing that ever happened for poor hard working men and women" (275). As for mountain top removal, she says she "would be afraid to express my real feelings" because many of her nephews support their families through mining. Nevertheless, her anger over the practice is clear:

> My heart aches at the sight of a black slug of muck that used to be a clear sparkling brook. Our beautiful mountain tops changed into scarred "tattered hills." So many people prefer "greenback" to green leaves. Our lands were just beginning to recover from the slaughter our grandfathers gave it by repeatedly cutting and destroying the woods to farm our hillsides. They had no other choice, but these strip miners have a lot to answer for. I don't think God would have made our country so beautiful if he had not wanted it to have remained that way. It's not so bad for the ones who have no other way to live, but what about the ones that are destroying something only God can create, just to enlarge their bank account. (275)

The depth of her feeling resounds in the elevated language here, calling on God's creation. Thus, in a succinct way she voices the dilemma about mining that continues to this day. For some it is a way to make a living; for others it represents only wanton destruction of God's beautiful creation. Similarly, her concerns about government aid are also still heard today. In her time it was Black Lung Benefits, which she feels came too late for those who really needed it, but what she most objects to is the age-old and still contemporary complaint that many who deserve aid cannot get it and many get it who do not deserve it.

For Slone and other mountain people, accepting aid is

problematical — even when it concerns her children. Slone herself always wanted an education, and she certainly wanted it for her children — so much so that the family moved closer to the school so that the children would not be stymied by the creek they had to cross to get there. And then there was the community school that became Alice Lloyd College. Slone admits that Mrs. Lloyd helped many of her students finish college by sending them on after the two years she provided and that she would probably have helped with Slone's five sons if Slone had asked: "but I did not want to be beholden to anyone" (278), a sentiment that threads its way throughout the book and is seen in the common practice of working for one's food and lodging during visits.

By the time she is writing *Common Folks*, Slone is well aware of the distinctive characteristics of her dialect. She puts regional expressions in quotation marks and explains the meaning of words, and she often makes a point to tell how her friends and kin pronounce words. For instance, she writes, "Sally Watts was a midwife, or 'Granny Woman' as we called them" (243). Sometimes, of course, we can gather the meaning from the context: writing about how hard it is to wash quilts, she remembers, "We 'most always took them to the creek to 'wrinch' them" (237). Of her mother-in-law she writes, "She really used the hillbilly way of talking. [. . .] She pronounced the word child as 'chal'" (240). Slone shows herself to be carefully attentive to language and aware of the differences between mainstream English and what is spoken in Appalachia. Given that she never travelled out of her area and that her formal education ended at the eighth grade, her sensitivity to language, her understanding of standard English, and her affirmation of eastern Kentucky dialect are impressive.

Common Folks is indeed the rich treasure trove of Appalachian customs and practices of common folks that Slone intended: "Folks," she writes, "who never did any great deeds, never became president [. . .] but were just common folks, loved by their families, and did the very best they could with what they had to do with" (203). Folks whose grandchildren will remember them now with pride: "Brave, sturdy, hard-working, God-fearing people, misunderstood by outsiders because their customs and speech belong only to them" (203). *Common Folks* goes a long way toward rectifying those misunderstandings.

How We Talked

A third book, *How We Talked*, published in 1982, is a linguist's dream, for it catalogues words and phrases, gives pronunciation guides, etymologies, and social and historical contexts for language, idioms, and speech patterns that are rapidly disappearing. As with her earlier books, Slone writes not only to explain but also to memorialize the distinctive language she grew up with. Also similar to her earlier work is her visceral awareness of the changes that time brings. Words here are merely the door to the beliefs, customs, traditions, and practices that Slone loves so well and whose passing she regrets.

One chapter that stands out with information not apparent in her earlier books is her chapter on "Food — Grub or Vittles" (80). Although prior books mention food a good deal because gardening and harvesting, cooking and canning, were the primary, time-consuming occupations for women, here she lists food item after food item and for each, she gives preparation instruction. In this chapter her venture into linguistics results in a cookbook! Almost everything she cooks, it seems, uses greater and lesser quantities of lard, and she swears by the virtues of pork grease, making her recipes unsuitable for today's fat-conscious housewives. Nevertheless, while the "recipes" are no longer appropriate, her work enables us to begin to understand something more important — the social value of food in this community, its ability to bring people together, to cement family life, and to connect humanity with the rhythms of the earth. In so doing, she emphasizes the differences between her time period and ours in this fast-food nation, where only the trendiest of chefs are now beginning to promote what mountain people did in their farm-to-table lifestyle.

Most readers also enjoy her explanations of clichés and dead metaphors, some of which are still heard today. Scraping the bottom of the barrel is one such idiom she explains: "We bought our flour in one-hundred pound barrels. By the time we used this much, what was in the bottom was no good" (23). So now we know why "scraping the bottom of the barrel" indicates that something is not good. Slone may not have known that the phrase is called an "idiom," but she instinctively knew that many outsiders would find it very interesting to learn where the phrase came from.

Other sections of the book cover what she calls "Old Sayings," names, words associated with moonshine and alcohol, school, religion, children's rhymes, their toys, snacks, and games, weather, medicine and cures, superstitions, and words related to work and tools. In all these areas Slone goes far beyond simple definition to make her language divulge the customs and practices of Appalachia. *How We Talked* shows the same love for her region, its people and its ways, as her other books, and it shows she was smart enough to recognize the position of language in this culture.

Rennie's Way

With *Rennie's Way,* Slone takes a giant step forward in crafting her material so that it seems to tell its own story. Indeed, her first work of fiction is a novel worthy of national literary distinction. *Rennie's Way* is Slone's first major work of fiction, rendering her earlier works apprenticeship to this higher stage of aesthetic achievement. While the novel carries forward the cluster of values, attitudes, and perspectives that distinguish Slone and that appear in her earlier works, here the historical and social contexts are of a piece, melded into a work of art that appears so easy and natural that readers do not realize they are being "lectured" to or deliberately being "taught" the many laudable customs and habits of mountain people of the twentieth century.

Perhaps the mature tone of the novel comes from the fact that this work is more — both consciously and unconsciously — a reflective reworking of material than anything written before. Here she allows herself not only to write from her heart (*What My Heart Wants to Tell*) about the people and culture that she knows so well (*Common Folks*) in the distinctive language of

Appalachia (*How We Talked*), but to bring all together in a believable fictional world that draws in the reader by its seemingly inevitable trajectory through human life. *Rennie's Way* touches all the major events of humanity despite the accidentals of education or location or socio-economic status: birth and death, violence and community, religion and spirituality, loss and gain, pessimism and hope, defeat and triumph, love and hate.

Slone's first attempt at this novel was *Sarah Ellen*, published in 1982 by a small local press from Pippa Passes, Kentucky, in Knott County where she lived. She revised and expanded it for publication as *Rennie's Way*, brought out in 1994 by the University Press of Kentucky. In the change of title and the revision she found the true focus of the earlier work, for the real story is the hard work and lifetime rhythm of difficulties and accomplishments experienced by Rennie, the mountain girl/woman limited by education and location and choices, rather than in the story of Sarah Ellen, the child Rennie raises and who eventually earns a scholarship to go off to college in Ohio. In the first book, focusing on Sarah Ellen, the woman who leaves the mountains, Slone permits the outsiders' view that making it out of the mountains constitutes "success" for the mountain woman. In *Rennie's Way,* Slone keeps the focus on Rennie, who likes her life in the mountains just fine, and who finds in Sarah Ellen's achievement the fulfillment of her own dream without making her leave the home she loves. *Rennie's Way* may be different from that of many mountain women, and it is surely different from what outsiders might expect, but it affirms the mountain woman's choice of a life of hard physical work, of helpfulness to others, a close relationship with the land that nurtures and sustains, a sense of belonging and responsibility and community, and indeed, a feeling that life is rich with purpose and fulfillment, and that contentment can be achieved at home.

Slone's mastery of her craft can be seen in *Rennie's Way* in that she promotes many of the same values and ideas as in her earlier work, but she engages the reader in a more subtle manner because we are drawn to the character of Rennie and simply want to follow her through the days of her life. In describing the main characters' lives Slone shows them participating in the common daily activities she writes about in *What My Heart Wants to Tell* and *Common Folks*, but those activities are not objectified in *Rennie's Way*. Instead, what Rennie does seems inevitable, not surprising; they are familiar and immediately understood, not needing explanation, although Slone often gives it. In *Rennie's Way,* Rennie follows the rhythm of the day as she tends to the cows and chickens and cooks the meals, and the rhythm of the seasons as she sows and harvests, makes jams and jellies, dries and stores away fruit, and happily participates in the community events of stringing beans and husking corn and stirring molasses.

A theme that emerges strongly in *Rennie's Way* is the centrality of women's work in mountain culture. We learn about how Rennie spends her days, caring for her sister Sarah Ellen and managing the household after her mother's death from complications of childbirth. Although her responsibilities are daunting and exhausting at first, twelve-year old Rennie rises to the challenge. Still a child herself, she steps into a woman's role without a second thought, and she never looks back. It is a role that suits her, and far from being the unrealistic event it may be in reality, in Slone's fictional world Rennie's tacit acceptance and her developing competence seem the only right and credible behavior for Appalachia. *Rennie's Way* may well be Slone's fictional wish-fulfillment for what might have been her own life if her father had not remarried after her mother's death.

In *Rennie's Way,* Slone does not state outright that outsiders' views of work and poverty in Appalachia as demeaning and demoralizing are incorrect; instead, she shows the joy and contentment characters feel when their work pays for accommodations or food, when their work for others ensures they are not indebted to anyone, and when their work is a source of pride and a mechanism for neighborliness and community spirit. While her woman's work is unceasing, it is never presented as drudgery. Over and over again Slone makes the point that work is enjoyable, even play. In a conversation between Rennie and Johnnie, Rennie admits she doesn't understand why it is that although they pick out the white ears for planting, when folks get together, there are always some yellow, some red, and some other colored corn in the midst. Johnnie explains, "That's so we can have fun when we shuck it"; at the first red ear a boy gets to kiss any girl he wishes, or another way to make a game of it is to keep points, with the highest score winning something at the end of the evening. Johnnie concludes, "It makes fun out of all that work" (97). Rennie reflects on other ways mountain folks make fun out of work: "bean stringin's, apple peelin's, corn shuckin's, quiltin' bees, hog killin's, barn raisin's, and a lot more" (97-98). And she shows it, too, in Rennie's happy anticipation and enjoyment of such events as they play out in the novel. Even the children work/play: Sarah Ellen and Hank "cleaned out the chicken house and spread the manure over the garden, having as much fun working as if it were play," Slone writes (152).

Slone's insistence on the fun of work suggests the efficiency of mountain life in that two aspects of life are accomplished in one event. Although she doesn't refer to it as efficiency, Slone makes a point of the fact that nothing is wasted in mountain life — no food, no fabric, no resources. Perhaps the most obvious area where waste is avoided is food. Rennie always cooks plenty — always enough to include guests or invite anyone who happens to be around — stranger or kin. Anything extra can always be given away or exchanged with neighbors, especially food that is canned and preserved. Cooked food not needed for a given meal is fed to the animals. Fabric and clothing are used over and over again. Clothes are passed down from one person to another, worn until worn out, and then patched for further use, if possible, and eventually made into quilts and other household items. Even magazines are used in two ways – they are read, the pictures admired, and then the pages are torn out and used on walls for decoration. When Rennie does these things in *Rennie's Way*, she is doing what all Appalachian folks do, simply showing the ways of the folks amongst whom she lives. Slone offers neither apology nor boast. Nevertheless, her novel offers an effective answer to those who see only the poverty of Appalachia. Shelter, warmth, clothing, food – where is the poverty in that? Creative re-use of materials? How effective and rewarding. In Slone's depiction, it is a rich life, and she lives in the mountains the "Economy" Henry David Thoreau advocates in *Walden*. Like his book, Slone's impresses upon the reader different understandings, Appalachian meanings, for the words "rich" and "poor" and "cost," and they have little to do with cash.

We might wonder why — in this era when sustainability and farm-to-table food is so trendy — Slone's model has not been held up for emulation, or why her book has not received more widespread acclaim. Mountain folk of her generation were simply ahead of their time, although through necessity rather than choice. Their habits were the advance guard for today's recycling movement. Slone lived through the Depression as well as the decades that represent perhaps the height of American consumerism in a marketplace of waste and destruction and poor stewardship of limited environmental resources. *Rennie's Way* offers an alternative life. Despite the hard work, Rennie takes deep joy in living and working as she does. In an unusually reflective passage, Slone describes Rennie's contentment in preparing the garden that would produce their food for the winter:

> Rennie loved the smell of the freshly turned earth, the feel of it against her bare feet. She would stop frequently to lean on her hoe and just suck in the smells of spring by the lungful. She didn't think of what she was doing as work; it was something she enjoyed to the very depth of her soul. For generations, year after year, her womenfolks had made a garden here in this same earth, and now she too was a part of that life. To plant and grow food for your

body was as natural as breathing. It was so much a part of her life that she didn't think about it or ask questions. She just enjoyed it. Had a stranger passed by, he might have thought that he had seen a deprived little girl doing work that was drudgery. He would not have understood — nor could Rennie have explained. (44)

Rennie couldn't, but Verna Mae Slone managed to convey this deep satisfaction with living intimately within the earth's natural rhythms, not dominating nature, but sharing its bounty.

Although *Rennie's Way* does not read as protest literature, Slone clearly advocates Rennie's way of life. She dwells on a positive portrayal rather than the negatives often associated with Appalachia, although she presents those as well. We see the repugnance of mountain people to the government, for example. Rennie's father, a preacher, tries to warn his brothers making moonshine about the coming "revenuers." Only he gets caught, however, and he goes to prison for ten years rather than turn in his brothers, the true moonshiners. Not only does the incident function as a plot device that enables Slone to focus on the lives of women in Appalachia, but it also suggests why mountain folk looked on strangers and the law with such suspicion. Everyone knew that Rennie's father didn't even drink, never mind make moonshine, but the outsiders seized upon him anyway, then wrongly imprisoned him, and their action forced Rennie's mother to raise her first baby and to keep a farm alone. By presenting the context, readers can come to understand why mountain folk tend to distrust the law and the government. Similarly, Slone was not a friend of coal, but this issue, too, she skirts gingerly. Rennie's cousin Johnnie shows up to live with the family because he prefers farm life to mining. Other cousins, he says, are all miners, "just kind of livin' hand-to-mouth." But for Johnnie, "I never liked workin' in the mines. I love the smell of outdoors" (51). And so he stays and learns a different way of life that he takes to easily. Later, Johnnie participates in another main way Appalachia has been exploited — the timber industry. But he does it only because he needs cash in order to pay his taxes on the property his father had left. By then, Johnnie is no longer a constant presence in Rennie's life, and so the timber industry touches the novel only tangentially.

Slone was not opposed to "progress." Her husband earned his living for many years clearing roads so the coal trucks and lumber trucks could get in to the "hollers" of eastern Kentucky. She had close relatives who lived in the coal camps. Strident protest was all around her; one of her sisters carried a protest banner during a union strike. But Slone chose to focus her writing on the positive life style of Appalachian small farmers rather than express her anger at the exploitation of Appalachian resources, natural and human.

In a similar vein, one would hesitate to call Slone a "feminist." She would no doubt reject the term for the image it conjured up in the '60s. Nevertheless, *Rennie's Way* is a highly developed affirmation of woman's competence and the sustaining function of women's community in the mountains. Slone devises ways to render Rennie's father ineffective. First he is wrongly imprisoned, but accepts the punishment rather than turn in his brothers because he feels he is in a better position to suffer the consequences than his brothers. This self-sacrifice for family makes him an absentee father and husband for Rennie's childhood years, but it's a kind of noble absence. When he gets released and returns home, Rennie's mom soon becomes pregnant, leading to her second child and the complications of pregnancy that end her life. Rennie's father is then portrayed as older and physically unable to do what most men would do for their families, expecting the young Rennie to step into her mother's shoes and manage the household. Another way Slone renders John Slone ineffective and absent is through his profession. Just as Papa in Louisa May Alcott's *Little Women* is respectably absent from his family of women by virtue of service as a chaplain during the Civil War, in *Rennie's Way* John Slone is absent much of the time as he travels to preach and respond to the spiritual needs of others. Rennie is not a card-carrying feminist, but Slone has created a female character and community that testify to the quiet courage and competence of mountain women.

SLONE'S LEGACY

Slone did not set out to be a writer. It came to her just as softly and naturally as the mountain life she depicts in all her works. One wishes she had begun to write earlier in life because the development of her talent is clear in each succeeding work. Mastery of her craft comes with *Rennie's Way*, where she takes advantage of the liberties offered in fiction to construct memorable characters, the events of whose lives keep us turning the pages. While Slone writes about the same geographical area and the same generations of mountain folk in all her books, fiction offers Slone the opportunity to create a work that invites the reader inside this world, to experience it as Rennie experiences it, and to watch Rennie as she matures into an adult and becomes a wise and respected woman.

While Slone still cares intensely about the value of the lifestyle and mountain ways she describes in all her writing, in *Rennie's Way* the reader comes to appreciate it as one is drawn to Rennie and the few characters who surround her. Slone adds a romantic sub-plot with the advent of Johnnie, who makes the story more credible as there is now someone to help with the work usually done by the man in the household. And she uses Johnnie to depict some of the less desirable characteristics of mountain people, such as their innate distrust of "brought on" people, outsiders. Johnnie, for no good reason at all, dislikes the frontier nurse who comes into the area, Miss Rose. Rennie appreciates her good service, but Johnnie never warms up to her and for most of the novel, simply disappears when she arrives. Slone manages to get in her punches against outsiders, however. When Rennie cooks up a good dinner of squirrel, green beans, tomatoes, cucumbers, onions, peppers, cornbread, and coffee, Miss Rose says, "I can't get over it." She continues, "You mountain folks have so much to eat, yet you raise it all yourselves." Johnnie intrudes, "Not the poor, starvin' people ye expected to find?" (71). His pointed comment is Slone's attack on the Appalachian stereotypes she resisted, but rather than its coming off as her own protest, as she would have done earlier in her writing career, she puts it in the mouth of her fictional character, from whom the perspective seems credible. Then table discussion moves on, as it does in real life.

Another clear sign of Slone's mastery of her craft is how she manages mountain dialect in *Rennie's Way* as opposed to earlier works. *What My Heart Wants to Tell*, her 1979 memoir about her father, is replete with mountain dialect and regional expressions that Slone encases in quotation marks. The effect is to emphasize the oddity of the expressions and to make them seem very awkward. She often defines terms, as when she writes that "nicknames were a 'must do,' or necessity" (25). A reader would probably understand the expression from the context without its being branded as different by the quotation marks and explanation. In *Rennie's Way,* Slone actually uses more mountain dialect than her earlier works, but it comes across as perfectly natural instead of being an oddity, and readers understand it because we have been drawn in to Rennie's world. Rather than seeming awkward and difficult to understand, this language with pronunciation-spelling and without quotation marks seems as natural as it is clear. In *Rennie's Way* Slone's craftsmanship allows her to show us rather than to tell us why Appalachian language and why Appalachian ways are worth remembering.

Perhaps Slone's novel should be read alongside Harry Caudill's *Night Comes to the Cumberlands* (1963), the monumental work that brought national attention to Appalachia, for it offers the inside human story of lives touched in greater and lesser ways by the social, economic, and political movements Caudill reports. But it also goes beyond Caudill's work, for Slone makes us see how the world might be a better place if Appalachian values and traditions were adopted outside the region. And hers is a story of hope, a story of how the world can be made better by one individual, one by one, each doing his or her part. Surely, rather than merely looking at a lost past, Slone offers a way forward to a better future — a remarkable vision for an uneducated, mountain woman from an isolated Kentucky holler.

Works Cited:

Slone, Verna Mae. *How We Talked* and *Common Folks*. Lexington, KY: The University Press of Kentucky, 2009.

____. *Rennie's Way*. Lexington, KY: The University Press of Kentucky, 1994.

____. *What My Heart Wants to Tell*. Lexington, KY: The University Press of Kentucky, 1979.

Clockwise from top left: Winifred, Ronald, Julie and Franklin Osborne.

THE OSBORNE FAMILY
A BAND OF BROTHERS AND SISTERS

By James M. Gifford

Looking back on Appalachia's role in American military history, it is easy to overemphasize the popular heroes like Andrew Jackson, Davy Crockett, and Alvin York and not provide enough praise for the thousands and thousands of other men and women who served their country. This essay salutes unrecognized heroes — like the Osborne family from Floyd County —who served their country quietly and bravely.

Maryland "Crow" Osborne was the youngest child of Buck and Julie Osborne of Hite in Floyd County, in southeastern Kentucky. After a tour with the Army in the early 1920s, Maryland returned to Martin and worked with his brothers in the restaurant business. In 1925, he met and fell in love with Allie Taylor, who had recently moved to town to work and attend school. According to his own account, Maryland "chased away Allie's other suitors," and they were soon married. The newlyweds moved in with Crow's mother, Julie Martin Osborne, and lived with her until she died. In 1926 Crow and Allie's first child, Winifred, was born.

Seventeen years later, in 1943, Winifred left her Appalachian home and traveled to Mississippi to work in a shipyard during World War II. The next year, she worked in a defense plant in Indiana, so she could be closer to home. Pictures of her in her Rosie the Riveter outfit show an attractive young woman with raven-black hair, dark eyes, and flawless complexion. After the war, she returned home and married Henry Hale, a US Navy veteran. Winifred's efforts during World War II encouraged her other siblings. Her four brothers were career military men and her two sisters were nurses in the United States Air Force.

Sadly, Maryland died of tuberculosis in 1942, at the age of 38, and did not see his children realize his patriotic dreams for them. The remarkable patriotism of the Osbornes brings great honor to their family. At the same time, the Osbornes represent thousands of other Appalachian families who have, from the very beginnings of American history, played a major, but unrecognized, role in fighting for and defending America's freedom.

HISTORICAL BACKGROUND

From colonial times to our current war against terrorism, Appalachian men (and in recent years, women) have been at the forefront of battle. Soldiering was easy for mountain boys because their life experiences often provided the skills necessary for survival and success. They came from a rugged, agrarian background that prepared them for the hardships of military life. Most were able marksmen who could outmarch and outride their urban counterparts. They were comfortable out of doors and accustomed to living off the land. In many respects, soldiering was easier than the life of grinding work and economic privation they returned to at the end of every war.

In the Revolutionary War, "the over mountain men" from the Watauga settlement helped to defeat the British at Kings Mountain. The Colonists won their independence on fields of battle, and Appalachian marksmen contributed to every American victory. Four decades later, America fought another war for independence. Although history books often present the War of 1812 as the military version of a comic opera, the fact remains: we were fighting the British again. If they had won, we would have lost our hard-earned freedoms and probably returned to a colonial status. Andrew Jackson, the hero of the War of 1812, was a prototypical backwoodsman who symbolized a new age in American history and rode the wave of his popularity as the hero of the Battle of New Orleans to the White House in 1828.

As the antebellum period continued, men from Appalachia continued to play a major role in our military efforts. In 1836, the heroes of the Texas War for Independence were men like Jim Bowie and Davy Crockett. Ten years later, Uncle Sam beat the drums of war, and a new generation of mountain boys marched forth to help us win the Mexican War. Tennessee is called the Volunteer State because of the high incidence of volunteerism that began with the Mexican War and continued into the twentieth century. Many eastern Kentucky counties met their draft quotas in World War I and World War II entirely through volunteers.

The Colonial wars, the American War for Independence,

and the continuing military conflicts of the antebellum period paled to insignificance compared to the Civil War, which was often fought in the heart of Appalachia. Mountain boys served with bravery and distinction on both sides, including three representatives of the Osborne family. Donald Osborne reports that his grandfather, Ambrose Taylor served with the Confederate army as did his great grandfather, Captain Adam Martin. Another great grandfather, Sergeant William Osborne, served in the 39th Infantry of the Union army.

When the war ended, no section of America had suffered more than Appalachia. Before the Civil War, the people of Appalachia had been prosperous, independent, prideful, and literate. The Civil War and various post-war discriminations greatly undermined the quality of life in Appalachia. By the beginning of the twentieth century, Appalachia was an island of poverty in a national sea of plenty.

Historical circumstances worked against our region in the nineteenth century, but historical events of the twentieth century would help Appalachia rebuild its quality of life. For example, World War I provided gainful employment for tens of thousands. As was often the case, an Appalachian soldier became the hero who captured the popular imagination. Alvin York, a mountain boy from Tennessee's Cumberland Plateau, went out on patrol in 1918 and singlehandedly killed twenty-five Germans with twenty-five shots and returned with 132 German soldiers whom he had captured. The men who surrendered to York had twenty-five machine guns among them. When York marched his captives to division headquarters, his commander remarked, "Well, York,

I hear you have captured the whole damn German army." York saluted and modestly asserted, "No sir, I just got 132 of them."

Kentucky produced a number of heroic WWI soldiers like Alvin York. Sergeant Willie Sandlin of Leslie County assaulted three entrenched German machine gun nests. Armed only with grenades and a rifle, Sandlin fought and killed all the occupants, captured a battalion headquarters, and created a hole in the German lines. Like Alvin York, Sandlin was awarded the Congressional Medal of Honor.

Another Eastern Kentuckian, Peter McCoy of Pike County, fought his way into a German trench, killed seven enemy soldiers, and captured seventeen more. At the end of the battle, his uniform and the pack on his back bore 177 bullet holes. McCoy was one of eight men from his company who survived this battle. For his valor, McCoy was awarded our country's second highest military honor, the Distinguished Service Cross.

Three decades later Appalachian men and women helped America fight a two-front war that spanned the entire globe. Franklin Sousley, from Fleming County, was one of the six men who raised the flag on Mount Suribachi at Iwo Jima. Sousley was killed in action three weeks later, but many of his Appalachian brothers and sisters returned to a hero's welcome. More importantly, they derived the educational benefits of the G.I. Bill, and used their education and training to revitalize the quality of life in their Appalachian homeland.

Another (indirectly) famous Eastern Kentucky soldier of the World War II era was Robert Lee Stewart of Letcher County. Stewart served in "F" Company, 27th Infantry regiment of the 25th

Infantry Division. Soldiering with him was James Jones, a young man from Robinson, Illinois, who later wrote a famous trilogy of WWII novels: *From Here to Eternity, The Thin Red Line*, and *Whistle*. In each novel, a principal character is a heroic rifleman from Appalachia. Although Jones gives him a different name in each novel, all three were modeled after Stewart. In a letter to his editor, the great Maxwell Perkins, Jones saluted Stewart's alter ego, Robert E. Lee Prewitt, as a man of "intense personal pride." Later, he described the Stewart/Prewitt character as an example of Appalachian men as great combat soldiers and observed, "I have seen such men do absolutely unbelievable things in combat." Through his fictional persona, Robert Lee Stewart became a symbol for the Appalachian soldiers of World War II, just as Alvin York and Willie Sandlin represented mountain soldiers of World War I.

When Winifred Osborne worked in the war industries during World War II, she became part of a generation of American women who proved that "the woman's place" was not necessarily in the home. In 1880, 2.5 million women were gainfully employed. By 1920, that number had doubled, and by 1940 it had more than doubled again. In the national workplace, women replaced men who were serving during World War II. Women like Winifred Osborne worked in ammunitions factories, shipyards, and aircraft assembly lines. They made victory possible for America and her allies, who depended on our factories to produce "the arsenal of democracy." Women, for the first time in American history, also served in non-combat jobs in the armed services. More than 250,000 women served as Wacs (Army),

Spars (Coast Guard), Waves (Navy), and in the Marine Corps. The "girls behind the men behind the guns" were machinists, storekeepers, clerical workers, and radio operators. They drove jeeps and trucks. They flew airplanes in non-combat roles and they served as nurses in combat field hospitals. Many of these women died for their country. Like the Osborne women, many American women had worked in the fields beside the men in their families. During the 1940s, they extended their support and played an active role in winning a two-front war that spanned the globe. By the end of World War II, thanks to the brave efforts of women like Winifred Osborne, there were few jobs in America that were completely closed to women.

Sadly, the war to make the world safe for democracy and the war to end all wars did not eliminate international warfare, and throughout the rest of the twentieth century Appalachian men continued to march forth in service to their country in Korea, Vietnam, and the Middle East.

THE OSBORNES GO TO WAR

The Osbornes were especially involved in the Korean War and the War in Vietnam. The oldest son, Donald, enlisted in the Army in 1947, at age 16. Three years later, he reenlisted and was sent immediately to Korea. The first day in Korea, Donald was issued winter equipment, a sleeping bag, two blankets and told to find a place to sleep until he could join his unit the next day. That night Don slept in a tent with some South Korean soldiers and "nearly froze to death." He soon learned that he should have put his blankets on the ground, not on top of his sleeping bag. He also learned that his boots — once removed — had to be put inside his sleeping bag at night to keep them from freezing. The intense cold led to foot problems for many American soldiers in Korea. Foot inspection by the medics became part of a soldier's routine, and Don learned to keep a dry pair of socks inside his shirt. Baths were infrequent and personal hygiene was a problem for the American soldiers.

As with most combat soldiers, the inconveniences Don suffered paled to insignificance when compared with the dangers. In April of 1951, the Chinese launched an offensive with an estimated 500,000 troops that attacked in constant waves. The Chinese flanked Don's 3rd Division, which fell back to a defensive position about two miles north of Seoul, South Korea. The Americans dug in there. That was as far south as the Chinese got for the rest of the war.

Mine removal was another dangerous job for Don Osborne and the soldiers of the 3rd Infantry Division. Removing mines by American or United Nations troops was a difficult job, because the mines were often not plotted or recorded. If this was the case, Don and his fellow GIs had to probe with bayonets to find them — an extremely dangerous job. Combat soldiers often experience recurrent feelings of sadness and regret. More than sixty years after his service in Korea, Don Osborne still has battle memories that plague him.

Yet, even in the midst of war, Don captured some positive memories. Once the 3rd Infantry Division was moved to Korea's east coast to reinforce the 2nd Infantry Division. One night on guard duty, he heard someone approaching. Rather than an enemy soldier, it was his platoon leader bringing Don's brother Ron out to visit him. The brothers visited for two days before Don's unit moved back to Korea's west coast. On another occasion, while Don was enjoying some R & R in Seoul, someone tapped him on the shoulder and Don turned around to see Billy Howard, a boy he had grown up with and known since he was five years old.

Don served in Korea as Squad Leader with the 15th Infantry from February 1951 until March 1952 and from October 1952 to January 1954 in Germany. He and his brother Ron served in Korea at the same time, though not in the same unit. Ron had enlisted in the U.S. Army in March 1948, when he was 16 years old.

Don Osborne and his younger brother Ron survived the Korean War; 868 Kentuckians did not. Five were killed near Osan on July 5, 1950 in the first battle of the war. The war appeared to be over in November 1950 when Chinese armies, hidden in the mountains of North Korea, nearly overran U.N. forces. Captain William E. Barber, whose home in West Liberty lay an hour's drive to the west of the Osborne home, won the Medal of Honor for defense against the attacking Chinese. Barber and a company of Marines held a mountain pass open for six days and allowed the 1st Marine Division to escape annihilation at the Chosin Reservoir. By the next year, the battle lines were drawn near the 38th Parallel and the war dragged on for two more years. During that time period almost 200 Kentuckians were taken as POWs and a fourth of them died from murderously inhumane treatment. Of the 868 Kentucky battle deaths in Korea,

21 came from Floyd County the Osborne's home area.

While Don and Ron Osborne were serving in Korea, their sister Janice Lee served in the United States Air Force Nurse Corps. Janice had graduated from Martin High School in 1947 and entered the Huntington (WV) School of Nursing. After completing the program to be a Registered Nurse, she returned to eastern Kentucky and worked as an Operating Room Nurse at Paintsville Hospital. In 1951, Janice was commissioned as a 2nd Lieutenant in the USAF Nurse Corps. She was initially assigned to the 314th Medical Group and later transferred to the 137th Fighter-Bomber Wing at Alexandria, Louisiana, where she served the remainder of her military duty.

While she was in Alexandria, Janice Lee met and married Major William Paul who was then a special agent in the Air Force OSI. After they were both discharged from the service, they settled in Atlanta where Major Paul served in the USAF National Guard JAG Corps and established a law practice. They had three children and six grandchildren. After retirement, Bill wrote a WWII novel, *The Road He Chose*. He is now working on a sequel while Jan keeps busy with her garden.

Following the Korean War, Ron served in Panama, Germany, and Vietnam, where he was wounded in battle. He was promoted to Command Sergeant Major of the First Infantry Division Forward in Germany and also served as CSM at Fort Hood Texas until his retirement in 1977. A highly decorated soldier, Ron died in September 1998 of multiple melanoma, a cancer that was probably caused by exposure to chemical agents while serving in Vietnam.

The next Osborne child was Julie, born in 1934. She graduated from Prestonsburg High School and Louisville General Hospital School of Nursing and entered the USAF Nurse Corp as a 2nd Lieutenant in 1956. She was first assigned to Cannon AFB in Clovis, NM and later promoted to 1st Lt. and transferred to Etain AFB in France for the remainder of her tour of active duty. In 1957, Julie married a USAF fighter pilot, 1st Lt. Laurence Daniel Biediger, and they had four children. Ten years later, then Colonel Biediger was shot down over Hanoi. He was presumed to be a POW until his remains were found by the North Vietnamese and returned to the United States for burial in 1983.

Maryland and Allie's next child, Franklin D. Osborne, was born in 1936 and enlisted in the U.S. Army in December 1953, shortly after his 17th birthday. After basic at Fort Bragg and AIT at Fort Benning, he served two tours in Korea with the 2nd Infantry Division. In 1958, his older brother Ronald persuaded him to transfer to the 2nd Armor Training Regiment. Both brothers then served as SGMs at posts within 50 miles of each other in Germany. Later Franklin served a tour in Vietnam as an advisor to Vietnamese Armor Forces and later served with the 1/5 Tank Company.

He was extremely proud of his service and accomplishments and distinguished himself with numerous awards for meritorious service and bravery in combat. He was awarded the Bronze Star with "V" Device for Valor and the Vietnamese Cross of Gallantry for his actions on November 11, 1965 (his birthday). On this date, while acting as Senior American Advisor to the Vietnamese 2nd/10 Armored Calvary Troop, the unit became heavily engaged in a series of three running battles in which they were surrounded by a superior Viet Cong force and in imminent danger of being overrun. Frank's forceful leadership and expert tactical advice steadied the panicked Vietnamese troop commander and rallied the troops to mount a strong defense. Finally, after a fierce day-long battle in which Frank called in American air and artillery strikes and after suffering more than 50% causalities, SGM Osborne and the remaining members of the troop broke through the enemy encirclement and reached friendly lines.

Following the model set by his older brothers, James Maryland "Merle" Osborne joined the US Army on November 19, 1957, two days after his 17th birthday. Merle did his basic training at Fort Knox and was stationed for two years at a NIKE Air Defense Missile Base in Michigan. He reenlisted, went to Military Intelligence School, and spent the remaining 20 years of his military career in various positions in the intelligence field, including overseas service in Korea, Japan, Germany, and Vietnam. His tours in Vietnam included Special Ops assignments with various Marine Corp, Air Force, Army Infantry, and Special Forces units. Merle retired from the Army as a Master Sergeant in 1978. Ron, Franklin, and Merle were among 125,000 Kentuckians who served in Vietnam from 1961-1975; 1066 Kentuckians were killed or listed as missing in action.

Research by East Tennessee State University's Pat Arnow and Bert Allen, a professor of Psychology at Milligan College, indicates that Appalachian soldiers in the Korean War comprised eight percent of the fighting force and received eighteen percent of the Medals of Honor. In the Vietnam War, Appalachian soldiers were awarded thirteen percent of the Medals of Honor, although only seven percent of the fighting forces were from the Appalachian region.

John M. Trowbridge, a freelance military historian, has compiled a list of ninety-two men with ties to Kentucky who have been awarded the Congressional Medal of Honor; twenty are from the Appalachian counties. In the Korean War, all five of Kentucky's Medal of Honor winners were from Appalachia: Captain William E. Barber of Morgan County; Corporal John Walton Collier of Greenup County; First Lieutenant Carl H. Dodd from Harlan County; Private David M. Smith from Rockcastle County, and Private First Class Ernest Edison West from Greenup County. These statistics testify to the significant role that Appalachian people have played in America's military history, but statistics alone can never capture the enormous contribution these men and women have made. That's why individual stories — like this one about the Osbornes — are so important.

THE OSBORNES RETURN TO CIVILIAN LIFE

The children of Maryland and Allie Osborne remained active public servants after they retired from military service. The oldest child, Winifred, who was almost always called Penny, worked in her husband's office when he was the sheriff of Floyd County. After her children were grown, she served as a postmaster at her local Blue River, Kentucky post office. She and Henry raised six children. Their son James Henry Hale was a fighter pilot who retired from the Air Force as a Lt. Colonel. Penny died March 1, 2014.

The oldest son, Donald, returned to civilian life and married Drema May of Belfry, Kentucky. Don enjoyed a 35-year career with the United States Postal Service; the last ten years as Prestonsburg's Postmaster. He retired in 1991. Earlier, in 1985, Don had retired from the Army after 6 years of active duty and 32 years in the U.S. Army Reserve as First Sergeant. Drema was an R. N. for 40 years, retiring in 1995 as Director of Nursing at Highlands Regional Medical Center. Don and Drema had three children: Martin Lee, an attorney, Julie Victoria, a dental hygienist who taught at Prestonsburg Community College, and Donald Gavin who is an auto mechanic in Prestonsburg. Julie Victoria, her son Max, and husband Herman Lester were killed in a plane crash in October 2005. Drema died in May 2012 after a long battle with cancer.

Ronald married Rhoda Lafferty of Prestonsburg in 1951 and they had three sons who are living in Texas. Ron died in 1978 of cancer caused by exposure to chemical agents while serving in Vietnam. His wife Rhoda died two years later. Ronald and Rhoda had two sons who each served three years in the Army.

Following her husband's death in Vietnam, Julie Dolores Osborne raised and educated four successful children and advanced her own education, too. She made a 20-year career in the field of nursing management, before retiring in 1994. Today she lives in Universal City, Texas, near her four children and seven grandchildren.

Franklin Osborne married Carolyn Sue Evans of Ashland, Kentucky in 1960 and they raised two daughters who are both attorneys. The oldest child, Crystal, continued the family military tradition by serving twelve years as an Intelligence officer in the US Army; she is currently a Major in the USAR. After Franklin retired from active military service, he and Carol made their home in Sarasota, Florida, where he worked for 19 years with the U.S. Postal System.

The youngest child of this remarkable family, James M. Osborne, retired from the Army as a Master Sergeant in 1978. He then earned an accounting degree from Eastern Kentucky University in 1980 and began a second career as an accountant, holding positions in both government and private practice. Now retired, he lives with his wife Margie and granddaughter Amber in Prestonsburg. The Osbornes were successful in civilian life because of what they had learned as soldiers and nurses. They applied hard-earned lessons of cooperation and initiative that had been forged in the furnaces of war-imposed self-discipline and responsibility. The result was a family of men and women who knew how to work and took pride in a job well done.

CONCLUSION

Another century of American life began with many of the same sad themes of our past. Americans continue to fight for the freedoms that we won on the field of battle in 1776. Hopefully, the model of patriotic service provided by the Osbornes will inspire others to military service. Someone has to do it. Freedom isn't free.

All of us owe a great debt to men and women like the Osborne family. Every one of us should make a list of the freedoms we enjoy and the comforts we love. Look at your list. It's a copy written in ink. The original was written in the bright red blood of an American soldier.

The Osbornes are important because of what they accomplished, and they also stand as symbols for millions of unrecognized veterans, extraordinary people who won wars and, like the Osbornes, returned home to live responsible and productive lives. Many went to college or built homes through the G.I. Bill. Their military experience, combined with additional education as civilians, enabled them to improve our nation's transportation and communication systems, advance American healthcare, improve our educational system, and lead us into our current high-tech age. Generation after generation of soldiers returned home and built an America that offered all Americans the hope for a brighter future.

We are losing thousands of those veterans every day. The men and women who gave so much and asked so little in return are quietly departing a country that owes them a debt that can never be repaid. This chapter thanks the Osbornes and all of our veterans for their service and their sacrifices. It also encourages all Kentuckians to express their gratitude. A hug or a handshake often means more to a veteran than a war memorial, a museum exhibit, or a statue.

Clockwise: James, Janice Lee, and Donald Osborne.

Eula Hall at Eula Hall Health Center, 1987.

Eula Hall's 1938 school picture, Pike County.

Patients at Mud Creek Clinic, 1974.

EULA HALL

By Brenda Evans

Eula was five and too young, her father said, for the birthing room. She had two choices: the creek where she could wade and wait for the birth of the fourth Riley baby, or the porch where Grandpa Ned Justice would amuse her with a stem-winder about her mother who was in the throes of delivery.

It was summer, hot and sticky either inside or outside their four-room house on Greasy Creek in Pike County, Kentucky, but heat didn't matter to Eula. She wanted to be inside with her mother. She wanted to witness the birth of their new baby.

At eight o'clock that night, a granny woman arrived, the midwife her parents had hired to attend the birth. In the bustle of comings and goings, Eula sneaked in, climbed onto a chair and peered through a square opening between the kitchen and her mother's bedroom. In the gray and dusky light, Eula saw her mother, thrashing and gasping and groaning in pain and blood, her arms splayed out and held down on each side by relatives.

The midwife cried out, "I can't deliver this 'un, Mr. Riley. There's too much blood. You get help or we'll lose her." Greasy

Creek in 1932 had no medical options. The nearest doctor and hospital were 15 winding miles away in Pikeville. But no matter, Eula's father had no car to get there and no money to pay even if he did. He ran through the hollow, anyway, to the storekeeper who had a truck. "Get us a doctor and pay him what he asks," he begged. "In the morning, I'll bring you a milk cow and a hog, and we'll be square." His old neighbor agreed.

Four hours later, Dr. Scott arrived from Pikeville in a black Model A. The bleeding had finally stopped, and Eula's mother was alive. But the baby was stillborn, probably smothered in its own mother's blood, Dr. Scott said.

That dark night, for the first time, Eula faced death and need: her family's poverty, her mother's suffering, her father's desperation. That vision never left Eula Riley Hall. "From then on, I held onto one dream," she said. "That someday I would be somebody, do things, change lives for people in hollers like ours on Greasy Creek."

At nine, Eula contracted typhoid fever. For four weeks, the disease ran its worsening cycle. Homemade remedies were available — kerosene and sugar for croup, chimney soot for cuts, turpentine for earaches — but no herb or bark or root would cure typhoid. By the fourth week Eula had lost her hair, but not her life. In September of that year she was well enough to enter elementary school for the first time. Four years later, she graduated eighth grade but went no further. High school was miles away. No buses ran along Greasy Creek. Formal education was over for Eula, but poverty, death and disease were still with her.

"Oh, Lord, I dreamed a lot," Eula said. "I didn't want to be trapped forever, not have nothing, and others around me not have nothing. I wanted to reach as far as I could. I just didn't know how to get there." In 1942, fourteen-year-old Eula lied about her age and signed up "to go to war," as she told her parents. The next day, recruiters put her and her brother Buster on a train to Ontario, New York. From there, Buster was sent to basic training and Eula went on to a canning factory that packaged food for the military.

Almost immediately, Eula knew she was in another Greasy Creek, except this one was up north and was a government-contract factory. The work was grueling: squalid conditions, erratic pay, 13-hour days, master-over-slave management. Within a month, Eula found a new voice, a roar of protest. She called a secret meeting and asked others to join her in a strike for consistent, adequate pay. First strike day, police arrived with riot gear and billy clubs. "It was scary as hell, and electrifying," Eula says. Men were backed against a wall, slapped, and frisked. Women, including Eula, tried to flee, but evasion was brief. They were handcuffed, arrested, and charged with instigating a riot. The strike had lasted two hours. Later that day, a police officer challenged Eula's age, ripped up her arrest papers, and put her on a train headed south to Pikeville, Kentucky.

But Eula had, at least for a few hours, found power to be somebody. For the first time, she had felt free: free to speak, free to protest, free to oppose people and institutions who claimed power over her. A mulish self-determination took deep hold. She could fight the fight, strengthen the weak, rouse the dead, if she had to, and would never again admit impotency. "Things don't always happen the way they should," she later said. "You've got to make them happen."

Back home, Eula was determined to make things happen. She took jobs as a "hired girl," the kind of domestic help that lived-in, cooked, cleaned, served meals, and did laundry for $1.50 or $2 a week. She often had to sleep with the women of the house to protect herself against lustful menfolk, but she was earning money.

Three years later, a swaggering young man fresh out of the army wooed her into marriage. McKinley Hall was tall, handsome, fun-loving, and a life-of-the-party fiddle player. Eula wanted a good husband, a good worker, a good partner. She wasn't certain that McKinley was that kind of man, but his singing voice was "as sweet as pie," and after their first date Eula was captivated. At seventeen and dreaming of a better life, she again lied about her age and married McKinley.

Eula and McKinley moved into living quarters above his mother's store, up a hollow called Big Mud off Route 979 near Harold, Kentucky. McKinley would get a job. Eula would keep house. McKinley would be the bread winner. Eula would be a good wife and mother. But from the start, McKinley boozed on moonshine more than he worked. Occasionally, she drank with him, but one November night while she and her mother-in-law sewed by the fire, they were startled by a violently slammed door. McKinley's mother put down her sewing. "Ease down under the stairs to the basement, Eula," she said. "When he's like this, he's capable of hurting ya." Her mother-in-law's voice trailed off into a whisper: "He's capable." But Eula believed she could take whatever McKinley had to give. She was his wife. She was pregnant with his child. She was free. She had a voice.

"What in the hell were you doing out drinkin' so late?" she howled when he staggered into the room. Without warning, McKinley hurled an empty liquor bottle. It exploded into a thousand pieces against the wall behind her. Stunned, she lurched down into the basement. Over the years, McKinley continued to both verbally and physically terrorize Eula: knifings, broken ribs, an arm twisted out of its socket, split lips, crushed eye socket and cheek bones, broken jaw. Often, the verbal abuse rivaled the physical.

From age fourteen in the canning factory, Eula believed that the power and freedom to protest were her moral right, but from McKinley, her drunken, violent husband, she learned that protest had to be governed by shrewdness. "McKinley was one person sober, another person drunk. When he slapped me or pulled my hair, if I run my mouth, I'd make it worse," she said. Eula learned to walk away or work more hours, or if he was sober, push him out. "When McKinley was gone, it was paradise. When he was there and drunk, it was hell," she said. Eventually, a new job, an iron will, a small silver pistol, and her growing activism led her to end her marriage to McKinley. But that would have to wait for 32 years and five children, birthed at home without a doctor. By the time it was finally over, Eula said, "I figured I had done four life sentences. If I had killed him — and I did think about it — I'd get at least eight years and then maybe a parole. I stayed 32 years, took the bad with the good. I figured I did my time four times over."

One afternoon in 1962, Eula got a call from Claydeen, a young woman in a bad marriage and eight months pregnant. "She was laid up in bed, sure as coffee is black, that her baby was coming," Eula said. Claydeen's husband was at work and had told her that she'd have that baby at home just like his mother and grandmother did. "It was like he thought giving birth was easy as dropping an egg," Eula said.

She knew that Claydeen was in trouble. She also knew that her midwifery skills were inadequate for a premature birth and that McKinley did not allow her to sit in his old truck, let alone drive it. But McKinley was at work and so drive she did, picked up Claydeen, then headed down US 23 to Pikeville Methodist Hospital. They were summarily turned away. Claydeen had no doctor there, and anyway she couldn't pay, they said. Back on US 23, Eula headed north to Our Lady of the Way Hospital in Martin, Kentucky, and again was turned away. Eula had one last hope, McDowell, Kentucky, where Appalachian Regional Hospitals (ARH), had recently opened a tiny hospital. The receptionist again was prepared to send them away, but Eula cut her off. "Don't you start that with me! This woman ain't going back home in this condition." She leaned in close. "You better git her a damn doctor, 'cause we ain't leaving till you do. You can call the police; you can call whoever you want to, but if you do, I'll call the *Floyd County Times*." Two hours later, Claydeen held a healthy, squalling baby in her arms.

Word of the Claydeen episode spread through the hollows. Eula had spoken up and her advocacy had gotten medical help for a neighbor. The next week, Eula was invited by a disgruntled

ARH employee to show up at their retreat at Jenny Riley State Park. Eula "fluffed out" her hair, put on her Sunday dress, and went. ARH dignitaries were the silver-spoon crowd, "Eastern Kentucky's high society," she said. She planned to be invisible, sneak in, look like one of the crowd, and assess what was going on. The manager of the McDowell Hospital spoke, as others had, from a pink fact sheet. Eula was "burning right up" by the third line: *ARH provides adequate health care to everybody regardless of race, creed, color, or ability to pay.* She tried to calm her boiling mind, hold back her words, but as the McDowell speaker started to leave the podium, Eula moved out of the middle of the pack where she had been hiding and waved the fact sheet: "May I ask who's responsible for this so-called fact sheet? The way I see it--no bigger lie ever was printed on a piece of paper than this. That's right, you don't give a damn what color they are, as long as they got *green*. I wish I had this fact sheet when I brought that lady in to give birth last week." The speaker rebuked Eula, but she pressed on, making certain the newspaper reporter she had spied in the crowd heard every word.

The next morning at a 7:00 a.m. meeting with the director of McDowell, Eula tried to be civil. She had promised herself she would be, but when the director spoke of the hospital's courage to operate a place like theirs, she fumed: "What's courage when people are suffering? You need to train those receptionists not to be bitches, allow doctors to see people in emergency situations, do more work in the community to assess needs." Over the next thirty minutes they went back and forth. Eula kicked against the hospital's blindness. Poverty-stricken people in the hollows of

Floyd County were suffering, ignored and untreated, she said, no matter what any fact sheet claimed. She left the meeting knowing only one thing: she had spoken and the director had heard her voice for poor people. The question was, would that voice make a difference?

Eula had learned two principles. One, don't sit down and shut up just because someone in authority tells you to. And, two, bring in the media because someone needed to tell what was going on in the hollows of Mud Creek. She had watched Martin Luther King and the Civil Rights movement and privately cheered them on for their boldness and determination in the face of injustice. King's 1963 March on Washington and "I Have a Dream" speech further inspired Eula. That same year she also read Harry Caudill's "righteous diatribe," *Night Comes to the Cumberland*, that had come out the previous year. Caudill's words were "intoxicating," she said. He put words to what she had intuited: there was "a vague wrongness," a dark flaw in the healthcare system of her county because haves could get it and have-nots could not. Whether the poor were casualties of neglect or exploitation, Eula wasn't certain, but she intended to find out. Besides, she rejected the idea of victimhood, always had, always would. Victims cowered or fled. Eula did neither.

The harsh nights of 1964 became the winter of Eula's discontent. President Lyndon Johnson had declared a war on poverty in his inaugural address in January, but by then Eula was preoccupied with her personal war on cold. In the summer, she had plucked duck feathers to make additional quilts and featherbeds. In the fall, she restitched her children's shoes where seams and soles were coming apart. In deepest winter, she stoked her tiny cookstove with bucket after bucket of coal, but even the blackest bituminous lumps could not keep out the icy wind that howled through the hollow and roared through the cracks in Eula's house. Along with the cold, a blast of new issues swooped into Eula's life. McKinley's cash-producing moonshine business that Eula had helped with in the past few years had all but dried up, and so had their cash. On the other hand, Eula's fame had flared higher because of the Claydeen and ARH episodes. People sought her advice on how to ratchet up their courage or navigate paperwork. Others urged her to start organizing. "*Organizing*? You mean talking to your neighbors? Since when did that become organizing?" she retorted. But Eula did want to do something, always had. As a child she watched for chimney smoke at an elderly neighbor's house. No smoke meant trouble, and she would run for help. Years later, Eula still reminded people that the best form of activism was being a good neighbor. Paying attention made a difference, and Eula wanted to make a difference.

Over the next months, Eula decided that making a difference required joining with likeminded warriors. Appalachian Volunteers (AV) formed in Berea, Kentucky, that year to focus on schools and education. VISTA, Volunteers in Service to America, an anti-poverty program that was part of President Johnson's War on Poverty, was also getting established in the area. East Kentucky Workers Rights Organization (EKWRO) was a late-1950s nation-wide movement of union-minded folks that had aroused from inactivity by 1964 and along with AV had established the local 979 Community Action Council. The 979 CAC focused on clean drinking water, paved roads, reliable electricity among the twelve or so hollows along Route 979 in Floyd County, Eula's neighborhood. But Eula was most keen on EKWRO. They were the hell-raisers, she had heard. To her, raising hell was not just a complaint or a whimper. It was a reasoned fight for right, and it might get loud. EKWRO was bent on fighting political and social power, and Eula was ready for a fight, in this case, a food fight.

After their school day at the new John M. Stumbo Elementary School near the mouth of Mud Creek, Eula's children sometimes came home hungry. When Eula probed, they talked about lunch. In the cafeteria, which also served as a theater for school events, poor children with no quarter for lunch were shunted onto the stage overlooking the children who did have a quarter. Eula's children usually had a quarter, but the have-nots — and there were many — watched the haves enjoy a warm noon meal while they had none. Stumbo was a bright spot in the community, brand new, clean, almost a mansion, as Eula saw it, but Stumbo was marginalizing poor children, literally pushing them to the periphery. Eula saw it clearly: poor children were hungry watchers, forced to see, hear, smell, but not touch and not taste. Poor children were shamed and set apart on the stage to watch. They got the message: go to the outskirts of regular society where you belong; your parents are poor.

Eula was furious. "If I had known, I woulda robbed that kitchen and fed them children every day. Lord, it takes a devil to do that to kids." Free or reduced lunches had not yet been federally legislated, so it was not a big government issue. Eula also decided that this went beyond the Stumbo staff although she knew from her own elementary years that staff often favored those who had money. But Eula knew that, ultimately, the problem lay with the local school board which, like many, was a tiny political fiefdom where the priority was, in her words, "who got elected, and how they would get re-elected." So it was easy enough to point her finger in the right direction: school lunches at Stumbo Elementary was a Floyd County Board of Education issue.

A few nights later, Eula went to her first EKWRO meeting to see whether the organization lived up to its reputation for raising hell. Leaders opened with a secrecy pledge, followed by a recital of their mission. Next, members voiced their distrust of corrupt politicians and "the ruling elite." After a few speakers, Eula stood and used storytelling skills she had learned from her Grandpa Ned Justice. "People," she began, "the schools are starving our poor little children." Then she spun out the story of what went on every day on the stage at Stumbo. Finally she said, "We gotta do something." Reaction was swift. Older members stomped their feet; others yelled in agreement. In the end, the group elected Eula to lead a five-member committee to write up a school lunch policy to present to the Floyd County Board of Education.

The next Friday morning, the committee and sixty parents arrived outside the board of education's office in Prestonsburg, Kentucky. Superintendent Charles Clark was on the steps with of a cluster of board members and supporters, some with baseball bats and helmets. The superintendent had been tipped off, and he was adamant. The protesters would not be allowed inside, let alone be allowed to speak to the school board. Young AV and VISTA workers were there as well and had alerted the media. Board members with weapons against unarmed parents was an enticing photo event. Within ten minutes, however, someone threw a punch and an EKWRO member shoved a board member. A brawl ensued. When someone thumped the superintendent in the face, as Eula remembers it, everyone on both sides realized they had gone too far. Police arrested the man who provoked the melee, and the school board quickly met with the EKWRO parents. Weekly deliberations followed and, in the end, the board brought out a new policy. No student would be shunted to the stage, all would sit together, and the board would provide a basic lunch for every child at Stumbo Elementary.

Eula was elated. Unlike the failed canning-factory strike when she was just fourteen or the Claydeen episode which was a one-woman protest that changed nothing, Eula had helped make a difference in the lives of the poor and voiceless along Mud Creek in Floyd County, Kentucky. "If we can get a school lunch program, maybe we'll take on *anything* that we think ain't right," she said.

After any fight, Eula tried to take away a lesson, even if that fight was with McKinley. After this food fight, Eula saw that collaboration among like-minded people was powerful, but not easy. Eula was independent, determined, single-minded. She went after what she wanted, and she preferred to lead. Even at age five, she would take charge. That night during her mother's bloody travail, Eula wanted inside, and she schemed and waited, and finally made a way to see her mother, splayed out in her own blood, waiting helplessly for a doctor who might come or might not. Eula never forgot her mother's being at the mercy of some other person. Nor did she ever forget what persistence can accomplish.

But Eula was a pragmatist: if something worked, it was good, like the moonshine-making project that she helped McKinley with. She hauled sugar, stirred the pot, fed the fire, and bottled the powerful elixir in Mason jars. That money put food in her children's bellies, shoes on their feet, coats on their backs. When her children were hungry, food trumped legality. Besides, Eula liked the independence she felt when they ran the moonshining business, but if collaboration with other activists would work, Eula decided, she would collaborate and she would have the media there to witness it.

Another lesson came to the front for Eula at the school board melee. Activists should not go out alone. They needed to take real people with them, people who had actually been disenfranchised. Exploiters should have to look into the faces of the those they had wronged: the sick, the suffering, the hungry, the hopeless. The poor must not remain invisible.

Two months later Eula formally aligned herself with VISTA and AV. McKinley ranted and demanded that she quit "running around acting like a communist." But Eula got on a plane, anyway, and headed south to a VISTA training session in the red clay of Georgia. During that trip, Eula admitted for the first time that something important was about to be sacrificed: for a time at least, her children would take second place to her activism.

After Georgia, Eula felt armed for battle. She was a professional with a paycheck, and she was determined to take on the establishment. The AV program that focused on cultural and educational change had been folded into VISTA whose purpose was more political and economic: wrest power from those in control and share it with the poor. The federal War on Poverty gave state governors control over VISTA, and Kentucky Governor Ed Breathitt quickly handed that control over to county governments. Floyd County Fiscal Court adopted the view that VISTA workers were communists, "a bunch of damn long-haired beatniks and hippies running around town up to no good," and ousted it. In addition, Governor Breathitt defunded AV. Undaunted, Eula and a group of local VISTA workers sought and gained designation solely as Appalachian Volunteers (AV) through Berea College. The change meant less funding and a lower profile, but it also meant that workers were once again Appalachians, and they could organize and carry out the agenda they chose.

Eula was ready. She had a purpose and transportation. AV had provided her a beat-up red and white Ford Bronco with a stick shift rising through rust holes in its floorboards. She was prepared to take two enormous steps forward: a step toward better healthcare for her Mud Creek neighbors and a step away from McKinley's oppressive brutality. These fights would be large-scaled and hard-fought, but she would not stop until she had won both.

Eula and two of her AV colleagues leaped feet-first into healthcare, a monstrous Hydra with multiple, intimidating heads: poverty, hunger, unemployment, polluted water, inadequate education, greedy powerbrokers, corrupt politicians, and unresponsive healthcare corporations. They decided to begin with a healthcare survey and knocked on every door, up every hollow, gravel road, and walking path in Little and Big Mud Creek. But people were wary. Half the doors were unanswered, and others were opened with a sneer or a shotgun. If a man was home, the woman would not speak. If a woman was alone, "it was like a loose fire hose that you couldn't cut off," Eula said.

A week and a half later, the compiled statistics were dismal: poverty, hunger, isolation, abuse, dirty drinking water, and shame up every hollow. Women and children were the most bruised and hurting, not that Eula was surprised that others lived like her and her children. Clean water, they decided, would be the place to begin. They tested open wells, 75 percent of which were contaminated with animal excrement and other pollutants, organized the Mud Creek Water Board, and lobbied the governor to declare Route 979 an emergency area. He agreed and the federal Office of Economic Opportunity funded a new water system for the area. As chairman of the water board, Eula led a multi-year fight against local powerbrokers over every well-drilling and pipe-laying project along Route 979. In the end, Mud Creek got clean water. "I really paid a price for being the person that I was," Eula said. "But I hung on."

Then in 1967 a handful of Floyd County health officials and political leaders petitioned Washington's OEC to fund a healthcare program. With the backing of Seventh District Kentucky congressman, Carl D. Perkins, the Floyd County Comprehensive Health Service Program (FCCHSP) was funded and soon operational. Eula was optimistic. Finally, those in power had come together to do good for the poor. Three years later, Eula found herself before the FCCHSP board with a long list of complaints. "We're being shafted," she said. "The clinic's purpose is to benefit the poor, but the poor are just being shuffled through and sent away, not treated." The clinic had become a referral service, she said, benefitting those with insurance who could go on to a doctor or hospital, but doing nothing for the poor who had no insurance. And it wasn't just Eula's word. OEC reported mismanagement, underperformance, physician in-fighting, conflicts of interest, and failure to make a dent in the overall health of the Mud Creek community. OEC gave Eula, EKWRO, and a new director temporary control to try to save the clinic. With good funding they would refocus the clinic's purpose and function, reallocate resources, and bring genuine healthcare to Mud Creek. But the dead horse could not be resurrected, and OEC withdrew funding.

Eula was devastated. Feeling discouraged and betrayed, Eula turned back to her home life where things were no better, especially with her oldest son, Randy, who was heading to the military. Before he left, Eula wanted to mend their relationship. But like McKinley, he knew how to show both love and torment, and there was no reconciliation. Eula and McKinley's relationship continued on the precipice, as well. He drew veterans' disability benefits and blew his check on booze. Outwardly they fumed or engaged in physical scuffles. Inwardly, Eula considered using her silver pistol to kill him. Once again Eula made a divorce plan, but once again it would have to wait. After the clinic failure, she had begun working for AppalRED, a legal aid office founded and operated by John Rosenberg, but her salary would not feed the children and provide a place to live apart from McKinley.

Although Washington officials defunded FCCHSP, they had left the door open for a new proposal. Shortly, Eula gathered her small cadre of war-weary activists and with the help of John Rosenberg wrote a grant application for a new clinic in Mud Creek. It would be "a clinic for the people, by the people," Eula said, and only community activists would comprise the board. Their grant application was swiftly rejected. It was a savage defeat and seemed to be the end of Eula's healthcare dream.

It was 1971 and another dream, divorcing McKinley, had to be deferred as well. Eula put her pistol away for the time being, but resolved that in one year, she would take the kids and be on her own. She put back every penny she could spare. Even McKinley contributed a disability check or two to help buy an old house with a trailer off to the side in Teaberry on Upper Mud Creek. For a while, house repairs took her mind off her failed dreams. She opened the trailer to abused women, the elderly, and University of Kentucky medical students who came to Mud Creek for a health fair sponsored by EKWRO. In a one-week blitz, the students gave 481 full check-ups and taught residents how to purify their water and do simple first aid. They also completed follow-up surveys. Nearly 90 percent of residents had never seen a doctor, and many surface wells were still contaminated.

By the end of the summer, Eula's old dream rose again. With $1400 in grant money, she and a few EKWRO volunteers spruced up the trailer by her house, built a welcoming front porch, and opened a bare-bones clinic. It was possibly illegal, Eula knew, but she didn't need a license to counsel, educate, and care for small things that didn't require a doctor. Within a month, two doctors came twice a week, for a dollar a day. "We didn't pretend, or intend to do anything improper, we just saw patients, did home visits and other work we could do without a license. The need was tremendous," Eula later recalled. Medical records, a supply room, and pharmacy quickly followed. "I knew I was doing right, but I was scared to death that I didn't know what the hell I was getting into."

Eula did know that she was facing three fights: one with McKinley, for a divorce, and two for the clinic for financial support and legal certification. She began with McKinley, bought the biggest padlock she could find, grabbed essentials from the house, took her youngest son Dean and granddaughter Eulana, and made the trailer clinic their new padlocked home. "We ain't a pair no more," she told McKinley. At first, he didn't put up a quarrel. Later, his rages began again. At night, Eula packed the kids and her gun into the Bronco and drove down U.S. 23 to a nursing home parking lot in Pikeville to get a night's sleep, and later, when police questioned her, she and the children slept in front of the police station. When the divorce and a restraining order were finalized, McKinley checked himself into the Lexington veteran's hospital, and Eula moved back into the Teaberry house.

Revenue for the clinic was another matter. Money was collected from patients on a sliding scale: the more you made, the more you paid. Those who could not pay were treated free. But that income was not enough, so Eula asked UMWA Local 17 for a financial lifeline, and, in turn, offered a healthcare lifeline to the miners. "I'm tired of watching good folks like you work day in and day out without the promise of health care. So I want a safety-net clinic, one that is always free for those that ain't got nothing," Eula told them. The union voted unanimously to divert a portion of their healthcare and retirement fund to the clinic. Active miners would pay higher fees; disabled or retired miners would pay less.

After the financial agreement with the Local 17, John Rosenberg guided Eula through the clinic's certification process. By 1973, they were legal. A volunteer painted a small wooden sign to hang out front: Mud Creek Clinic. Right away, Eula began greeting fifty patients a day at her small front desk. Physicians and a medical team worked for small wages, and volunteers got no pay. In rapid fire, Eula took on the role of counselor, advocate, psychiatrist, social worker, and fundraiser. The scope of Mud Creek's healthcare needs was enormous, and by 1974 Eula gave up her three-bedroom house to make a larger clinic. Her living room became a waiting room; the kitchen, a nurses' station. The three bedrooms were divided into six examining rooms, and an enclosed front porch became a doctor's office. The pharmacy was in the middle of the house, the safest place, in what had been Eula's family room. Eula figured it was the only pharmacy in Floyd County with a fireplace.

Other fights would follow. Eula continued her political activism and was elected president of Kentucky Black Lung Association. During Washington negotiations on new legislation, Eula was the sole woman at the table. She argued for benefits for miner's widows, but was stymied by a fellow Appalachian negotiator. Outside the meeting room, Eula put her fist in the man's face and said, "Now I want you to go back in there and shut up! You don't know what I see up those hollers; you don't see the women left behind taking care of four kids. Think about what your wife would say to you. You better straighten up or you'll get it in the mouth and I'll make sure everybody knows." Back at the table, the man yielded and the group quickly agreed on final terms. The proposal was sent on to Capitol Hill and passed a few weeks later.

One night shortly after the Washington trip, McKinley showed up. "You shouldn't be here. We're divorced. There's a restraining order," she warned. In the darkness, McKinley swung a whiskey bottle across the left side of Eula's face and left her with a broken jaw, crushed eye socket, and split lip. After stitches, plastic surgery and weeks of recuperation, Eula pulled out her silver pistol again, plunged back in at the clinic, continued black lung advocacy, and added miners' safety, including picketing at the deadly Brookside strike in Harlan County, and in 1975 Eula received national recognition. The American Public Health Association awarded her their annual Presidential Citation Award for her work for community healthcare. It was the first of many prestigious awards.

Another financial crunch came by the end of that year. UMWA funding dried up because of strikes and bad management, so Eula and the Mud Creek Clinic board made a wrenching decision. "We ain't gonna sell out," she assured her staff, "but we have to have money." A deal was struck with Big Sandy Health Care (BSHC). "We don't want you, but we need you — and your money," Eula told BSHC. The Mud Creek board maintained 51percent of the clinic, their board, and all the staff. Eula's title changed to patient advocate. "I got everything I wanted. They could call me the janitor as long as they let me work," Eula said. The clinic continued to treat the whole patient: general medical care, referrals, mental health service, transportation, food, clothing, and shelter. In addition, they got a new fetal monitor, EKG, X-ray, ultrasound, and one-bed emergency room.

Five years later, at age 55 on a perfect June night, Eula fought the biggest fight of her life. Half the blue-black sky throbbed with a smoky orange glow and at the center dazzling yellow tongues licked up into the darkness. Mud Creek Clinic was burning. Eula, her daughter Nanetta, and granddaughter Eulana frantically shuttled bucket after bucket of water, along with bedsheets, rugs, anything to smother the flames. Dogs barked. Horses bolted from their stable. A crowd gathered. One man described the scene: "Within twenty minutes, the roof caved in, and screams of horror rang out. ... Medical records, supplies, drugs, and equipment ... the desk Eula had worked at just hours before were reduced to ash.....The clinic Eula had risked her life to build was gone. Eula knelt...stared into the smoke and ash and cried uncontrollably, something she had not done in decades."

Eula woke early the next morning. Twenty people were already gathered at the smoldering ruins by a picnic table and weeping willow that had escaped the fire. More came, talking arson, layoffs, and revenge. "What we should be talking about is our patients," Eula said. "Some folks might die if we don't get up and running." A pickup truck roared into the gravel driveway, and an old woman stepped out. She was there for her morning appointment. Eula looked at the woman and at the weeping willow. "Let's get a phone line on that tree and get our clinic back," she said. And so she, the staff, volunteers, and the board began again with a picnic table and a phone line strung on a weeping willow tree. The cause of the fire was never determined.

Two years later on a sunny day in 1984, a new clinic opened. From the first clinic in a tiny trailer in Teaberry to a modern, well-equipped 5,200-square-foot brick clinic on Route 979, Mud Creek Clinic and Eula's childhood dream to be somebody and do something had come a long way. And the dream goes on. The clinic has expanded even farther with a 1800-square-foot dental clinic, clothing room, food pantry, mental health counselor, and scholarship fund. In 2006, Kentucky legislators officially renamed Route 979 the Eula Hall Highway, and, today, Mud Creek Clinic sees more than 15,000 patients a year. No one is ever turned away. The clinic has a new name as well. The sign out front reads: Eula Hall Health Center. In addition, Eula still works and dreams. At age 87, she is at her desk in the clinic eight hours every day and speaks of another dream: "I want a nursing home here on Mud Creek. Maybe someday."

Eula Riley Hall has kicked, clawed, cursed, planned and collaborated to realize her childhood dream to be somebody and to do something, and she has succeeded. Three honorary doctorate degrees, along with more than 30 other national, state, and local awards, line her office walls. But she herself admits that she is not perfect and never has been: not as a woman, not as a wife, not as a mother, not as an activist. She also admits her work has never been about perfection. It is about an indefatigable will, imagination, and, most of all, determination. "I'm not a show person, and I don't scare easily. So when I have something to fight for, I fight," she said recently. Eula is still utterly committed to doing what is right for people who can not do it for themselves.

Ironically, McKinley Hall, her former husband, may reveal the deepest truth about Eula. After McKinley's death, his new wife did not claim his body, so Eula and her children put together money for a copper casket and proper burial. "It was respect for another human being," Eula says. And perhaps that best shows the real Eula Hall: a woman who respects the human being she sees inside the best and the worst of us.

As she says, "If it ain't right, make it right." Eula, at age 87, is still at the clinic every day, making things right for the people on Mud Creek.

AUTHOR'S NOTE

Mud Creek Medicine: The Life of Eula Hall and the Fight for Appalachia, a 2013 biography by Kiran Bhatraju, has been invaluable as a detailed study of Eula Hall's life and work. In addition, I found *Back Talk from Appalachia: Confronting Stereotypes*, edited by Dwight B. Billings, Gurney Norman, and Katherine Ledford, along with Ronald D. Eller's *Uneven Ground: Appalachia Since 1945*, very helpful for information on Big Sandy Valley social activism in the last half of the twentieth century. I also have consulted many on-line articles and essays and talked with four Appalachian scholars who personally know Eula Hall: George Brosi, Gurney Norman, Loyal Jones, and Ron Eller. Finally, my interview with Eula Hall on August 1, 2014, in her office at Eula Hall Health Center in Grethel, Kentucky, was the most illuminating of all my sources.

BILLY C. CLARK

THE CHRONICLER OF
THE BIG SANDY VALLEY

By James M. Gifford

The great Kentucky writer, Billy C. Clark, began life in storybook fashion.

On December 29, 1928, Bertha Clark, who was pregnant with her seventh child, went to Huntington, West Virginia, to shop for second-hand clothes for her six children. While shopping, she experienced labor pains. Quickly gathering her purchases, she boarded a streetcar and headed home. One thought occupied her mind: she was determined that her child would not be born a "foreigner."

The streetcar ride brought more pains. As Mrs. Clark gritted her teeth and searched for the Big Sandy, the driver noticed her. "Something wrong, lady?" he asked as he stopped the streetcar to let a passenger off.

"I'm going to have a baby," she said..

"Not here in the streetcar!" the driver yelled. "Hold it! Hold it!"

"How far till we cross the Big Sandy?" she asked in desperation.

"Not far," the driver answered. "How far do you live from the end of the bridge?"

Below the mouth of Catlettscreek," she said.

He pushed the streetcar as fast as it would go. The rest of the passengers shouted and quarreled as the driver passed their stops, refusing to let them off. Now and then he looked over at Mrs. Clark, "Hold it, lady! Hold it just a little longer!"

When Billy Curtis Clark was born on Kentucky soil that day, he seemed to be just another child born into Appalachian poverty. Billy's father, Mason, was a cobbler and mountain fiddler. His mother Bertha took in washing and "scrubbed until her hands bled," but she often gave to needier families.

Billy left home when he was eleven years old, and for the next five years he lived on the third floor of the City Building in Catlettsburg while he worked his way through high school. "I cleaned the men's and women's jails," he remembered, "wound the town clock, and served as a volunteer fireman." He also fished, trapped, picked berries to sell, and worked at odd jobs.

After high school, an almost three-year stint in the Army made Billy eligible for educational benefits under the G.I. Bill, and he enrolled at the University of Kentucky in the fall of 1952. For financial reasons, he left college without a degree in 1955 and proceeded to publish five books with New York publishers: *Song of the River* (1957), *The Trail of the Hunter's Horn* (1957), *Riverboy* (1958), *Mooneyed Hound* (1959), and *A Long Row to Hoe* (1960).

Billy C. Clark

In 1956, Billy was home and working for Ashland Oil when he met and married Ruth Bocook, also a native of Catlettsburg. Billy's second cousin Jesse Stuart and his wife Deane "stood up with them" when they married in July. In 1963, he returned to finish his coursework at UK, served as writer-in-residence, and published three more well-received books: *Goodbye Kate* (1964), *The Champion of Sourwood Mountain* (1966), and *Sourwood Tales* (1968). He graduated in 1967. Then he became a professor and writer-in-residence at Somerset Community College for eighteen years. There he founded *Kentucky Writing*, a magazine primarily for high school students. In 1985 Billy and Ruth moved to Farmville, Virginia, where he served as writer-in-residence at Longwood University and founded *Virginia Writing*. He left Longwood University in 2003 for Hampton-Sydney College.

Clark's books had been out of print for almost two decades when he signed a letter of agreement in 1991 that gave the Jesse Stuart Foundation the exclusive rights to republish and market his out-of-print books. The following year, the Stuart Foundation republished Clark's autobiographical classic, *A Long Row To Hoe.* That fall, the city of Catlettsburg proclaimed September 5th "Billy C. Clark Day," because the state of Kentucky named the bridge leading from Catlettsburg to Kenova, West Virginia, the "Billy C. Clark Bridge." Billy also served as Grand Marshall of the Catlettsburg Labor Day Parade that year. A mural on the floodwall in Catlettsburg now depicts Billy C. Clark and his books.

The gradual reissue of Clark's books created a renaissance of interest in his life and works that resulted in new publications: *To Leave My Heart At Catlettsburg* (*JSF*, 1999), *By Way of the Forked Stick* (UT Press, 2000), *Creeping From Winter* (Persimmon Hill, 2002), and *Miss America Kissed Caleb* (UPK, 2003). His work defined the river culture of Appalachia.

Like most successful writers, Billy Clark published extensively in periodicals and participated in numerous writing workshops, literary festivals, and book fairs. Billy was still professionally active in his last years. In 2007, Wind Publications published two new Billy Clark books: *To Find a Birdsong* and *To Catch an Autumn.* That same year, the Ashland Community and

Technical College Theatre premiered "River Dreams," Betty Peterson's stage adaption of *A Long Row To Hoe*.

Clark died on March 15,2009. Now he belongs to the ages. It is easy to imagine the old muskrat hunter in well-worn fishing garb talking with his heavenly Father: "Lord, I know you've been listening in on some of those stories that my Catlettsburg friends have been telling on me. Now here's what really happened . . ." And the Lord smiles, wondering if eternity will be quite long enough for Billy Clark to complete his report.

Billy C. Clark rose from poverty to become a nationally famous educator and author. Thanks to his mother's courageous journey in 1928, the Commonwealth of Kentucky lists him as one of its finest writers.

THE CHAMPION OF SOURWOOD MOUNTIAN

By John H. Spurlock

Billy C. Clark's novel, *The Champion of Sourwood Mountain*, first issued in 1966 by G.P. Putnam's Sons, is one of the great rite of passage novels in American literature. The reader accompanies a young boy on his beginning journey down the long and winding road of self-discovery. Clark's narrator, thirteen-year-old Aram Tate, lives with his father and mother — Nathaniel and Martha — at Elkhorn, a coal-mining town on the Big Sandy River. Knowing his parents' dream of buying a farm beyond this mining area and seeing his father brought home injured after a cave-in at the mine, Aram decides that he will never work in a coal mine.

With his parents, he celebrates their purchase of a log

cabin home and farm on Sweet Water Creek, at the foot of Sourwood Mountain, where his father will cut timber and farm for a living — far from the coal mines — and where Aram may realize his dream of owning a hound pup, one from great bloodlines.

At his new home, Aram meets Eb Rington, the self-proclaimed "champion" of Sourwood Mountain, a berry picker, keeper of hounds, varmint hunter, seller of roots and herbs, fisherman, trapper, teller of tales , owner of the great "lion dog" Thusla, and one of the greatest con men in American literature — ranking squarely with Mark Twain's King and Duke.

As caretaker of the community cemetery, Eb lives in a shack nearby, and, during the early days of their relationship, Aram wonders why so many old men come to visit the graveyard, where no one has been buried for years. Much later, Aram watches through a hole in the stone fence of the cemetery as Eb and a visitor retrieve a white vinegar jug filled with moonshine from one of the straw-lined graves. Having saved five dollars from doing various chores for neighbors, Aram is ready to make a down payment on a pup from a highly regarded redbone hound known as Tweedle, owned by Rile Feder. Eb convinces the boy he can double his money by betting on Napoleon, a legendary fighting game rooster, but Aram loses his five dollars as the great Napoleon collapses and feigns death at the beginning of the fight.

Later learning that Eb can neither read nor write, Aram decides to abandon his mentor and friend, until his mother tells him she is ashamed of him for judging the man so harshly, after all the worthy things Eb has taught him about the natural world around him. She tells her son that schools in the mountains were scarce in Eb's day and that Aram's father had only a first-grade education and she finished only the third grade. She encourages her son to renew his friendship with Eb because everyone needs to be loved. Aram and Eb strike a bargain in their renewed friendship: Eb will teach the boy to run a trap line, and Aram will teach Eb the alphabet. Both succeed and Eb is overjoyed to be able to write his name for the first time in his life. At the end of the novel, Aram receives "pick of the litter" from a new litter of Tweedle's pups. Some stranger had miraculously unbarred Tweedle's gate, while she was in season, and she escaped in the mountains, where she was joined by Eb's great dog Thusla. Later, as Eb and Aram visit Rile Feder's home and observe Tweedle's new puppies, Aram first chooses one beautiful in conformation, a mirror image of Tweedle, then reconsiders and selects a pup the "spitting image" of Thusla — not a great hound, but a great friend and companion, a dog great of heart.

Through Billy Clark's expert use of Aram as a native narrator, the lad becomes all young boys in all places at all times, and Aram takes his place alongside, Mark Twain's Huck Finn and Jesse Stuart's Sid Tussie, two other immortal youth cut from the same homespun cloth of American literature.

LEFT:
Julianne and
Chad Perry.

BELOW:
Chad Perry receives the
O.T. Dorton President's
Award from the Johnson
County Chamber of
Commerce, 2010.

G. CHAD PERRY, III

By James M. Gifford

When Paintsville attorney Chad Perry died on November 4, 2010, newspapers across the state praised him and his wife Julianne "Judy" Williams Perry for their lifetime of hard work and philanthropic support of education and improved health care for their eastern Kentucky homeland. Perry's successful life began in a strong, two-parent home in Paintsville. He was born April 21, 1929, in Johnson County, Kentucky, the son of the late George C. Perry Jr. and Eula Preston Perry. George worked for C&O Railroad and Chad's mother Eula ran Carolyn Clay dress shop for many years.

With financial assistance from his parents, Chad Perry worked hard to obtain a good education. He graduated from Paintsville High School in 1947 and attended Kentucky Wesleyan College, before earning his law degree from the University of Kentucky College of Law in February, 1951.

After law school, he immediately entered the military service and served as a First Lieutenant in the United States Air Force JAG program from 1951-1953. For the next twenty-five years, he continued in the USAF Reserves and rose to the rank of major. After leaving the reserves in 1976, he maintained his USAF relationship for many years by serving as Kentucky's liaison officer with the Air Force Academy in Colorado Springs, Colorado and recruiting high school graduates for the Air Force Academy. One of his recruits, Clay Bailey, became a three-star general.

After he left active military service, Chad returned to his hometown of Paintsville, married Julianne "Judy" Williams on November 11, 1957, and practiced law for more than fifty years. The decision to return to Johnson County was easy. "It was home," he said. As a partner with Perry, Preston, and Miller, he practiced in the area of workers compensation, medical malpractice, and general litigation. On two occasions he served extended periods of time as City Attorney, was elected to the City Council, and on occasions served as a special circuit judge. Many lawyers agree that America's legal system is inefficient, and that irked Chad Perry, who was, according to his friend and partner John David Preston, "the Master of the efficient use of time and resources." For example, motion hours often led to much wasted time. "To combat this problem, Chad came up with an unbelievable series of reasons why he should go first on any given docket. Much to my amazement," remembered Preston, "he got away with this much of the time."

Compulsive workers are often seen as "dull and boring" to their friends and colleagues. Not so with Chad. He had a vibrant personality and a great sense of humor. Once when Jim Todd was practicing in Pikeville, he and Chad were working a case together. Jim sent Chad a letter about the case with this hand-written inquiry, "Any news?" John David Preston wryly observed this was Jim's "attempt to avoid damaging the English language by overuse." Responding in similar fashion, Chad copied the letter, scribbled the word "no" at the bottom, and returned it in a hand-addressed envelope.

Chad Perry was as loyal to his school as he was to his country. He lectured on administrative law to continuing education groups at both the University of Louisville and the University of Kentucky. He served on the UK College of Law Visitors Board and was a member of the visiting committee of the College of Law. He was class agent for the College of Law Class of 1951. Mr. Perry was a University of Kentucky Fellow for over 25 years and a member of the Lafferty Society. In 2006, he was elected to the University of Kentucky Alumni Hall of Fame, and the following year he was elected to the Alumni Hall of Fame at Kentucky Wesleyan College.

Mr. Perry became the most financially successful attorney in Johnson County history. As his career prospered, he became more active in promoting the economy and the quality of life in eastern Kentucky. He was a Director of the Bank of Blaine and Vice President and Director of the People's Security Bank of Louisa. He served on the Board of the First National Bank of Paintsville and also served as general counsel for the Big Sandy Area Development Authority.

Perry's service to his eastern Kentucky homeland progressed from promoting the region's economy to helping develop educational opportunities for eastern Kentuckians. He was elected to the Board of Directors of Pikeville College and received an honorary doctorate from that institution in 2001. He also served on the board of the Appalachian School of Law and Pharmacy in Grundy, Virginia. In recognition of his many accomplishments, Perry was named "Outstanding Private Citizen" by the Eastern Kentucky Leadership Conference in 1999. The Perrys were constant advocates for higher education for the young people of their eastern Kentucky homeland, and they took special pride in local graduates who attended professional school. "We have no children of our own," said Perry, "and Judy and I look upon these graduates as our own children. We get pleasure in seeing others succeed."

Late in his life, Perry launched his most ambitious educational endeavor. He founded the Pikeville School of Osteopathic Medicine in 1996. The project began in 1993 when the Perrys proposed building an osteopathic medical school in Paintsville, their hometown. To initiate this project and to reinforce their serious commitment to it, they pledged a one-million dollar personal gift. A group of community leaders was then formed to promote Chad and Judy Perry's dream of a medical school in eastern Kentucky. Incorporated as the American College of Osteopathic Medicine in 1994, the name was later changed to the Southern College of Osteopathic Medicine (SCOM), which formally filed an application and feasibility study with the American Osteopathic Association in 1995. However, by that fall, local fundraising efforts had not reached necessary goals and a new plan emerged: to merge SCOM with nearby Pikeville College. The merger was successful. In May 1996, the Pikeville

College School of Osteopathic Medicine became a reality. The following fall, the new medical school began accepting students.

This medical school was created to train physicians who would work in the Appalachian region. At the beginning of this century, Appalachia had only one primary-care physician for every 1,200 people, and the standard for urban areas in America was one for every 900 people. Although this medical school was the brainchild of the Perrys, who donated the first million dollars to the project, it was quickly embraced and supported by the people of eastern Kentucky. A number of private and corporate donors contributed to the hospital inception, along with financial support from the Appalachian Regional Commission. Paul Patton, the co-chair of the ARC, called the emerging hospital "a Kentucky effort ... and a Kentucky success."

The Pikeville College School of Osteopathic medicine held its inaugural commencement in the spring of 2001 at the Mountain Arts Center in Prestonsburg. Almost 90 percent of the graduates were from the mountains. Like Jeff Potter, Chris Bailey, and Jason Rice, they planned to remain in Appalachia and open family practices in medically under-served communities.

Potter, Bailey, and Rice were among the first to achieve what would have been impossible without Chad Perry's vision and leadership. Potter, a Pikeville native and Bailey, from Prestonsburg, voiced similar sentiments. "Our grandfathers would never have believed it," said Potter. "They would have never thought it possible," said his classmate Chris Bailey. Both had attended Alice Lloyd College, near Hindman. After graduating from medical school, they did their residencies at Pikeville

Methodist Hospital and began medical practice in the mountain-ous section of southeastern Kentucky.

Jonathan and Heather Hutchins followed a similar course. Jonathan, from Chattanooga, and Heather, from the small com-munity of Blackberry in Pike County, met at the medical school in Pikeville and married before they graduated. They later went through residency together and opened a family practice in Appalachia. What had seemed impossible had become a reality because of Chad and Julianne Perry. After Chad Perry's death in 2010, Johnson County Judge Executive Tucker Daniel praised the medical school in Pikeville as "Chad Perry's brainchild." Daniel said that the school "rightfully belonged here in Paintsville" and only the opposition of "a few shortsighted local individuals caused us to lose that opportunity and Pikeville now reaps the benefits."

Mr. Perry served as a director or trustee for several chari-table, educational, and cultural organizations. He and his wife Julianne were active in many other civic and community organi-zations.

His last major project was an attempt to help Midway College establish in Paintsville a new school of pharmacy, which was projected to generate $30 million dollars annually in economic activity in Johnson County. For the second time, the Perrys wrote a one million dollar check to launch an ambitious professional school in eastern Kentucky. After two years of work, plans for the pharmacy school unraveled. In December 2011, the college ended its pursuit of a pharmacy school and early the fol-lowing year the college voluntarily withdrew its application for accreditation.

Even though the Pharmacy School never materialized, Chad Perry never stopped working toward future successes for eastern Kentucky. In 2010, the year of his death, he was again looking to the future and hoping to see an Optometry School established in Paintsville, because there were, according to Perry's research, no optometry schools in Kentucky, West Virginia, or Virginia. "Unfortunately, this requires huge sums of money for a building and equipment," he said. Perry was, nevertheless, optimistic. "I hope someday to receive a call or calls from people who would contribute large sums of money for such a venture."

Perry's vision for progress in Paintsville mirrored his ambitions for eastern Kentucky. "I see the pharmacy school and the medical school and the dream of an optometry school as a regional thing. What's good for one county is good for the entire region."

Looking back on his long years of public service and philanthropy, Chad Perry observed that his success was fueled by hard work. "I don't pretend to have been successful in making a lot of money quickly. I just worked a lot of hours over a long period of time," he said. "If you come to work an hour earlier — at 8 instead of 9 — and stay until 6 instead of leaving at 5, and you eat lunch at your desk, it gives you more hours that add up over the years." Perry's commitment to hard work was shared by his wife, Julianne, who was his sole general practice law office manager for more than forty years. Chad and Julianne had shared a life of hard work, vision, determination, and generosity.

Most people who knew Chad Perry had a story to tell about his almost complusive commitment to work. In 1985, Chad's firm moved its office from Main Street to its present location on College Street, where Chad practiced law until his death. For most firms, office relocation would result in significant downtime. "Not so with Chad," observed his partner John David Preston. After closing their office at the usual time of 2 pm on Saturday afternoon, Chad and his colleagues began their move. "Chad went to the pool hall and drafted all the able-bodied loafers into a moving gang. There were so many guys moving stuff across the parking lot it looked liked a trail of ants." By Monday morning at 8 am, the firm was "fully operational" in their new location.

Chad Perry's service to eastern Kentucky was a heartfelt mission that he pursued to the very last day of his life. For example, on January 19, 2010 — the last year of his life — he accepted an appointment to the Board of Trustees of the Paul B. Hall Regional Medical Center, and faithfully served that institution until his death later that year. His many years as an attorney had made Chad acutely aware of the problems and needs of his eastern Kentucky friends and neighbors, so Chad used his abilities and his influences to promote the hospital, and the many other projects he enthusiastically supported. His dedicated service brought better heath care and a better quality of life to the people of his beloved eastern Kentucky homeland. Chad Perry was always modest about his accomplishments. "I have a little entrepreneurial spirit," he once admitted. "I have the ideas and sometimes I help a little with the money."

For many years, Chad Perry and John David Preston had

privately complained to one another about the myriad interruptions to the practice of law. Their pet peeve was the fact that the courthouse shut down when someone died. On the day of Chad's funeral, Judge Janie McKenzie Wells called Judge Preston to ask if the Judicial Center would be closed for the funeral. "The thought had never crossed my mind," Preston reflected and then pointed out that "Chad would be most upset with me if I ordered the courthouse closed." Chad Perry never retired, and he worked to the end of his life. "He worked right up to the very last day, which is the only way that would have suited him," concluded his law partner and close friend.

George Wolfford

GEORGE WOLFFORD

By John Cannon

George Wolfford, born July 3, 1935, in Carter County, enjoyed a distinguished, 40-year career as a reporter and editor for Ashland's daily newspaper, *The Independent*. He had his first taste of the newspaper business when he was a young boy in Grayson, delivering papers for both the *Louisville Courier-Journal* and the *Ashland Daily Independent*. A good student and industrious worker, Wolfford worked three years as a guide for cave tours while he was a student at Prichard High School in Grayson. "My time at Carter Cave was a great job that helped mold me into what I am today," says Wolfford. "I think I learned a lot of the people skills that served me well as a journalist on those tours," Wolfford adds. "I learned to talk to groups of strangers ranging in age from toddlers to senior citizens, and I did it all while I was still in high school. You can't beat that for experience." Wolfford grew up in a depression-era family that valued education. His father, Earnest Earl "Joe, " was a high school principal and teacher, and his mother Ethel was also a high school teacher.

"They never discouraged me from trying new things. They expected us to excel," says Wolfford.

As a boy, Wolfford idolized his paternal grandfather, G.W.E. Wolfford, a circuit judge who presided over criminal and civil cases in Carter County from 1927-1940 "I wanted to be just like him," George says today. After graduating from Prichard, Wolfford enrolled at Eastern Kentucky State College where he became involved in campus politics. Wolfford was the first person elected Vice President of the Student Government Association at Eastern State. After earning a Bachelor's degree in English, Wolfford still had ambitions of following in his grandfather's footsteps and was accepted into the University of Kentucky College of Law. He seemed well on his way to realizing his dream.

However, soon after he graduated from college, he married Wanda Jackson, a Harlan County native and former EKSC classmate. The pressures of going to law school and caring for his young wife proved too much for young Wolfford. He left law school after one year, and George and Wanda moved to Ashland where George found a good job at the Ashland Works of Armco Steel. The job paid well; Wolfford enjoyed it and he thought he would continue to work at the steel mill until he retired. But then the United Steelworkers at the Ashland Works went on strike, and Wolfford suddenly found himself with no work and time on his hands. He began looking for temporary employment.

His search brought him to the *Ashland Daily Independent* where he applied for a short-time job as a reporter or copy editor to earn some money during the strike. Coincidentally, a young reporter was about to take a maternity leave. Wolfford expected that by the time she was ready to return to her job, the strike would be over and he could return to his job at Armco. However, by the time the strike ended, he was enthusiastically hooked on his new career as a journalist

Wolfford's first day on his new job was scheduled for March 3, 1958, so, with nothing else on their calendar, George and Wanda left Ashland on February 28 to take a leisurely drive "up the Big Sandy" on U.S. 23. When they reached Prestonsburg, they encountered a number of emergency vehicles and learned that a Floyd County school bus carrying 45 elementary and high school children had hit the rear end of a wrecker and plunged down a steep embankment into the cold waters of the Levisa Fork of the Big Sandy River, where it was quickly swept downstream.

Wolfford immediately realized that this was going to be a major story for his new employer, so he left Wanda waiting in the car and began gathering information by listening to interviews, talking to emergency responders, and carefully observing what was taking place. In the right-hand corner on the front page of the Feb 28, 1958 *ADI* was a short story headlined "Independent Reporter Hears Interview With One Survivor." The story was right below two Associated Press stories about that morning's school bus crash.

That marked the first time George Wolfford's name appeared in *The Independent* in connection with a news story. During the next four decades, it would appear thousands of times. As years passed, Wolfford became a popular and well-known journalist. But on that cold, final day in February, 1958,

George Wolfford was an unknown rookie reporter trying to gather details about a school bus crash that had killed 26 students and the bus driver.

Although he had played an important role on the day of the crash, Wolfford was deemed too inexperienced to write the follow-up stories on this tragic accident. Instead, Burl Osborne, who had grown up in Ashland and was working at *The Independent* while earning a journalism degree at Marshall University, was assigned that task. Despite his youth, Osborne was a rising star in print journalism who went on to become head of the Associated Press and executive editor of the *Dallas Morning News*. Wolfford called Osborne "one of the nicest men you could ever hope to meet." In the days after the bus crash, Wolfford learned from Osborne and other colleagues how a small daily newspaper with a small staff should respond to a major national story in its own backyard. Those lessons proved invaluable in Wolfford's coverage of two other major disasters in the years ahead.

One occurred at 7:36 pm on November 14, 1970, when a Southern Airlines DC-9 carrying 37 members of the Marshall University football team, eight members of the coaching staff, 25 boosters and five flight crew members crashed into a hill just short of the runway at Tri-State Airport. The small newsroom crew on that Saturday immediately went to full alert. Reporters who were not scheduled to work that night were called in to help with the coverage. In the aftermath of the school bus crash, several days passed before fatalities were clarified. In this crash, the death toll was known immediately: All 75 on the plane were killed instantly when the plane hit the hillside. Regional reporter Jim

Todd wrote the lead story on the crash for Sunday's *Independent*, and George Wolfford added a number of feature stories.

The third major disaster Wolfford covered during his long career occurred on May 28, 1977. The Beverly Hills Supper Club in Southgate, Kentucky, burned, killing 165 people and injuring more than 200 others. Sadly, *The Independent* began its report on the fire by incorrectly reporting its impact on members of the Tri-State Roadrunners Club, based in Ashland, who were visiting the huge night club just across the Ohio River from Cincinnati on the night of the fire. There was a six-column story on the front page of the Sunday, May 29, *The Independent* with this headline: "No Ashlanders Known Dead In Beverly Hills Fire." That was welcome news to local residents, as 81 members of the local Roadrunners had boarded two chartered buses at Ashland Community College on Saturday afternoon to begin what they thought would be a night of good food and fellowship, followed by a concert by singer John Davidson. On Monday, which was Memorial Day, Wolfford wrote the story accurately giving the names of the 18 Roadrunners who had perished in the fire.

Early in his career at *The Independent*, Wolfford did something that now is banned for members of the newspaper's editorial staff: He ran for and was elected to a four-year term on the Boyd County Fiscal Court. At the time he filed as a Republican candidate for county commissioner, Wolfford said everyone told him that he had no chance of being elected. But he surprised everyone by defeating the incumbent commissioner that November. It was a credit to Wolfford's popularity, gained mostly through his work at Armco and *The Independent*, that he was able to win a countywide race after only being a resident of Boyd County for a few years. His political popularity did not last. When Wolfford ran for re-election four years later, his friends assured him of victory. But Wolfford failed to win re-election. "I won the race everyone said I had no chance of winning and lost the race they said I could not lose," Wolfford now laughs. "I'm not sure what that means." After his term on the fiscal court, Wolfford was appointed to the zoning board in Ashland and that prompted *The Independent* to impose a policy barring editorial employees from serving on public boards. A debate over a zoning issue became so heated that Publisher Jim Norris ordered Wolfford to immediately resign from the planning board. At the same time, Norris also resigned from his service on several public boards.

George Wolfford wore many different hats during his four decades at *The Independent*. He served as regional editor and as head of ADI's news bureaus in Prestonsburg, Greenup, Catlettsburg and Grayson. His four-year stint as head of the bureau in Prestonsburg required that he make the round trip from his home in Ashland to the bureau four days a week.

Wolfford's favorite job at *The Independent* changed little during his four decades at the newspaper. "I always liked getting out and meeting and talking to people and helping them tell their stories," Wolfford says. "I think that is what I did best because it is what I most enjoyed. I like to tell people's stories."

Mark Maynard, *The Independent*'s current editor, worked closely with George Wolfford for nearly 30 years. "George was a great reporter because he knew what a good story was and how to get it," says Maynard. "Many times he would leave the newspaper and be gone for three or four hours. He would always come back with three or four stories to write." "You never had to worry about finding something for George to do because George knew where to look for news and find it on his own," Maynard said. "George knew just about everyone and had so many great sources that no one else seemed to have." Now that Wolfford is retired, he remains a valuable source for today's reporters and editors. "If you need to know about something that happened in the past, reporters know to call George Wolfford," Maynard says of his former colleague. "Chances are that George can either tell you the information you need or direct you to someone who can. Sources like George Wolfford are invaluable and can't be replaced. We're so lucky to have George just a phone call away. He's a real treasure."

Wolfford also spent time as the first and so far only male Today's Living editor of *The Independent*. Lee Ward is the current Lifestyles editor of *The Independent*, the same job Wolfford had when he was Today's Living editor. She has known Wolfford for more than 20 years.

"I have only good things to say about George Wolfford, and there aren't very many people I can say that about," Ward says. "George was so easy to work with because he always did what he said he was going to do and did it so well. He was so dependable and pleasant to work with."

George and Wanda Wolfford recently celebrated their 60th anniversary. They have lived in their home on Carr Street in Ashland since 1961. Early in their marriage, the couple jointly decided that Wanda would be a full-time, stay-at-home mother, a career in which George says his wife has performed with great skill and wisdom. The couple has four children, two boys and two girls, and each has enjoyed a successful life.

Wolfford served for 30 years in the U.S. Naval Reserves, retiring as a lieutenant commander. The military service required that he be out of town on Naval duty for one weekend a month and for two weeks each summer. Wolfford was one of several *Independent* employees serving as "weekend warriors" either in the National Guard or in the Army or Naval reserves. Wolfford said he always felt he had the full support of the management of *The Independent* in performing his military duties even though it sometimes left the newspaper a little shorthanded. As for Wolfford himself, his time in the Naval Reserves provided him with excellent leadership training and "enabled him to see the world," Wolfford says, adding that his Naval Reserve pay strengthened his family's economy.

Wolfford has always had a passion for genealogy and wrote and published excellent histories of Carter and Lawrence counties. While both volumes are now out of print, they remain valued and trusted sources of information, especially for genealogists.

Lee Ward says she will never forget her first extended conversation with George Wolfford. He asked where she was from and where she went to school; then he asked about her family members and where they were from. Conversations like that are vintage George Wolfford. Numerous people have had the same type of conversations with George Wolfford. George was not being nosy. He just has an insatiable appetite to learn more about

ABOVE: George and Wanda Wolfford.

LEFT: Wolfford served for 30 years in the U.S. Naval Reserves, retiring as a lieutenant commander

our region's people. He is always trying to find links between family trees in this region. George Wolfford's love of genealogy is a natural extension of his love for people. "He was never malicious in anything he did. He loved people so much that he wanted to know as much as he could about them," Ward says. "That thirst for information is what made him a great reporter," and one of the true hidden heroes of the Big Sandy Valley.

DONNIS BUTCHER

By Linda Scott DeRosier

In the 1940s and 1950s, high school basketball in Eastern Kentucky gave an identity and a sense of common purpose to  the region's small towns. High School basketball became an instrument for survival and a positive centerpiece and rallying point for small communities whose schools were too poor and/or too small to field football teams. Basketball so dominated the culture that many small towns enjoyed lasting distinction on the basis of their high school team's accomplishments in a regional or state tournament, and the boys who comprised the varsity basketball teams became genuine community heroes. In this setting, basketball games became the major social activity of the school year for both the adults and children of the community. These get-togethers provided inexpensive, family-oriented socialization and were carefully scheduled so as not to conflict with church activities, the other focal point of small-town life. The importance of athletic teams in Eastern Kentucky's small towns contributed to a community reluctance to accept large, consolidated county high schools.

Donnis Butcher, who played both basketball and baseball for Meade Memorial High School in Johnson County, was one of the Big Sandy Valley's most successful athletes during those pre-consolidation days. He was also representative of many young men from the Big Sandy Valley who went on to enjoy recognition at the collegiate level. Unlike most, however, Donnis Butcher's glory years did not end with his college career. He went on to play basketball for two professional teams—New York Knicks and Detroit Pistons—and he is the only eastern Kentuckian to coach an NBA team.

Donnis Butcher, one of the Big Sandy Valley's most successful athletes, was born number fifteen of Ollie and Beecher Butcher's sixteen children on February 8, 1936 in the front room of the home place on TwoMile Creek at Williamsport, Kentucky, where he lived the first nineteen years of his life. All Beecher Butcher's sons not only played basketball, they were good at the game; Donnis, however, was exceptional because even in high school, he played harder than anybody else. In the summer of 1955 following his graduation from Meade Memorial High School, the entire community was consumed with the story of Adolph Rupp, legendary coach of the Kentucky Wildcats coming to Two-Mile Creek after the favorite son. Rumor had it that Rupp drove a big convertible into the hills—no small task in those days of winding back roads that took about ten hours from Two-Mile to Lexington—and signed Donnis and Johnny Cox to the 1959

Kentucky squad. Johnny stayed in Lexington, played four years, and became an All American basketball player at UK, but Donnis got homesick and came home in a matter of days.

After a few days at home, Donnis left for Dayton, Ohio where he got a factory job with National Cash Register. This scenario was quite common in those days when the "three Rs" for eastern Kentucky high school graduates were reading, 'riting, and Route 23 to the north. Playing for the NCR team, Donnis met another soon-to-be-lifelong friend, Vern Woods, who accompanied him when Donnis came home and enrolled at Pikeville College in the fall of 1958. This announcement generated a great deal of excitement among students, faculty, and people throughout the region, because the college team would have two "big" men. Donnis, at six- foot-three, coupled with six-foot-four Vern provided formidable opposition to the majority of small college teams whose players were smaller and less gifted athletically.

Donnis played the 1958-59 season at Pikeville College for Coach W. R. Daniels who was replaced the next year by Paul Butcher, Donnis' older brother and former high school coach. In Donnis' first year of collegiate play, the Pikeville College team won the Kentucky Intercollegiate Athletic Conference (KIAC) championship and then went to the National Association of Intercollegiate Athletics (NAIA) post season tournament in Kansas City. According to fellow player/guard Everett "Big June" Hall, Jr., "under Paul Butcher's coaching the Pikeville College team functioned as a family." He went on to say that those years taught him and his teammates respect, self-discipline, and good work habits. According to former teammates, coaches, and other friends, Paul Butcher's coaching had a very positive effect on his little brother. Big June remembered, "Coach Butcher was not only a good basketball coach; he was a good man. His treatment of his players on and off the court had a profound impact on those he coached, so he deserves some credit, not only for his little brother's skill at basketball, but also for the solid values that made Donnis a successful human being.

Pikeville College cheerleaders raised money to go with the team to the NAIA tournament in Kansas City by having bake sales and going around to the high school district tournaments where they carried an open blanket through the stands at halftime so people could throw in contributions. In Donnis's home district, his wife, Delorise, put on a cheerleading uniform and walked through the crowd with the cheerleaders, and they collected enough money to pay their travel expenses to the tournament. Flying from eastern Kentucky was impractical in 1959, so team members and cheerleaders rode the regularly scheduled train from Pikeville to Ashland. That trip takes not quite two hours to drive today, but in 1959 it was a full day's journey by train. The traveling squad and cheerleaders connected in Ashland with another train to Cincinnati. There they caught a Cincinnati-St. Louis train; from St. Louis they went directly to Kansas City. Nobody—coaches, players, cheering squad, fans—nobody had a bed; they chugged along sitting straight up, stopping only to change trains. Some members of the travelling group recall the trip taking about three days and exhausting everyone involved. But they were young and many—perhaps most—had never been out of the hills of Kentucky and at least one member of the group retained proof of where they changed trains. Some members of this merry band discovered that every layover station along the way included a picture-taking booth similar to the one in G. C. Murphy's Department Store back in Pikeville, so they took advantage of those four-for-a-dollar photo opportunities to chronicle their trip westward. Donnis, along with most of the "first five" players, was too embarrassed to take part in the photo gig; "he was cool even then," remembers one of his classmates. Pikeville College lost its first game in Kansas City, but Donnis was selected Little All American that year.

After his college basketball career ended, Donnis was drafted by the New York Knicks in the 7th round of the 1961 NBA Draft. He lived three years on Long Island in New York while he played for the Knicks. From 1964 until his death on October 8, 2012 he lived in Michigan where he played for the Detroit Pistons, later coached the Pistons, and finally became an executive for Converse, a company that makes basketball shoes and other athletic equipment.

Unlike many famous athletes and many current NBA players, Donnis Butcher was a dependable and loving husband and father. Don and Dee's first child, Debra Lynn, was born in Ohio on February 7, 1958. Pikeville College alum's from that era recall little Debbie toddling around the Pikeville College campus wearing a small black shirt with an orange bandanna. Four decades later, on May 21, 1996, grown-up Debra was cutting her dad's hair at her parents' house near Detroit when a thunderstorm swept over the area. She rushed out to the driveway to close her car windows and was struck by lightning and killed instantly.

Donnis and Delorise had two sons, Don Russell (Donnie) born in Kentucky on August 10, 1963 and Dennis Keith (Denny Mac) born in Michigan October 25, 1968. Both boys played high school and college basketball and both became career coaches. A 1986 newspaper article from a Michigan newspaper, the *South Lyon Herald*, features a picture of Donnis and Denny "enjoying the sunshine while playing a game of one-on-one." In this article, reporter Matt Seidl suggests the fifty-year-old Donnis "comes across like a 25-year-old. He's energetic, he's happy, and most obvious, he's satisfied with his life."

Seidl quotes Donnis as saying, "I wouldn't trade this job [with Converse] for anything in the world. I really enjoy it and because I am still so close to the game of basketball, I really don't miss playing or coaching." Donnis goes on to reflect on a night in Philadelphia he considered the highlight of his professional playing career, when he had "24 points, 14 rebounds and nine assists from his guard position to lead the Knicks past Philly and Wilt 'the Stilt' Chamberlain." Despite averaging 30 points-per-game in high school and 24 points-per-game in college, Donnis didn't consider his offensive game to be his greatest strength. In his view, he excelled on defense by playing the game hard from start to finish and always giving 100 percent. He told Seidl that he never saw himself as a star but always felt like he was just one of the guys: "I just want to be myself... I've had my moments. Now I just want to enjoy life. I love working and I love playing golf. I'm real happy with the way things are right now." He went on to tell the reporter that his wife, Dee, deserved all the credit for his satisfying middle age years, "I couldn't have done anything without her."

Perhaps the greatest tribute to Donnis Butcher's character can be seen in the number of extended family members dedicated their lives to education and coaching with the desire to build character among their players. Both Donnis's sons and several nephews became successful coaches. Nephew Steve Butcher followed in Donnis's footsteps at Pikeville College, and he later taught, coached and served as Superintendent of Schools in Wolf County Kentucky.

Everett Horn, Jr., who was a starting guard with Donnis, went directly from Pikeville College to coach his *alma mater*, the Inez Indians. In those days Inez basketball was much bigger than the 600-member town would indicate. Due to the legacy of renowned coach, Russell Williamson, each year Inez was able to schedule a couple of games with big schools (primarily Louisville, Lexington, or Maysville) outside of Eastern Kentucky. In 1962, when Donnis was playing for the New York Knicks he found out his old teammate Big Junior Horn's Inez team was going to be playing a game in Louisville the night before the Knicks played the Cincinnati Royals. Since Cincinnati was fewer than 100 miles northeast of Louisville, Donnis invited the whole Inez team to the pro game in Cincinnati. Coach Horn says it was a transformative experience for Inez players, who sat right up front at the pro game and were invited into the locker room afterward to meet Donnis' team. This sort of generosity, both of spirit, time and money, was characteristic of Donnis Butcher.

Over the years a number of people who went to school with

Donnis at Meade Memorial or Pikeville College—now the University of Pikeville—or who encountered him later in life passed along stories of how "old Donnis never changed a bit." Donnis was always the boy from Two-Mile Creek, who came home at least once a year for a fishing trip accompanied by his brothers, sons, nephews, and a whole pack of good old boys who were life-long friends. Junior Horn, who visited him several times in Detroit remembered Donnis had a very impressive office as Pistons' Head Coach and later as an executive at Converse, but his personality never changed.

When Donnis played in the NBA he was a hero to the folks back home. His games were not televised and not even broadcast on radio in eastern Kentucky. His brother Doug figured out a way to get the games over the radio and friends and their families gathered at Doug's home to listen. After the game if Donnis could manage to get away, he would call and recap it with his brother. Doug's son Steve Butcher, who spent a great deal of time with his uncle over the years, tells the story of Donnis calling brother Doug after a record setting pro game, saying "had a great night tonight; between Wilt and me we scored 110 points." That was Wilt Chamberlain's record setting 100 point game on March 2, 1962. Donnis went on to say, "Yeah, Wilt got 100 points; I got ten." Donnis was a fierce competitor but he was always ready to laugh at himself.

People remembered Donnis with fondness, respect, and pride. His son Donnie said: "He has been the rock of our family for his entire life. Anything that I have done, or my brother or sister has done, we always looked to him for guidance, in all

matters. Obviously, he is a legend for what he has done athletically. But spiritually, our maturity is due to him." After Donnis died,
Ron Branham, who also attended Meade School observed:

> I was listening to the game the night Donnis fouled
> Chamberlain, and Chamberlain made the free throw
> that was the 100th point. He [Donnis] was from our
> small school at Williamsport, and he would come down
> occasionally when in the area, and us players were in
> awe of him because at only 6'2" or so, he could dunk
> the ball. We didn't have one player who could do that
> and we had one guy who was 6'6" tall. I listened to all
> his games I could pull in on an old Buick car radio that
> had been converted to electric. Our thoughts and
> prayers go out to the family. We have lost a good'n.

Although Donnis Butcher spent the majority of his life "up
north," folks from the Big Sandy Valley said he never truly left
eastern Kentucky. All who knew him would agree that his basketball success, his stellar career as an executive with Converse,
and his solid family values and great personal leadership made
Donnis Butcher one of the hidden heroes of the Big Sandy Valley.

Ira Potter

DR. IRA POTTER

By Nicole Wells

Ira Blaine Potter is one of the Big Sandy Valley's far-sighted leaders. For more than forty years, Dr. Potter has led, and continues to lead, a personal crusade to improve healthcare in his eastern Kentucky homeland.

Like many Appalachian people, Potter overcame poverty to achieve success. He was born in Letcher County on May 15, 1942. The second of six children, Ira had a rough childhood. His mother, Alora Andersen Potter, hoboed a train at age thirteen and was discovered in a boxcar in Louisville. The next year, Alora married Levi Potter, a coalminer who was a heavy drinker. Their marriage deteriorated, ending in divorce when Ira was six. Young Ira began living with his paternal grandparents, Ira and Kate Potter, at Shelby Creek in Pike County when he was nine months old. The white frame house with lap siding and a tin roof was built in 1890, and the outhouse was "too far or too close to the house depending upon the season."

"At six years old, I was probably the youngest bootlegger

in all of Kentucky," Ira Potter often jokes. His grandparents were hillside farmers who supplemented their income by moonshining whiskey. A child makes an ideal bootlegger because no one watches children carefully, so if law enforcement officers are surveilling a house and a child goes to the barn with a bucket and comes back with a bucket, it doesn't alert much suspicion although that bucket may contain a quart jar with moonshine whiskey in it. As a boy, Ira went up and down the creek looking for discarded whiskey bottles that he brought home and washed. His grandfather gave him a nickel for every jar or bottle that was usable. A stopper was made from a corncob. His grandfather never sold any other type of alcoholic beverage. He stopped making moonshine in his mid-sixties but continued to sell moonshine that was delivered by other dealers to his house.

Ira's difficult childhood made him undisciplined, and he refused to study in school and neglected his homework. Rather than participating in class, he sat at the back of the room and read all of the books in the classroom, including the encyclopedias. Despite dedicating little effort to academics, he consistently scored well on the county's annual achievement tests that determined if a student was qualified to pass on to the next grade level. Reportedly, he only continued his elementary education because of the strong, sometimes physical, insistence from his grandmother. After completing the eighth grade in 1955, Potter pledged an end to his formal education.

However, at the beginning of the next academic year, he enrolled at Dorton High School and attended with no family encouragement and only meager financial support from his

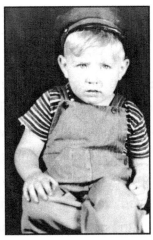

Ira Potter, age 2, 1944. Dr. Potter with his grandmother, Kate Johnson Potter, at his medical school graduation.

grandmother. Although Potter was not a very good player, he was on the high school basketball team and possessed a deep passion for the sport. His coach, Monroe Hall, was also a talented science teacher. Hall inspired Potter through impressive scientific demonstrations, luring him to the front of the class. Consequently, the awed student built his own laboratory under the floor of his grandparents' house, assembled a projection microscope, and examined a wide range of animals he caught in the woods. After obtaining formaldehyde from the school, he preserved a variety of creatures, mounted them, displayed them in wooden frames, or contained them in jars. His thirst for knowledge soon trans-ferred to other subjects, and Ira Potter emerged as the valedictorian of his graduating class in 1960. Additionally, Potter won the top awards in science, math, English, and social studies.

After graduation, Potter sought closure with his parents. He had known his father for years from a distance, but they were not close. He traveled to Detroit to see his mother. This act sparked a drive for independence. He searched for a job, but refused to consider coalmining or hillside farming; not many additional opportunities were available. His principal Charles Wright and several other teachers encouraged him to pursue college, but that seemed financially impossible to Ira. Nevertheless, he received promotional materials from many universities, and often sat on the porch, reading them and imagining the possibilities of higher education.

One day while plowing behind a mule, he stopped for a water break. As he sat on the ground and stared at the old mule, he had an epiphany. He told the mule, "you're a mule and you have to do this for the rest of your life. I'm not a mule, and I'm not doing this for the rest of my life. I will find a way." So on the day of freshman registration at Morehead State College in the fall of 1960, Potter climbed into his jalopy that he and his grandfather had purchased for $200, and drove to Morehead, Kentucky. In the 1950s, the Soviet Union had launched Sputnik and the Space Race was on with the United States. Consequently, the NDEA provided loans and scholarships to students who excelled in science and math. These scholarships did not cover all of Ira's tuition and expenses, but he was determined to earn a college degree. He worked at a sawmill, drove a laundry truck, and briefly mined coal. Hard work and a diet consisting of not much more than saltine crackers and water carried him through his college years. An honors student, Potter graduated in 1964 with majors in mathematics and biology. He also received a secondary education teaching certificate. While in college, he married Anna Burke, his high school girlfriend. Because she had not finished high school, employment opportunities for her were limited, but she took babysitting jobs as often as she could to help with the family expenses.

After graduation, Potter taught mathematics at Millersburg Military Institute in Millersburg, Kentucky. However, he was soon drawn back to Pike County to teach algebra, trigonometry, geometry, biology, chemistry and physical science at his alma mater, Dorton High School. As Hall had done for him, Potter inspired several of his students to successful careers, including law and political leadership.

After two years at Dorton, Potter concluded that teaching was not his ultimate goal, and began to ponder different options for his future. He decided to pursue medicine, and enrolled in the University of Kentucky School of Medicine. In 1966, he packed his wife and two children in a Corvair and moved to Lexington, Kentucky, into student housing. He received support from the Rural Scholarship Fund, which provided approximately $2,500 per year toward medical education. The scholarship required him to return to an underserved area in eastern Kentucky for four years after he finished his medical training. He also received other smaller scholarships and worked his first summer at Eastern State Hospital in the psychiatric wards, helping with patients as well as doing physical examinations for the psychiatrists. Anna was busy with children, but she continued babysitting as often as she could to help support their growing family. Four years later, in 1970, Ira Potter graduated with honors in medicine and pharmacology. He was among the top ten students in his class.

After medical school, Potter continued his education at the Memorial Medical Center in Savanah, Georgia. While in Savannah, he did a rotating internship with an emphasis on family practice. In the early 1970s, physicians received broad training because many went to rural areas where they would not expect to receive specialized assistance from other physicians. Potter's training included giving transfusions to RH babies, delivering babies, doing difficult birthing procedures, and assisting in neuro and cardiac surgeries. Dr. Potter left Savannah in 1971 and returned to eastern Kentucky to work for a mandatory four-year period to repay the money from the rural scholarship program that had helped him underwrite his educational expenses. In 1975, he also became board certified in family medicine.

His marriage to Anna Burke ended in a friendly divorce in 1979. Shortly after their divorce, Anna earned a Masters degree in Sociology and worked in Lexington as a social worker until her death at age fifty-four. Dr. Potter was a single father of three children for almost a decade before marrying Patricia Johnson Tackett in 1992. Dr. Potter helped Patricia raise her son. Dr. Potter credits Patricia for being "the prime factor" in all his successes.

Despite attractive offers from various institutions, medical schools, and clinics, Dr. Potter remained in eastern Kentucky to serve the people of his Big Sandy Valley homeland. He founded a private medical clinic in rural Floyd County and funded it with loans and hard work, plowing the majority of the income back into the clinic. The clinic was located on Beaver Creek in Floyd County near the Floyd/Knott county line. The original clinic was a group of trailers that were hooked together to form a compound. This arrangement worked satisfactorily for a while but the sheer numbers of patients soon made the quarters too cramped. When the abandoned Lackey Elementary School came up for auction, Dr. Potter purchased it for about $15,000 and razed the old building. Initially the clinic he built was about 5,000 square feet of space but that eventually became inadequate and 2,500 square feet of extra space was added. This later also became inadequate and another 4,000 square foot building was built adjacent to the clinic. Initially, the clinic did not have a name, but patients began calling it "Potter's Clinic." Ultimately it was formally named the Potter Medical Clinic, located at 77 Millard Allen Dr., Lackey, Kentucky.

Forty-three years later, the clinic continues to operate on private funds in a two-building complex. Dr. Potter and a staff of twenty offer a variety of medical services including: x-ray, cardio-vascular studies, pulmonary studies, drug addiction counseling, minor surgical procedures, and a full laboratory operated through Quest Laboratories. His medical clinic has mentored multiple physicians including local doctors Jeff Potter, Chris Bailey, Terry Hall, Tim Wright, and Jodi Johnson. Over the years, Dr. Potter and his staff have treated numerous ailments and injuries, including shootings, stabbings, and automobile accidents. In an age of increasingly impersonal healthcare, physicians from the Potter Medical Clinic still make house calls, attending to patients who are unable to travel to the clinic.

Acknowledging further need for medical advancement and educational opportunities in eastern Kentucky, Dr. Potter assisted Chad Perry in creating the Paintsville Clinic and also helped Perry develop the Pikeville School of Osteopathy. He has served on many committees and counsels, alongside distinguished state and national politicians. As a community service, Dr. Potter founded the Children's Christmas Program, a charitable organization to provide toys, clothing, and other necessities for the region's underprivileged children. In the 1980s, with the assistance of the Garrett Fire Department and Maytown Fire Department, Dr. Potter began to take Santa Claus and gifts out to the homes of underprivileged children. At first this was referred to as Toys for Tots. Charitable donations provided toys, clothing, and other necessities. Ultimately the program became so large that the Potters could not get to all the needy children so the program changed to the Children's Christmas Program and used the local Elementary School gymnasium where the children received gifts and enjoyed entertainment by local bands, musicians, and magicians. On one occasion there were so many children in the gymnasium that the floor began to sink. Fortunately the fire department was assisting with the program and they evacuated the building and no one was hurt. From then on the program was held in the high school gymnasium.

Dr. Potter has served on the staff of Highlands Regional Medical Center for forty-two years and has served on multiple committees in the hospital including the Credentials Committee and the Executive Counsel. Dr. Potter is a life-time member of

Dr. Potter with Patricia Johnson Potter on his right and his office manager of 40 years, Priscilla Prater, on his left.

the American Medical Association and the American Academy of Family Physicians. He is board certified in family practice and addictionology. He has worked many years with counseling and treating drug addiction and alcoholism, both serious issues in eastern Kentucky. Aware of his service and leadership, in 2014 *USA Today* interviewed him about the impact of the Affordable Care Act on medicine in eastern Kentucky.

Currently, Dr. Potter remains in full-time practice at the age of seventy-three. He and Patricia have four children: Alora, Scott, Martha, and Devin and five grandchildren: Shannon, David, Jared, Laken, and Grace. They also have three great-grandchildren: Joseph, Jacob, and Lyla. The Potters love to travel, and they have visited more than sixty countries. Today Dr. Potter continues to dedicate much time in studying healthcare, so that he can continue to provide excellent medical care to the people of the Big Sandy Valley.

Sam McKinney

SAM MCKINNEY

By Jonathan Jeffrey

No artist can truly escape his roots. The places and people from an artist's formative years indelibly stamp his psyche and inevitably mark his creative products. Sculptor Sam McKinney exemplifies the artist whose creativity has been inspired by his native landscape and culture. Except for short periods, McKinney has never strayed far from his Appalachian homeland, and he admits that the area molded his perceptions of beauty and form as well as his ethics and values. In Appalachia, eking out a living in the coal mines, the forests, a factory, or even art requires adaptability, ingenuity, and hard work. Blessed with a curious mind and a creative bent, McKinney has produced works which grace halls of state, majestic homes, museums, sculpture gardens, and commercial buildings. Although known chiefly as a sculptor, McKinney doesn't allow his creativity to be so narrowly defined. He paints in all mediums, creates multi-media pieces, draws, and produces etched glass and stained glass works. Even his sculpture is varied in subject and medium. "An artist," Sam judges, must possess "a curious mind that is so curious it cannot get stuck in one rut. I love exploring all mediums, all expressions, from abstract to figurative reality." This teeming curiosity coupled with his multiple artistic talents allow McKinney to flourish as an artist in Appalachia.

Sammy Ray McKinney was born on April 6, 1951 to Woodie and Billie Lorraine (Holcomb) McKinney in Lexington, Kentucky, where Sam's father, a World War II combat veteran, received training in electrical engineering under the GI Bill. Woodie and Billie both grew up in Letcher County and never left the region for extended periods, except for Woodie's military service and education. Woodie served with the 101st Airborne Division during World War II and parachuted into Normandy on D-Day. Although Woodie rarely talked about his military service, Sam and the Fleming-Neon community recognized him as a hero, even asking him to serve as the Grand Marshal for the Neon Christmas parade in 1996. For fourteen years, Woodie worked for an independent electrical business that serviced the coal mining industry in the Knott County area. Later, during one of the slumps in the coal industry, Woodie established his own business. He performed many types of electrical and mechanical work in order to provide for his family. His father's adaptability and flexibility did not go unnoticed by Sam, who would later employ the same traits with his artwork. Sam notes that seeing his father's entrepreneurial spirit "was a great influence" and adds that it allowed him "to see that it was possible to be your own provider." He established a good work ethic at an early age, motivated by the fact that work was usually rewarded. He picked blackberries and collected walnuts to sell, mowed lawns, and chopped kindling for retail.

Sam was also influenced by his mother's deeply held religious beliefs, which were manifested by right living and regular attendance at the Fleming Baptist Church. He accepted the concept that a heavenly being had created a world filled with "divine beauty" which he found in abundance while wandering "his playground," the mountains and woods of Letcher County. He favored the tops of ridges peppered with ageless rock formations that had survived after "everything around them had melted away. I was struck," says Sam, "by the awe and beauty of the creation as I looked out to the layers of mountains beyond." Even as a youngster he internalized nature's beauty and wanted to express it. On these mountain ridges, Sam avers, "I first became aware of my creative self."

He expressed this creativity early in life. His first known art effort, at age four, was a three-dimensional figure fashioned from notebook paper and pink ribbon that his mother fortuitously kept, sensing, like most mothers, that this was something special. As Sam's creativity blossomed, his mother saved other art projects, eventually compiling a scrapbook of them that remains in the artist's possession. By fifth grade, Sam was confident that he would become an artist. Although art was not part of the formal curriculum in the region's elementary or secondary schools, certain teachers recognized his ability and requested him to prepare bulletin boards and posters, provide illustrations for the school paper and yearbook, and design and execute decorations for events. He notes with pride that he designed the themed decorations for four proms while in high school. Concurrently, he was executing portraits—"something a little finer than photographs"—for people in the community using a variety of mediums: oils, pastels, and charcoal. He vividly recalls his first paid commission, a painted drum head in psychedelic colors for which a local rock-n-roll band paid him $75 in 1965.

Sam's decision to pursue art as a career was re-affirmed by the positive results of his work in a correspondence course with the Washington School of Art. As time approached for Sam to attend college, Woodie was dubious about his son making a living as an artist. The duo compromised when Sam agreed to pursue a teaching certificate in addition to art training, so that he would have "something to fall back upon." Nearby Morehead State University possessed a highly respected art department, so Sam enrolled in the fall of 1969. The pragmatic, "empowering" professors, such as Gary Hoover and Doug Adams, who not only understood theory but could explain how to mechanically improve and finesse an artist's skills, impressed McKinney. Hoover also embodied the engaged academic, who while teaching still actively executed commercial and private commissions. Sam enjoyed all his art classes at Morehead, particularly his studio work, and graduated with an art degree in 1973.

Before graduating, Sam married Martha Karen Stuart, a girl he had known since high school who had subsequently become a nurse. When they discovered they were expecting a child, Sam admits he experienced the "primordial urge to seek shelter" and began to plan and assemble his home which he calls a "site-specific, functional piece of sculpture." Nestled on a knoll outside of Elliottville, Kentucky, his home and studio is a marriage of three log structures. The residential portion of the structure is a modified reconstruction of an 1845 log house that Sam purchased in 1974. It was originally constructed as a home in 1845 for Doc Cockrell, a New England-educated physician and gentleman farmer who settled in Morgan County's Jericho community. The white pine logs were hewed in the Red River Gorge and finished at a saw mill that Cockrell constructed on the Red River in Wolfe County. True to his family's engrained traits of thriftiness and ingenuity, Sam salvaged the entire structure, even straightening and reusing the nails and rescuing the original tin roof. He added the studio and gallery space in the 1980s, using logs from a structure on the courthouse lawn in Carlisle and from an old house on Greasy Creek outside of Paintsville. The creativity and resourcefulness Sam utilized in constructing his home is also exhibited in his artistic endeavors. In naming the structure's working space Serendipity Studios, McKinney paid homage to the fact that many of life's greatest discoveries and inventions come by chance or in the routine of work.

Sam's first piece of commissioned sculpture was a life-size, stoneware Madonna and Child, fabricated using traditional coil construction, for St. Claire Hospital in Morehead, Kentucky. McKinney and partner, Jeff Burr, operated a pottery studio in the basement of their Morehead living quarters; they dug the clay nearby and built their own kiln. As envisioned, the sculpture was too large for the kiln, so the artist fashioned it in two pieces that were married after firing. After completion, the hospital installed the piece outdoors for everyone to enjoy. Unfortunately, the sculpture was soon vandalized and destroyed. Hospital admin-istrators re-commissioned the piece, and McKinney erected a larger kiln at his new home so that the Madonna and Child could be fired as one piece. Using drip burners and two old vacuum cleaners, McKinney fabricated a kiln that would heat with wood and heating oil to 2500 degrees. The sculpture's second mani-festation was installed in the same location as the original, and it too was destroyed, this time by an irate physician. Jesus Our Savior Catholic Church in Morehead re-commissioned the piece; when completed, church leaders safely ensconced the piece in a niche inside the church. Again the sculptor creatively used materials close at hand, heeding the ageless advice of his parents who had repeatedly admonished him to "work with what you've got."

In the mid-1980s, Letcher County Sheriff Ben "Buster" Taylor and a local veterans group bemoaned the fact that their county lacked a proper war memorial and challenged the county's citizens to donate funds so that one could be erected at the courthouse in Whitesburg. With funds secured, the group approached native son Sam McKinney about sculpting a repre-sentational piece for the project. The funds were inadequate for a traditional bronze sculpture, but the ingenious McKinney sug-gested a life-size soldier done in cold cast bronze, a process which involves blending bronze powder with epoxy resins and pressing it into a mold and reinforcing it with layers of fiberglass cloth. Using a Vietnam War veteran and friend as a live model, McKinney produced an emotive piece titled "Freedom's Price" in which a lone soldier laments a fallen comrade who is identified by a set of dog tags held in the soldier's hand and by an empty helmet at his feet. Because the memorial honored veterans from several wars, the soldier carried both World War I and World War II rifles. McKinney had the model wear his father's jump boots and used his father's own World War II dog tags for the mold. This piece of sculpture demonstrated McKinney's ability to work congenially with clients, to produce a quality product using innovative techniques, and to seek ways to personalize commissions for the intended audience. Art is highly subjective, but the artist must employ wisdom in making the art contextual and pleasing to the patron.

McKinney's next commission came from nearby Knott County. Family and friends of the region's beloved and influential Congressman Carl D. Perkins approached McKinney in 1985—shortly after Perkins' death—about sculpting a life-size, full figure representation of the legislator to be installed in front of the courthouse in Hindman. McKinney's grandfather had grown up with Perkins, so the artist was familiar not only with the man's reputation and accomplishments but with his character and personality. Again funds would not allow for a traditional bronze sculpture, so McKinney utilized the cold bronze cast method, capturing the Congressman's familiar gregarious smile and stance with left thumb hook in the waistline of his pants. When McKinney and Perkins' widow, Velma, unveiled the statue to the public, she was so overcome with the likeness she burst into tears. In recognition of Perkins' leadership in educational legislation, McKinney was commissioned in 1994 by the Department of Education and Labor to paint an oil portrait of Perkins that would eventually hang in the Sam Rayburn Building in Washington, D.C. Even later, the sculptor executed a bronze bust of Perkins for Morehead State University that was ultimately donated to the Carl Perkins Federal Building in Ashland. McKinney also painted a portrait of a seated Perkins for his family. The Perkins pieces illustrate McKinney's artistic range and his ability to endear himself to clients via his engaging personality and his ability to capture more than just an image of the person; indeed, he includes a hint of the person's soul in his work.

As McKinney's reputation widened in the 1990s, he received several commissions for bronze busts from commercial and governmental entities in addition to more affordable portraits. He also returned to Morehead State University in 1991 to pursue a Master's degree in art, which he earned the following year. As part of an assistantship, he was commissioned to paint a portrait of Appalachian scholar, author, and poet, James Still, which would hang in the Still Room in the University's Camden-Carroll Library. What started out strictly as an artist/subject relationship blossomed into a "mid-career mentorship" for McKinney. Although not an artist, Still was familiar with the creative process and possessed a wealth of "life lessons" that he shared with his new friend. As he prepared for and executed the portrait, McKinney spent a considerable amount of time with Still at the author's cabin on Dead Mare Branch in Knott County, familiar territory for Sam. Single again, the artist had time to confer with Still during the day and visit his nearby parents in Fleming-Neon at night.

James Still—in his late-80s when McKinney first met him—

possessed a keen mind interested in all types of subject matter. In addition, he enjoyed travel for research and recreation. One day Still inquired if McKinney would like to accompany him on a trip to some of the Mayan ruins in Mexico. McKinney, who also enjoyed travel, quickly accepted the offer. Over the next four years, the duo trekked to Mexico and Central America several times and once even ventured to Cuba. McKinney acknowledges that these "nurturing and empowering relationships" are an occupational by-product that he relishes. As an artist McKinney endeavors to inculcate the spirit of the subject in his work. When dealing with clients, he tries to "become involved with them, if they will allow it." The watercolor portrait of Still that McKinney painted employs a softer color palette than the artist typically employs. The painting perfectly captures the essence of the author's simple life. Wearing faded jeans and a white cotton shirt, Still sits in a caned rocker, book in hand, just inside his log cabin with the weathered, wooden door opened to allow in sunlight for reading. Shelves of books create a backdrop for the scene and within close reach is a cup of hot tea offering quick respite.

In 2000, King's Daughters Medical Center (KDMC), headquartered in Ashland, Kentucky, interviewed several artists about designing a fountain for their main campus adjacent to Central Park. Acting on a referral from the Ashland Area Art Gallery, McKinney submitted pencil renderings of four concepts for a fountain that incorporated a family interacting with water to a review committee. Captivated by the drawings, the group commissioned McKinney to design "Flow of Life," a small fountain that would include several life-size bronze figures. Administrators intimated that the organization was poised for future growth, but McKinney could not have imagined that this initial project would lead to a decade of KDMC commissions; modern, regional artists rarely enjoy such sustained patronage. The tableaux that McKinney proposed consisted of a young family frolicking with water and was to be located near the hospital's main entrance. The original design had the four-member family tightly concentrated on a round pedestal, the father holding his son out from his body while the mother and sister sat at the patriarch's feet. Water falls from a pail the boy is holding and playfully splashes the females below. The smiling expressions, the universal appeal of water play, and the tight-knit family were images that guaranteed smiles when entering and exiting the medical facility. Upon closer examination, admirers noticed the life-like qualities of the animated quartet and beautifully textured clothing that contrasted with smooth bronze skin. "Flow of Life" was the first piece of commissioned public sculpture in Ashland's history, so the hospital and the artist hoped to make a positive statement with this work. The public easily connected with the grouping once it was installed, and administrators were so enamored with McKinney's creation he received a bonus upon the project's completion. By this time, McKinney had married again—this time to Ingrid Leigh Prince—and the piece also represented a regeneration of family life for the artist.

When KDMC added the Heart and Vascular Center building to the Ashland campus, the hospital administration commissioned McKinney to create a larger fountain at that building's entrance. The new fountain contained a series of nested hearts constructed from brushed stainless steel. The exterior set of three connected hearts was stationary, while the two interior sets of three hearts were hung allowing for a degree of kinetic movement. The fountain captured the pleasant attention of hospital patrons and passersby, and it was highly symbolic. Obviously, the hearts suggested the function of the nearby building's activities, but that only hinted at McKinney's use of symbolism. The artist intentionally included three sets of three hearts and named his new piece "Trinity." A small plaque at the fountain educates the curious about the universal significance of tripartite relationships, i.e. the family: father, mother, child; primary colors: red, blue, yellow; state of being: mind, body, spirit; time: past, present, future. Metaphor and allegory have been intentionally used in sculpture throughout history; sculptors aspire to capture a concept such as beauty, fire, wind, progress, or omnipotence and manifest it in physical form. Like most of his predecessors, McKinney enjoys the process of using physical materials and forms to represent metaphorical concepts, no matter how problematic. As a matter of fact, McKinney declares: "The greater the challenge, the more inspired I become." He views the role of the artist as a problem solver, who must consider space, function, and purpose in his creative endeavors.

Each of McKinney's KDMC pieces radiates with inspiration, but his dangling "Healing Hands" fixture in the atrium of the Heart and Vascular Center triumphs in both form and metaphor. This piece consists of one large inverted heart joined to another similar sized hanging heart which symbolize the field of medicine practiced within the building. To express the importance of the human touch in the healing process, McKinney lined the stainless steel ribs that form the hearts with colorful acrylic hands, each lit from the interior with a single LED light bulb. The rows of hands metaphorically conveyed the idea McKinney desired, but he customized the concept further by actually taking castings of the hands of hospital administrators, doctors, and other health care professionals which he included in the piece. This heightened the staff's sense of ownership in the building and its function. The gleaming orb that rests in the center, and subsequently between the two hearts, represents healing, thus all the hands are reaching in that direction. The piece masterfully captured the essence of the building's function and creatively filled an otherwise staid space with a colorful and clever work of art for patients to admire and ponder. McKinney doesn't consider his art as just something beautiful; art should stimulate contemplation, meditation, reflection, and discussion.

From 2000 to 2012, McKinney produced nine pieces of artwork for KDMC at their main Ashland campus and at various branch locations. The pieces varied significantly in form, material, size, and subject matter. As KDMC expanded and as administrators' trust in McKinney increased, they simply provided the artist with the dimensions of an area in which they wanted to include an art feature and a budget. The sculptor then conceptualized a design which he presented to administrators for approval and subsequently worked with architects and contractors in executing it. "The mid-career patronage of KDMC," admits McKinney, "was a Godsend boon for my creative skills and secured my pursuit as an artist. Collaborating with Chief Executive Officer

Fred Jackson and President of Operations Howard Harrison, nine monumental projects were completed. The foresight, energy, tenacity, progressive thinking and trust in my abilities by these two men was one of the most inspirational and greatest working experiences of my life!" KDMC administrators acknowledged the significance of McKinney's artistic contributions. Howard Harrison, Vice President of Facilities at KDMC, states that the administrative team appreciated the healing aspect of art and intentionally included it in planning facilities. "Sam's vision for each of his creations," noted Harrison, "always amazed us…as we…told him what we wanted to accomplish with each project. Sam McKinney is passionate about his art; his creations themselves say all that need to be said."

McKinney continued to produce other art while fulfilling commissions for KDMC. Just after he completed "Flow of Life," he traveled to Italy for a much deserved vacation. When near Florence, he received a call from a representative of Pyramid Hill, a sculpture garden outside Hamilton, Ohio, informing the sculptor that his design for a representation of Adam, the archetypal first man, had been accepted. Many people consider this piece, titled "Adam's First Breath," to be McKinney's masterpiece. The artist himself declares it "the culmination of my artistic journey." Duncan White, an insurance company executive that McKinney serendipitously met after dealing with health insurance issues following a serious accident, commissioned the piece. An arts enthusiast and philanthropist, White wanted to commission a figurative piece for Pyramid Hill, which was otherwise crowded with abstract work. The duo agreed that the new sculpture should be a counterpoint to Eve, one of the only figurative pieces found in the sculpture park. McKinney already had played with the idea of creating an Adam figure in the past. White offered him the inspiring challenge to sculpt a manifestation of the first created man.

The base of "Adam's First Breath," consists of scattered volcanic rock from which elongated shards of polished pink granite extrude at an angle. The materials symbolize the basic elements from which God formed man and illustrate the steady evolution from loose igneous rock to granite which is formed from heat and pressure. The ultimate creation, Adam, forcefully emerges from the top of the granite formation like a powerful, but dazed, action hero. The masculine torso is expertly crafted. "The human form," notes McKinney, "is the epitome of beauty in form, proportion, countenance, psychology, intelligence, and expression." McKinney's Adam bears no navel, because he was not born of man and woman; divine deity formed him and breathed life into him. McKinney compares constructing the piece to jewelry making, where instead of a gem, the bronze piece precisely rests in the unforgiving granite setting. "With this piece," McKinney avers, "I achieved my vision, the moment of becoming, in every way." White and the owner of Pyramid Hill were so taken with "Adam's First Breath" and McKinney's skills, they commissioned the artist almost a decade later to produce a more modernistic piece honoring the tempestuous love of Romeo and Juliet titled "Wherefore Art Thou."

Although McKinney continues to receive commissions, he admits that the sustained patronage of King's Daughters spoiled him for a decade. Now, he must, like any entrepreneur, market his vision and skills. He accomplishes this through exhibitions, participation in competitions, through the websites of professional societies and design organizations, his own website, and through public relations. Such efforts have been fruitful. McKinney's work was featured in the 2012 trade publication *Masters in Landscape and Public Sculpture*, which recognized the works of leading sculptors worldwide. McKinney was particularly gratified when he discovered that the publishers chose "Adam's First Breath" to grace the cover. Having pieces installed in venues throughout the region also helps generate interest in his work and commissions.

Much of McKinney's sculpture commissions have been outdoor, public pieces. He recognizes the need to use quality material in his work that will stand the test of time and the environment. He has become even more cognizant of this principle after recently working on several restoration projects, including his own "Freedom's Price" in Whitesburg. A larger project involved removing, repairing, cleaning, and re-installing the Doughboy statue originally dedicated at the Rowan County Courthouse in 1929. The statue was one of scores of almost identical works credited to sculptor Ernest Moore Viquesney. There are slight variations amongst the World War I monuments, but the Morehead doughboy is typical with his rifle in his left hand and his right hand held high above his head clutching a hand grenade. What McKinney and members of the Rowan County Veterans Association had postulated was a poured bronze sculpture turned out to be pressed bronze sheets, thus the piece was much lighter than first expected. This work reinforced McKinney's notions on sculpture preservation, which is the reason he prepares a document for owners that outlines a maintenance schedule for his pieces.

McKinney will undoubtedly continue to produce beautiful, thought-provoking, quality sculpture and other artwork for many more years. "Retirement," he states, "is not even in my vocabulary. I love what I do. I'm impelled to do it. Whatever I do, I try to do it in a creative way. Art is not so much a career as it is a way of life, a way of living." Indeed! His artwork is innovative and results from a mind that can creatively accentuate a space with beauty and purpose. In a region whose natural beauty inspired him, McKinney has worked hard and ingeniously to make a living at art. Because this passion is also "a way of living," he's had no choice.

MAJOR COMMISSIONS

1981 Jesus Our Savior Catholic Church, Morehead, KY, _Madonna and Child_, Life size 5'6" stoneware-fired clay.

1986 Letcher County Veterans Association and public donation, Letcher County Courthouse, Whitesburg, KY, _Freedom's Sacrifice_, life-size full figure, 6'4" bronze.

1986 Knott County Courthouse, Hindman, KY, U.S. _Congressman Carl D. Perkins_, life-size full figure, 6'4" bronze.

1989 JLG Industries, Greencastle, PA, Mr. John L. Grove, life-size bronze portrait bust.

1990 Shippensburg University, Shippensburg, PA, _Mr. & Mrs. John L. Grove_, life-size bronze portrait bust.

1991 Johnson County Courthouse, Paintsville, KY, _Sheriff Gene Cyrus_, life-size bronze portrait bust.

1992 CSX Railroad, National Headquarters, Jacksonville, FL, _Senior Vice-President Don Rodriguez_, life-size bronze portrait bust.

1994 Department of Education and Labor, U.S. House of Representatives, Sam Rayburn Building, Washington D.C., _U.S. Congressman Carl D. Perkins_, life-size oil portrait 4'x6'.

2000 King's Daughters Medical Center, Ashland, KY, _Flow of Life_, life-size, four figures (two adults and two children), bronze fountain.

2002 Pyramid Hill Sculpture Park and Museum, Hamilton, OH, _Adam's First Breath_, figurative-130% life-size, 9' high, bronze, stainless steel, granite and volcanic stone.

2003 Kingsbrook Life Center, Ashland, KY, _Spirit of Love_, life-size figure bonze (child and ¾ adult)

2003 King's Daughters Outpatient Center, Ashland, KY, _Jubilance_, 16' x 25', stainless steel, thermoformed plastic and radiant light film.

2004 University of Kentucky Rural Health Center, Hazard, KY, _Unseen Forces_, 16' x 38', stainless steel, CAB and radiant light film.

2004 King's Daughters Medical Plaza B, _Rhythms_, 18' x28', Stainless steel, bronze, powder coating and fountain.

2005 King's Daughters Heart and Vascular Center, _Healing Hands_, 12' x 18', suspended stainless steel, acrylic, LEDs and micro wiring.

2006 North American Stainless Steel and the Kentucky Cabinet of Economic Development, Old Capitol Annex Building, Frankfort, KY, _Kentucky Wind_, 48" x 39", stainless steel and glass bead.

2006 King's Daughters Heart and Vascular Center, Ashland, KY, Trinity, 14' x 22', stainless steel fountain.

2007 King's Daughters Heart and Vascular Center, Ashland, KY, _Trillium_, 38" x 9', painted steel and glass.

2008 North American Stainless Steel and Humana Fightmaster Cup, _Fightmaster Trophy_, stainless steel and walnut.

2010 Pyramid Hill Sculpture Park and Museum, Hamilton, OH, _Wherefore Art Thou_, two 11'6" bronze figures attached to 15'x8", granite monolith.

2010 Finalist for Flight 1591 Memorial Commission, Lexington, KY.

2011 Mr. & Mrs. Paul Lyon, Salyersville, KY, _The Butterfly Effect_, two full-figure portraits, bronze.

2012 King's Daughters Hospital, Portsmouth, OH, _Buckeye Nation_, 14' x 13' three dimensional mural, aluminum and graphic enamel.

2012 Finalist for life-size bronze of Kentucky Governor Lawrence Wetherby, Middletown, KY.

2013 Papa John's Pizza International, Inc., Louisville, KY, _John Schnatter_, bronze bust for Founders Legacy Awards.

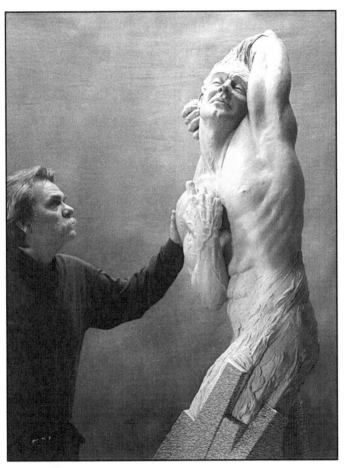

Sam McKinney with original clay model of Adam's First Breath.

NOTES ON SOURCES

All quotations unless otherwise noted are from an interview conducted with McKinney by the author on 19 Nov. 2014 at the artist's home outside Elliottville, Kentucky. The interview is archived at Morehead State University and at Western Kentucky University. McKinney's own website, www.sammckinneyart.com, is an invaluable visual and textural source about the sculptor's work. The quotes about "Adam's First Breath" are from Kathy Witt's article "Sculpting Life" found in *Kentucky Living* (December 2004).

FOLK MEDICINE IN THE VALLEY OF THE BIG SANDY

By Ernest Martin Tucker

Folk medicine encompasses medical beliefs and practices that have been learned through tradition — not in schools of medicine, tending to be outside the realm of scientific medicine. Before the formation of modern hospitals and clinical care in the 1950's, folk medicine played an important role in eastern Kentucky; because detailed medical manuals for laymen did not become widely available until the late nineteenth and early twentieth centuries. Folk treatments frequently involved plants and plant products that came from the woods and fields, while others were purchased in country stores or through the Parcel Post.

Just as the number three is significant in the Bible, the number three is also significant in home remedies: Draw the baby through it three times; three days; three large live toads; three leaves; say it three times. Many of these treatments involved healers, people with a reputation for being able to cure without the use of herbs, bandages, poultices or minerals. These treatments, and other equally strange and mysterious ones, abounded in the past.

A popular notion held that blood got thicker in the winter, so in the spring it needed to be thinned. Sassafras tea was by far the most popular of the spring tonics: "In the spring of the year when the blood is too thick, there's nothing so rare as a sassafras stick." The roots of the sassafras tree were gathered in the fall after the sap had fallen, the red being preferred. Sulfur and molasses was nearly as common a tonic as sassafras tea, but not as delicious or fragrant.

The most popular remedy for rheumatism was to carry a buckeye in your pocket. Another tale testifies that bee stings heal. Berries from the poke plant were also widely used for rheumatism treatments: "Pick the berries after the first frost, because it kills the poison in them. Wash them, and then strain the juice and mix with good 100 proof whiskey, half and half." Others would take a fruit jar full of earthworms, place them in the sun until they dried out, or fry them under a low heat until they produced grease. This oil then would be rubbed on the aching joints with good results. Finally, if nothing else worked: "When you hear the first whip-poorwill in the spring, turn over in bed three times."

For backache, find a person who was born feet first. After you've found such a rare person, lie face down on the floor and have him or her walk up and down on your back three times.

For sore muscles and sprains, "take three large live toads and drop them in water and cook until soft. Remove the frogs and add one-third pint of kerosene, three-fourths of a pound of butter, and one-and one-half ounces of ammonia, and rub it on."

For headaches, a wide variety of remedies have met with considerable success. Quite often, the sufferer simply tied a white cloth or handkerchief around his or her head very tightly, and left it on until the headache went away. Paper from a brown sack could be moistened with apple cider vinegar (sometimes combined with black pepper), and wrapped around the forehead, much like a treatment for sprains. Others would soak a brown paper sack in vinegar and pull it down over the head, for the added benefit of breathing the vapor.

A common treatment for earache involved blowing tobacco smoke in the ear, with some people specifying home-grown tobacco, although it might be pipe or cigarette smoke. A plug of cotton or a warm cloth usually followed the smoke treatment to hold in the smoke. The next most common remedy for earache was urine, sometimes called "chamber lye." Some claimed that the urine had to come from the person with the earache in order for it to be effective, and others said that the donor had to be of opposite gender than the sufferer. How much urine was required ranged from one or two drops to as much as a teaspoonful, while a few even advocated "peeing" directly into the ear! Dog urine, though difficult to obtain, was considered by some to be the best kind. Another bizarre remedy began with: "Kill a rabbit. Take the urine from the bladder and warm it over a coal oil lamp; then drop a little in the ear."

Skin problems constituted some of the most common and harmful ailments of the past. Heading the list in the winter months was scabies. One of the most common treatments for the itch was sulfur and lard. The mixture was usually one part powdered sulfur to two parts lard: "Grease all the body except the face every night, and don't change clothes for three days. Then bathe, and the itch should be gone."

Poke root had many supporters and could be used in a number of different ways; Some simply took the raw roots, broke them open and dabbed the juice on the affected places, while others would boil the roots until tender and pour the liquid into the bath water.

Boils seem to have been a much greater problem in the past than they are now, perhaps because people bathed less frequently. Raw fat bacon was one of the most common home remedies, tied on the boil overnight or at least until the soreness left. Any salty fat meat would do, and some even said that a layer of blue clay could be applied first for added drawing power. A small poultice made from the striffen, the thin white membrane found under the shell of an egg, also was a very popular remedy. Some used it raw, while some peeled it from a hard-boiled egg, but the results often were equally as quick.

Ringworm was thought to be an actual worm imbedded beneath the skin in the shape of a small circle. Actually, ringworm is no worm at all, but rather a fungus much like that which causes athletes' foot. Still, many of grandma's cures were based on the assumption that the culprit was a worm buried beneath the skin. For example: "If you can get it before it gets bigger than a thimble, press a thimble down over the area infected, and go clockwise and counter clockwise till it makes a red ring, and it will disappear."

The treatments for snakebite certainly reflected the terror

of being bitten. The pain could be so intense that a victim was willing to try almost anything in hopes of getting quick relief.

When a person had been bitten by a snake or by a mad dog, a stone would be soaked in sweet milk at body temperature, though other accounts said the stone had to be boiled in the milk. Then the stone would be placed directly on the bite, others said about one-quarter of an inch away. This treatment could take several hours. Cutting a chicken in half was an alternate remedy.

For bee or wasp stings, the victim could grab the nearest cooling agent, such as mud. Common baking soda made into a paste, liquid vanilla extract, and wet salt were popular treatments. Fresh wood ashes moistened with a little water and wrapped in a cloth around the bite or sting provided pain relief and aided healing. In addition, gasoline, kerosene and turpentine were frequently rubbed on a sting to relieve the pain and reduce the swelling. A chew of tobacco was also very popular in the treatment of insect stings; the instructions were to fold into one and one-half inch squares, wet with spit, and put it on the bite until the redness goes away.

Thrush is a mild inflammation of the mucus membrane in the mouths of young children, its name originating from its resemblance to the speckled breast of the bird which goes by the same name. A male or female could qualify as a "thrush doctor" in a number of ways, but the story heard most often was that it had to be a male: "the seventh son of a seventh son." Furthermore, a person who had never seen his father also had the necessary credentials. Any woman who did not have to change her name when she married, a Jones who married a Jones for example, also qualified, as did someone born with a "veil" (a thin membrane) over the face. The usual treatment called for the thrush doctor to blow into the mouth of the child.

A hacking cough in the middle of the night signaled the beginning of the croup, a term which covered a variety of throat conditions including acute laryngitis and diphtheria. Midnight croup attacked children between the ages of two and four. A teaspoonful of sugar with three drops of kerosene was frequently used to break up the phlegm associated with croup. Likewise, a little moonshine or castor oil in sugar could be effective, or you might roast, bake, or boil white onions and place them in a thin cloth. Then squeeze out the juice and take it orally in small doses. A pinch of powdered sulfur could be added, but that was optional. Poultices frequently were used for croup: "Fry onions in grease or lard and put them on the chest on a cotton cloth while they're still hot."

Some of the most interesting remedies for asthma had a strong folklorish flavor and required the passage of a good deal of time: "Go to the woods, cut a sourwood or a sassafras stick as tall as the youngster, and hide it. When the child outgrows the stick, the asthma will be gone." But, if the child found the stick before outgrowing it, "the spell would be broken." So you had to be careful where you hid the stick. A variation of this story said that instead of hiding the stick, you should hold it upright against the wall, paste wallpaper over it, and leave it there.

A red face and a rapidly rising fever might signal the onset of measles, after which the victim could expect a stiff dose of sheep manure tea, the most frequently mentioned folk treatment for measles. The sheep manure either boiled in water and strained or put in a clean cloth and dipped into boiling water like a tea bag. The dosage varied greatly from a teaspoonful to about one-half cup, usually unsweetened. The dose would be repeated regularly until the measles broke out, at which point the patient would be said to be well on the way to recovery.

Thousands of eastern Kentuckians, some only middle aged, remember the asafetida bag which at one time was worn by nearly every school-aged child in the hills during the winter months when colds and other communicable diseases were most likely to occur. Asafetida is a hard gum that looks something like brown beeswax. It was extracted from a tree native to India, so it had to be purchased from a general store or by mail order. It was worn around the neck in an innocent looking cloth bag. A strong odor kept people far enough away to prevent getting germs of any kind, or so it was thought. The onion poultice was certainly a favorite for chest colds: Fry, boil, roast or bake a few onions, according to a wide range of recipes, and apply them to the chest while still very hot. Sometimes the heated onions would be placed between two cloths or in a large cloth bag.

Some remedies were designed just to relieve a cough. Many were quite tasty, often including several delicious ingredients mixed together: "A handful of hickory bark, a handful of white pine needles, and a quart of water. Boil together until a stain appears and the water turns reddish brown. Strain. Add a handful of sugar and boil it all down til it makes about a teacup or is syrupy. Use as needed, or a tablespoon at night."

Turpentine was frequently employed in treating cuts and

bleeding, poured right on the wound as a disinfectant. In addition, granulated sugar or brown sugar could be placed in a cloth, dipped in turpentine, and tied over the wound. Often, sugar would be sprinkled directly onto the wound followed by the turpentine treatment, the turpentine and sugar being said to stop both the bleeding and the pain. Soot, taken from the fireplace chimney, from the stove flue, or from the chimney of a coal oil lamp, could be put on the cut to effectively clot the blood. Sometimes it was mixed with a little sugar, or with cobwebs or lard. The main drawback was the scar, which would often be permanently dark.

A woman said that her mother could stop bleeding. Then she said: "You're really not going to believe what I'm going to tell you now, but my mother can stop bleeding over the phone!" How did they acquire the power to stop bleeding? Some said that it could only be passed on by a mother to just one of her children. Others said that a woman could transfer the power only to a man, and a man only to a woman. Furthermore, a person's ability to stop bleeding would be lost should any of these rules be violated. Typically, such healers would hold the injured part of the body in their hands and repeat, either aloud or silently, from Ezekiel 16:6 in the King James Version of the Bible: "And when I passed by thee and saw thee polluted in thine own blood, I said unto thee, why dost thou waste in thine own blood, live ye. Why dost thou waste in thine own blood? Live!" Also, a freshly sharpened axe placed under the bed would "cut the flow."

Nosebleed was treated by placing a piece of brown sack paper, poke paper, a piece of cardboard or a penny between the upper lip and the teeth. Cold objects threaded on a string and hung around the neck or down the back of the neck were effective. These could include a piece of lead, a dime, a knife, keys or scissors. A nickel, held with the tongue to the roof of the mouth, would work for some. Cold water, cloths dipped in cold water, or a cold-water bath, were also relied upon to stop nosebleed. A variation of this treatment said: "Run to the spring; get cold spring water; put it on your face with a cloth, and lie on your side." You might try plucking a hair from the crown of your head, as some people did, for "quick results." Those inclined toward remedies with a more folklorish flavor could "Let three drops of blood fall on an axe and strike it into the ground." A slight burn could be treated with cold water, ice, or melted snow, either "the first snow to fall in winter" or "the last one," depending on the story. Holding the burn as close to a fire as possible, "to draw the fire out" was another popular a treatment.

Dysentery is an ailment of the large intestine characterized by severe pain in the abdomen, headaches, vomiting, extreme thirst, and the passing of blood and mucus, the "flux," all of which could render the patient dangerously debilitated. For "flux," or "bloody flux," dysentery, many hill people relied heavily upon the common blackberry plant to affect a cure. A handful of blackberry roots would be boiled in water to make a tea: "Drink as much as you can;" or, "three swallers after each meal and at bedtime." Or as one fellow said, "Find a blackberry bush which has made an arch and rooted itself, and crawl through: You're cured!" Folklorists report that this practice had ancient origins.

Internal vermin of various types were such accepted facts of life in rural America that it wasn't a question of whether but rather of when and what kind. A frosty, white powder around the mouth could signal their presence. There are a great variety of worms which could inhabit the human body, though most worm remedies were directed at the roundworm, the hookworm, or the legendary tapeworm, all of which would, as a rule, take up residence somewhere within the intestinal tract. For roundworm and hookworm, the remedies often were identical, with turpentine the most trusted weapon. The remedy could be as simple as a few drops of turpentine in a teaspoonful of sugar, though sometimes the formula was more specific. External applications of turpentine for worms were popular, also. Often, a little turpentine, "what you could get on the end of your finger after shaking the bottle," rubbed around the belly button would cause the worms to "let loose and pass."

For tapeworm, starve the worm and patient for several days. Then put a piece of raw meat between the patient's teeth. When the worm comes up the throat to grab the meat, you grab the worm! Less aggressively, some would boil cabbage, holding the patient over the kettle with mouth wide open to "cause the tapeworm to pass on."

Mystery surrounds the coming and going of warts, shingles, and sties. According to folk traditions, you get warts in only one way; by handling toads. The most common treatment for warts was some version of the "steal your mother's dishrag" tale. You stole your mother's dishrag and buried it without telling anyone, and when it rotted, your warts would be gone! There are two elements here that appear time and time again in wart remedies: the necessity for secrecy and the passage of time. Greasy or oily substances had their uses. Put grease on the wart and let a dog lick it off, "three times," or apply castor oil twice a day until the wart dropped off, a treatment still widely used. Another type of remedy employed the Irish potato: "Cut a potato in half, take the starchy white milk, and apply it to the wart," and of course, "don't tell anyone, and then forget about it." Bean leaves could be substituted for potatoes: Slip off into the bean patch and rub the warts with a bean leaf. Bury the leaf, and when the leaf rots, the warts will be gone.

Warts could also be bought off, charmed off, or "chanted" off. The "buying" story usually went like this: Someone would give the person who had the warts a penny (sometimes one penny for each wart) who then would rub it on each of the warts. The one with the warts was expected to keep the coins until the warts were gone. "Charmers" would always go through a little ritual such as rubbing the blade of a pocketknife over each wart while quoting something from the Bible.

Childhood measles predisposes adults to an attack of shingles. Still widely held in Appalachia is the idea that you should never allow the paths of the blisters to cross after encircling the body, because if you did the patient would die, or so it was thought. So every effort was made to keep them from crossing. Chickens, especially black chickens, played an important role in the treatment of shingles, and one woman told me she once had a terrible time with this affliction and had repeatedly gone to the doctor without relief until she became so desperate that, taking the advice of an elderly neighbor, she bought a "coal black hen," carried it in the dead of night out to the alley in back of her house, and wrung its head off, all the while in utter terror that one of her more sophisticated city neighbors would catch her in the act. She then proceeded, as she had been instructed, to rub the black chicken's blood all over the shingles. A variation to this story say to cut the toe off a black hen, and "let the blood run where the patient does not want the shingles to go," "Rub the blood all the way around yourself," or, "Draw a line or make an X at the end of each branch of the shingles to keep them from spreading and crossing." The blood of a black cat — the story usually said to cut off its tail — could be used instead of a chicken.

You get sties from "peeing" in the middle of the road, at the "forks" of a road, or even "by the side" of the road. There were many slight variations to the following story: Head for the forks in a road. Decide which road you want to take. Face that road and say: "Sty, sty, leave my eye, catch the next one passes by." Then, walk down the road you have chosen and don't look back. Some said that in addition to that routine, you should wrap a bean in a cloth, and when you finish saying the final line, throw the bean off to the side of the road and run as fast as you can: "The first person to come along will get the sty."

Pregnancy and the care of babies occupied a lot of attention, of course. "Drop a spoon, there'll be a new baby," and if you "dream of death," it is a sign that there will be a birth in the family. A pregnant woman should never, never, look at a dead person, or her child would be born "white as death." If she smelled turpentine, the baby would be stillborn. And, if she hung out clothes, the umbilical cord would "wrap itself around the baby's throat and choke it to death." And to prevent birthmarks, an expectant mother was cautioned not to pick strawberries, one of the most often repeated prenatal prohibitions.

In some localities, the new mother was advised to be careful about how much water she carried at one time because the amount she carried was said to be directly related to the amount of drooling her baby would do. One mother said that after the birth of her child, she would never carry "more than a thimble full" at a time. Her daughter made the mistake of carrying a mop bucket full, and her baby girl "did a great deal of slobbering."

If a baby had serious trouble sleeping, it could usually be blamed on the colic or teething. To prevent colic, "keep his feet covered at all times during the first year."

With teething, feverishness, vomiting, diarrhea, crying, swollen eyes, and sometimes convulsions might be the baby's lot. Often the treatment was simply to give the baby something convenient to chew on, such as a dime worn on a string around the neck. Certainly one of the most often used treatments of this type was a necklace made from burdock roots. Those fleshy roots would be broken into small chunks, strung on a string or ribbon, and placed around the child's neck, or put in a small pouch and hung around the neck.

The idea behind weaning a baby was simply to employ anything to make nursing as unpleasant for the child as possible, sometimes by using black shoe polish. Nor did it take long to get the idea when chicken manure, soot, or a combination of soot and castor oil, or soot and black pepper, were applied. Wild onions and castor oil might work, too.

Folk medicine survives today in The Big Sandy Valley, but not so much in practice as in quaint stories to be told by the elderly. A few still use traditional healing methods as inexpensive alternatives to costly modern medicine, but most have great faith in modern medical procedures, like most Americans everywhere. When they get seriously ill, they call the doctor. When they have babies, they want the most advanced care. The preparation and use of home remedies is simply too inconvenient and the results too unpredictable for most eastern Kentuckians today, and government sponsored health-care programs may well have eliminated forever the need for most home treatment in the Big Sandy Valley.

ABOUT THE AUTHORS

The authors of this collection of essays are a diverse group that includes English professors, journalists, a politician, two psychologists, a minister, several historians, a poet, a judge, an archivist, and a photographer. Like their subjects, the authors have a broad range of personal and professional accomplishments, but they are united in their commitments to eastern Kentucky's Big Sandy Valley.

JOHN CANNON

John Cannon retired in August 2014 after 45 years as a reporter and editor of newspapers in Ohio, Tennessee and

Kentucky. A native of Washington Court House, Ohio, he earned a bachelor's degree from Morehead State University and a master's degree in journalism from Ohio University. Prior to becoming city editor of *The Independent* in 1979, he worked as a reporter at daily newspapers in Gallipolis, Ohio, and Bowling Green, Kentucky, as Sunday editor in Clarksville, Tennessee, and as editor of a tri-weekly newspaper in Gallatin, Tennessee. He was named the first opinion page editor of *The Independent* in August of 1981 and stayed in that position until his retirement, winning many awards for his editorial and column writing. He lives with his wife, Lynda, a daughter and two granddaughters in Ashland. The couple also has two sons.

HARRY M. CAUDILL

Harry M. Caudill was an author, historian, lawyer, legislator, and environmentalist from Letcher County, Kentucky. Caudill served in World War II as a private in the U.S. Army and was elected three times to the Kentucky State House of Representatives. Later, he taught history at the University of Kentucky from 1976 to 1984. A common theme explored in many of Caudill's writings is the underdevelopment of the Appalachian region, which he attributes in large part to the rapacious policies of coal mining industries. He also produced several volumes of folklore and oral history, centering on Letcher County and Harlan County, Kentucky.

CATHY CORBIN

Corbin is a freelance editor from Morehead, Kentucky. She holds a BA Degree in English and Business Administration from Eastern Kentucky University, and a Master's Degree in Higher Education Administration and English from Morehead State University. Her professional career includes working as the Gifted and Talented Coordinator for Rowan County Schools, teaching English and supervising student teachers at Rowan County Senior High School, and working as a resource teacher in the Kentucky  Teacher Internship Program. Cathy and her husband, Tom, are members of the Martin County Historical and Genealogical Society, and they are the Coordinators of the Society's Himler Project.

KEVIN COOTS

Kevin Coots has worked over 25 years at Ashland Community and Technical College in a variety of roles, first as a member

of the English faculty, then as Chair of the Humanities Division and now as Associate Dean of Admissions and Records/Registrar. A resident of Ashland, Coots has been a strong supporter of the public library and the Jesse Stuart Foundation, both strong forces for literacy and education in our community.

LINDA SCOTT DEROSIER

Linda Scott DeRosier was born in the upper room of her grandmother's log house in Boone's Camp, Kentucky. She

received her B.S. degree from Pikeville College at age twenty, and earned a Master's degree from Eastern Kentucky University and one from Harvard. She went on to complete a cross-disciplinary doctorate (Ph.D.) in philosophy, education, and psychology at the University of Kentucky. She was the 1999 recipient of the Frances Shaw Writing Fellowship granted by the Ragdale Foundation, Lake Forest, Illinois, where she spent a summer in residency working on a novel. She is the author of *Creeker: A Woman's Journey* and *Songs of Life and Grace*.

BRENDA EVANS

A former English teacher, Brenda Evans lives and writes in Catlettsburg, Kentucky near the Big Sandy River. She has graduate and undergraduate degrees from Marshall University and University of Missouri. Originally from the red clay soil of middle Tennessee, for the past six years, Brenda has immersed herself in Appalachian poetry, narratives, and creative nonfiction. She hones her own writing skills each summer at Appalachian Writers Workshop at Hindman Settlement School in Knott County Kentucky. Among her favorite Appalachian authors are Barbara Kingsolver, Maurice Manning, Wendell Berry, Robert Morgan, Marianne Worthington, and Edwina Pendarvis.

JAMES M. GIFFORD

James M. Gifford is the CEO & Senior Editor of the Jesse Stuart Foundation, a regional press and bookseller headquar-

tered in Ashland, Kentucky. During his thirty years at the helm of the Foundation, Gifford has edited and published almost 150 books that focus on the history and literature of Kentucky and Appalachia. Dr. Gifford received the B.A. degree from Maryville College, the M.A. degree from Middle Tennessee State University, and his Ph.D. in history from the University of Georgia. He has published in historical, educational, and literary journals, and he has won professional awards as a teacher, author, and publisher. His *Jesse Stuart: An Extraordinary Life* was nominated for the Weatherford Award in 2010.

JONATHAN D. JEFFREY

Jonathan D. Jeffrey is the Department Head for Library Special Collections at Western Kentucky University (WKU) as

well as the Manuscripts & Folklife Archives Coordinator. In addition he has responsibilities as the curator for WKU's Robert Penn Warren Library. He received his B.A. degree from the University of North Texas, the M.A. degree from Stephen F. Austin State University, and an M.L.S. with an emphasis in archival management from the University of Maryland. Since coming to WKU in 1990, Jeffrey has written a number of scholarly and popular articles and monographs about local history, the Kentucky Shakers, historic preservation and library history. He has received WKU's public service award, a Jefferson Award for public service from the Bowling Green community, and an award of distinction from the Kentucky Museum & Historical Association.

LOYAL JONES

Loyal Jones, a native of Cherokee County, North Carolina, grew up on a mountain farm. He studied at Berea College and

 the University of North Carolina at Chapel Hill. He retired in 1993 from his long-time position as Director of the Appalachian Center at Berea College, where he taught Appalachian Studies courses and organized annual celebrations of regional culture. Jones is widely published on Appalachian life, and values religion, humor, and music.

PAULA KOPACZ

Professor Kopacz received her B.A. from Mount Holyoke College, her M.A. from the University of Connecticut, and her

 Ph.D. from Columbia University. She came to Kentucky in 1985 and quickly fell in love with the area and its culture. She teaches courses in Appalachian Literature and Early American Literature at Eastern Kentucky University, where she was named a Foundation Professor. She has published on American writers from Anne Bradstreet to Sena Jeter Naslund. She is currently editing a collection of letters to Jesse Stuart and writing about John Filson's Kentucke.

CLYDE PACK

Clyde Roy Pack is an award-winning newspaper columnist whose books include *Muddy Branch: Memories of an Eastern Kentucky Coal Camp, Coal-Camp Chronicles, Dear Hearts and Gentle People: Rural Americans at Their Best, The Overnight City: The Life and Times of Van Lear, Kentucky 1908-1947,* and *Pretty Babies Grow Up Ugly.* He retired in 1994 from the Paintsville Independent School System to become a writer and features editor at *The Paintsville Herald.* His humor column, "Poison Oak," has been syndicated in several weekly newspapers throughout the region. He lives in Johnson County with his wife, Wilma Jean.

EDWINA PENDARVIS

Edwina Dawn Pendarvis was born in Weeksbury, in Floyd County, Kentucky. Her mother's family is from Marrowbone, near Elkhorn City and the Breaks, the landscape that inspired Effie Waller Smith's poems and stories. Most of Pendarvis' poems, stories, and essays are about life in the Big Sandy Valley and elsewhere in central Appalachia. Her memoir, *Raft Tide and Railroad: How We Lived and Died*, is an informal history of her family's eventful life there, from the early 1800's to the late 1900's. Pendarvis's poems and essays are published in several Appalachian anthologies, such as *The Southern Poetry Anthology* and *Wild, Sweet Notes*, and in regional journals, such as *Appalachian Heritage, Appalachian Journal, Journal of Appalachian Studies*, and *Now & Then*. She co-edited, with James Gifford, *Appalachian Love Stories*.

JOHN DAVID PRESTON

John David Preston was born at Paintsville, Kentucky. He currently serves as Circuit Judge for the 24th Judicial Circuit. He received a B.A. in history from Harvard University and a law degree from the University of Kentucky. He practiced law for twenty-eight years with G. Chad Perry, III, before being appointed judge in 2005. He wrote the first edition of *The Civil War in the Big Sandy Valley in Kentucky* in 1984, the second edition in 2008, and has written numerous articles relating the history of  eastern Kentucky. In 2012, he began reprinting volumes of history and genealogy of eastern Kentucky under the name East Kentucky Press, Inc.

JOHN SPARKS

John Sparks is a writer, historian, and ex-minister living in eastern Kentucky. His published works include *The Roots of Appalachian Christianity: the Life and Legacy of Elder Shubal Stearns; Raccoon John Smith: Frontier Kentucky's Most Famous Preacher; Kentucky's Most Hated Man: Charles Chilton Moore and the Blue Grass Blade (nonfiction biography); The Last Dance of Gus Finley: a Tale of Eastern Kentucky Justice* (historical fiction)*;* and several short pieces in Ashley Parker Owens's *Kentucky Anthology* series of story collections. If he ever writes a memoir, he'll be sure to pay tribute to James Frey and call it *A Million Little Preachers.*

JOHN HOWARD SPURLOCK

John Howard Spurlock, a native of West Virginia, earned his B.A. at West Virginia University, where he studied under the great Stuart scholar, Ruel Foster. He subsequently completed an M.A. and Ph.D. at the University of Louisville. His doctoral dissertation on Stuart, directed by Stuart biographer Harold Richardson, was later published. Spurlock made a distinguished career as an English Professor at Western Kentucky University, retiring in 2005 after 38 years including 20 years on the Graduate Faculty  where he specialized in American and Kentucky Literature as well as linguistics. John devoted many years of service to the Jesse Stuart Foundation as a member of the Board of Directors, and he edited and introduced a number of important JSF publications. An enthusiastic outdoorsman and devoted patriot, John's happy days of retirement are spent reading, gardening, feeding the wildlife on his home acreage, and enjoying the company of his wife of 53 years, Elizabeth Sue Williams Spurlock.

ERNEST MARTIN TUCKER

Professor Tucker was born in Louisville, graduated from Georgetown College, received a Master's Degree from the Uni-

versity of Louisville, and completed the course work for a Ph.D. at the University of Kentucky. Recently retired, he had taught history at Ashland Community and Technical College since 1968. Coming from a big city background, early on he became fascinated with the history and cultural past of eastern Kentucky, including the folk medicine, the tools, imple-

ments, and devices which were used, and the home-spun humor.

NICOLE WELLS

A native Kentuckian, Nicole Wells earned her Bachelor of Arts in English/Teaching from Eastern Kentucky University. Pas-

sionate about travel and learning about other cultures, she received a full scholarship to spend a semester studying at the Istituto Europeo di Design in Milan, Italy. She has worked as an Editorial Assistant with the Jesse Stuart Foundation since summer 2014. Wells is now pursuing her Masters of Arts in English: Composition and Rhetoric at EKU, where she received an assistantship to work in the Noel Studio of Academic Creativity as Editorial Assistant for the *Kentucky Journal of Undergraduate Scholarship.*

INDEX

The stockyard at Catlettsburg, Kentucky. Photo courtesy of Caroline Wilson.

CPSIA information can be obtained at www.ICGtesting.com
Printed in the USA
LVOW01*1945220915

455282LV00003B/4/P